Contemporary India

Contemporary States and Societies

This series provides lively and accessible introductions to key countries and regions of the world, conceived and designed to meet the needs of today's students. The authors are all experts with specialist knowledge of the country or region concerned and have been chosen also for their ability to communicate clearly to a non-specialist readership. Each text has been specially commissioned for the series and is structured according to a common format.

Published

Contemporary India
Katharine Adeney
and Andrew Wyatt

Contemporary Russia (2nd edn)
Edwin Bacon

Contemporary South Africa (2nd edn)
Anthony Butler

Contemporary America (3rd edn)
Russell Duncan
and Joseph Goddard

Contemporary China
Alan Hunter and John Sexton

Contemporary Japan (2nd edn)
Duncan McCargo

Contemporary Britain (2nd edn)
John McCormick

Contemporary Latin America (2nd edn)
Ronaldo Munck

Forthcoming

Contemporary France
Helen Drake

Contemporary Spain
Paul Kennedy

Contemporary Asia
John McKay

Contemporary Ireland
Eoin O'Malley

Also planned

Contemporary Germany
Contemporary Italy

Contemporary States and Societies
Series Standing Order
ISBN 978–0–333–75402–3 hardcover
ISBN 978–0–333–80319–6 paperback
(outside North America only)

You can receive future titles in this series as they are published by placing a standing order. Please contact your bookseller or, in the case of difficulty, write to us at the address below with your name and address, the title of the series and one of the ISBNs quoted above.

Customer Services Department, Palgrave Macmillan
Houndmills, Basingstoke, Hampshire RG21 6XS, England, UK

Contemporary India

Katharine Adeney
and
Andrew Wyatt

First published 2010 by
PALGRAVE MACMILLAN

Palgrave Macmillan in the UK is an imprint of Macmillan Publishers Limited,
registered in England, company number 785998, of Houndmills, Basingstoke,
Hampshire RG21 6XS.

Palgrave Macmillan in the US is a division of St Martin's Press LLC,
175 Fifth Avenue, New York, NY 10010.

Palgrave Macmillan is the global academic imprint of the above companies
and has companies and representatives throughout the world.

Palgrave® and Macmillan® are registered trademarks in the United States,
the United Kingdom, Europe and other countries.

ISBN 978–1–4039–4312–5   hardback
ISBN 978–1–4039–4313–2   paperback

This book is printed on paper suitable for recycling and made from fully
managed and sustained forest sources. Logging, pulping and manufacturing
processes are expected to conform to the environmental regulations of the
country of origin.

A catalogue record for this book is available from the British Library.

A catalog record for this book is available from the Library of Congress.

10 9 8 7 6 5 4 3 2 1
19 18 17 16 15 14 13 12 11 10

Printed in China

For Hugo, Rosy and Jonathan

Contents

List of Illustrations, Maps, Figures, Tables and Boxes

Acknowledgements

We have enjoyed writing a book that examines the breadth of Indian experience and has given us an opportunity to venture away from our usual political 'beat'. The book includes details of the extreme diversity of India, but focuses on this diversity through the perspective of nationalism, nation building and change. This starting point makes the material on such a large and diverse country manageable.

Katharine's interest in India began at school where (probably because of the ethnic diversity of the area she grew up in) her education included many South Asian themes – the caste system in Geography, Hinduism, Islam and Buddhism in Religious Education and a memorable experience burning a *chapatti* in Home Economics! The seeds of interest were sown early, and she continued her interest at an academic level studying for a BA in Politics at Hull, where she was taught Indian politics by Subrata Mitra, and Gandhi's theories of political action by Bhikhu Parekh, both of whom were inspirational teachers. During her MSc studies she realized that too much of political science focused on European and American examples and ever since has striven to write about India within mainstream debates – rather than treating India as 'a case apart'.

Andrew was very fortunate to live and be educated in India. Chapattis (and *dal*) were part of an informal education which was complemented by various 'Asian' studies classes organized by Rosemary Wallis. Andrew's learning about India resumed at the University of Bristol in 1991. Highlights of his graduate study included field trips to India and Vernon Hewitt's memorable twenty-week lecture series on South Asia. Teaching Indian politics since 1998 has been a privilege and has made writing this book easier. His fascination with south India has developed during many trips to Tamil Nadu since 2000 that have also reoriented his culinary worldview around the delights of *sambhar* and rice.

In the writing of this book we have incurred many debts. Friends have discussed issues, and graciously read versions of chapters and made suggestions that improved the manuscript. We particularly want to thank James Chiriyankandath, Barbara Mitra, Kunal Sen, Carole Spary, Glyn Williams and John Zavos. Several anonymous reviewers made very valuable comments which helped us write a more comprehensive book. Steven Kennedy, our publisher, retained his good humour throughout our delays in completing the manuscript and also made several suggestions of ways to improve it.

The largest debt of gratitude is owed to our families. Katharine thanks Steve for his patience with this project as well as for reading several chapters. Their son, Hugo, whose birth in 2009 fortuitously delayed completion of the manuscript until after the 2009 elections, cannot be thanked for contributing to its completion, but Katharine dedicates this book to him and hopes that he will appreciate the wonders of India (and the rest of South Asia) when he is old enough to do so. Andrew thanks Mary for cheerfully supporting him while being frenetically busy with her own work. His two children, Rosemary and Jonathan, are well acquainted with *dal bhat* and are looking forward to their first visit to India.

KATHARINE ADENEY
ANDREW WYATT

Note: Illustrations 1.1, 1.3, 2.1, 2.2, 2.3, 2.4, 2.5, 3.1, 3.2, 3.3, 3.4, 4.3, 5.1, 6.6, 7.3 and 8.1 are the copyright of Katharine Adeney. Illustrations 1.2, 4.1, 4.2, 5.2, 5.3, 6.1, 6.2, 6.3, 6.4, 6.5, 6.7, 7.1, 7.2 and 7.4 are the copyright of Andrew Wyatt.

List of Abbreviations

AEC	Atomic Energy Commission
AIADMK	All India Anna Dravida Munnetra Kazhagam
AIR	All India Radio
AITUC	All-India Trade Union Congress
AIYM	All-India Yadav Mahasabha
APEC	Asia Pacific Economic Cooperation
AREDS	Association of Rural Education and Development Service
ASEAN	Association of South East Asian Nations
Assocham	Associated Chambers of Commerce and Industry
BIMSTEC	Bangladesh, India, Myanmar (Burma), Sri Lanka, Thailand Economic Cooperation
BJP	Bharatiya Janata Party
BMS	Bharatiya Mazdoor Sangh
BPO	Business process outsourcing
BSP	Bahujan Samaj Party
CBM	Confidence building measure
CENTO	Central Treaty Organization
CII	Confederation of Indian Industry
CITU	The Centre of Indian Trade Unions
CPI	Communist Party of India
CPI(M)	Communist Party of India (Marxist)
CPI (Maoist)	Communist Party of India (Maoist)
CPI(ML)	Communist Party of India (Marxist-Leninist)
CTBT	Comprehensive Test Ban Treaty
DMK	Dravida Munnetra Kazhagam
DTH	Direct-to-Home
EIC	East India Company
FDI	Foreign direct investment
FICCI	Federation of Indian Chambers of Commerce and Industry
FII	Foreign institutional investment

GCC	Gulf Cooperation Council
GDP	Gross Domestic Product
GM	Genetically modified
GNI	Gross National Income
HAHK	*Hum Apke Hain Koun*
HYV	High-yielding varieties
IAS	Indian Administrative Service
IAEA	International Atomic Energy Agency
ICS	Indian Civil Service
IIT	Indian Institute of Technology
IMF	International Monetary Fund
INC	Indian National Congress
INTUC	Indian National Trade Union Congress
IPS	Indian Police Service
ISI	Inter-Services Intelligence
IT	Information Technology
ITES	IT-enabled services
IUD	Inter-uterine device
LJP	Lok Janshakti Party
LTTE	Liberation Tigers of Tamil Eelam
MLA	Member of the Legislative Assembly
MP	Member of Parliament
NAM	Non-Aligned Movement
NBA	Narmada Bachao Andolan
NCAER	National Council of Applied Economic Research
NDA	National Democratic Alliance
NGO	Non-governmental organization
NPT	Nuclear Non-Proliferation Treaty
NREGA	National Rural Employment Guarantee Act
NRI	Non-Resident Indian
NSS	National Sample Survey
NTR	N.T. Rama Rao
NWFP	North West Frontier Province
OBC	Other Backward Caste/Class
OCI	Overseas Citizenship of India
PDS	Public Distribution System
PIL	Public Interest Litigation
PIO	Person of Indian Origin
PMK	Pattali Makkal Katchi
PMO	Prime Minister's Office
PPP	Purchasing power parity

RAW	Research and Analysis Wing
RJD	Rashtriya Janata Dal
RSS	Rashtriya Swayamsevak Sangh
SAARC	South Asian Association for Regional Cooperation
SAFTA	South Asian Free Trade Area
SC	Scheduled Caste
SDSA	State of Democracy in South Asia
SEATO	Southeast Asia Treaty Organization
SEWA	Self-Employed Women's Association
SGPC	Shiromani Gurdwara Parbandhak Committee
SHG	Self-Help Group
SLORC	State Law and Order Restoration Council
SMSP	Single member simple plurality
SP	Samajwadi Party
SRC	States Reorganization Commission
ST	Scheduled Tribes
TDP	Telugu Desam Party
UBG	United Breweries Group
UCC	Uniform Civil Code
ULB	Urban local bodies
UN	United Nations
UPA	United Progressive Alliance
US	United States
USSR	Union of Soviet Socialist Republics
VAT	Value Added Tax
VHP	Vishwa Hindu Parishad
WTO	World Trade Organization

Introduction

Contemporary India is a diverse and dynamic polity and society. It is a country of contrasts – and home to the second largest population in the world. Many different languages and dialects are spoken among a population of more than 1.1 billion people. India has a rich and fascinating culture which is shaped by several different religious traditions as well as the linguistic diversity of the country. Indian society is far from uniform and is heterogeneous. As well as extensive cultural variety there are important regional and class differences that help give Indian society its multi-layered character. Indian society is also marked by a system of social stratification known as caste which accords different groups high and low social status. Contemporary India has been decisively shaped by its history. Traders, visitors and invaders brought their own culture and priorities to India. The transition to self-rule in 1947 after a decisive struggle with the British Raj brought with it important changes. Most notably, Indian nationalists adopted universal suffrage and socialist-style economic planning. Since 1991, reforms have been made to this economic system which have created opportunities for business and investors, but also posed challenges as some economic inequalities have increased, notably between states of the federation.

We are both political scientists and we pay close attention to the way in which the political system is intertwined with India's complex society. However, we are acutely aware that while politics is important it does not define all of social life. The subject of contemporary India is complex. To bring focus to the book we have three key objectives. First, we provide a comprehensive but succinct account of India's diversity. We take a close look at several aspects of Indian society, including religion and culture. As will become clear in our discussions, religion is an important part of Indian society but it is not the only one. Secondly, we identify key social and political changes that have occurred since 1947. The pace of change has been extremely dramatic in the last twenty years, and even since both

1

authors started their academic engagement with the country. Looking at these two themes allows us to unpack the geographic, linguistic, religious and social complexities that make India such a fascinating country to study and visit.

Our third objective is to explain what it means to talk about India as a nation. This is a key issue for contemporary India. It still creates disagreement. The controversy about how a national community should be defined gives the impression, rightly or wrongly, that India is a relatively new nation. India is very self-conscious about its national identity (a fact revealed by frequent use of the prefix 'All-India' to distinguish national organizations from regional ones). These controversies are multiple but the most significant relate to the role that different religious groups should have within public life, demands from lower-caste groups concerning access to government jobs and education, as well as continuing calls for the creation of new states. Visitors to India who engage in conversations relating to these issues will hear arguments on either side of the debate vehemently and stridently expressed.

Taking a long view of Indian history helps reveal why the issue of the nation is so challenging. As we discuss in Chapter 1 – only rarely has the majority of the territory of the subcontinent been ruled by one government. As India came closer to independence from the British, reaching agreement on what it meant to be Indian proved to be difficult. Not everyone accepted – especially the British – the idea that the people of India were a single undivided group. Emphasizing differences encouraged the idea that several nations co-existed uneasily inside India, these nations often being defined along religious lines, particularly the differences between Hindus and Muslims. This was a point of disagreement in the political developments that led up to partition and independence in 1947. The Congress nationalist movement contested this view arguing that it represented all Indians regardless of their social or religious background. As noted above, in contemporary India many of these debates continue, and the success of Hindu nationalism as a political force since the early 1990s has made many of the debates (which include unfounded assertions against Muslims) 'acceptable'.

Despite its increased popularity, Hindu nationalism has not become a dominant idea. This is partially because, as we note in Chapter 2, India is physically as well as socially diverse. India's rapidly growing population, divided between city and countryside, lives longer and has migrated within India. Although India is strongly associated with

Hindu religious traditions, it is also home to followers of all the major world religions. It can easily be assumed that religion is the fundamental divide in Indian society but we show that other divisions cross-cut religious affiliations. Language is an important social marker and the profusion of languages spoken in India is a vitally important fact that is too easily overlooked. Language shapes culture given that folk stories, newspapers, literature and films use one language as a medium of communication. Most languages are spoken in a geographically defined area although, as the population of major metropolitan centres such as Delhi, Mumbai and Bangalore become more polyglot, they are becoming increasingly multilingual. Visitors watching TV in India are likely to be struck by the inclusion of many English words within the Indian languages. 'Hinglish' as it is known is most notably used in metropolitan Hindi-speaking areas, but has become popular all over India. Despite this, the linguistic diversity of India means that much culture in India is regionally specific. Thus people may well identify with the region in which their language is spoken and give this more priority than their religious affiliation.

The diversity of India made the design of governing structures a challenging task. We show how this is the case in Chapter 3. The controversy about the character of the Indian nation was reproduced in arguments about how powerful the central government should be. Many in Congress favoured a strong central government that would protect the nation against threats and have the wherewithal to build a modern Indian nation. Consequently many political institutions in India have a distinctly national orientation. Forces in some of India's many regions rejected this official nationalism. Some argued for better recognition of India's diversity and reforms to a heavily centralized federal system. These debates continue in contemporary India as the recent calls for the creation of a state of Telengana and Gorkhaland demonstrate. Just as important at the time of independence were debates over how to reform the caste system of social stratification. Caste refers to the placing of groups in a hierarchy – rooted in Hindu religious traditions that consider some (hereditary) occupations to be ritually pure and others to be polluting. The most ritually inferior groups were regarded as so polluting that they were deemed 'untouchable'. These groups have come to be known as 'Dalits', a term that literally means the oppressed. In Chapter 4 we show how the practice of caste has changed, partially through policies of affirmative action aimed at lower caste groups, but also how it continues to generate inequalities. Although the founders of the

Table I.1 Quick facts about India

Official name	Republic of India
Capital	New Delhi
Area	3,287,240 sq km
Population	1,176 million (2010 estimate)
Population density	325 per sq km (2001)
Population growth rate	1.93% (2001)
Languages	Hindi and English official languages; 22 national languages – recognised in constitution (see Figure 2.1 for breakdown)
Religions (2001)	Hindus 80%, Muslims 13%, Christians and Sikhs both 2% (see Table 2.2 for breakdown)
GNI (2008)	$1,215 billion
Per capita GNI	$1,070 (when adjusted for PPP $2,960) (2008)
Distribution of GDP	Agriculture 15.7%, Industry 28%, Services 56.4% (2008/9 estimate)
Urban population (2001)	28%
Literacy	65% (75% for males, 54% for females).
Sex ratio	933 females for every 1000 males
Infant mortality	58 per 1,000 live births (2005 estimates)
Life expectancy	66 (64 years males, 67 years females)
Government type	Federal parliamentary republic
Administration	Federal
Executive	President, Prime Minister and Cabinet
Legislature	Bicameral. Lok Sabha, currently 543 members directly elected to renewable 5 year terms except for two members of the Anglo-Indian community directly appointed by the President; the Rajya Sabha, currently 233 members indirectly elected through single transferable vote by the state legislatures plus 12 members nominated by the President. One third of the membership of the Rajya Sabha is indirectly elected every two years
Party structure	Multiparty. Six official national parties, multiple regional, caste, religious parties
Judiciary	Supreme Court is the highest court in the land
Head of state	President Pratibha Devisingh Patil (2007–)
Head of government	Prime Minister Manmohan Singh (2004–)

Please note that these data do not reflect important regional variations, for example in the sex ratio or literacy rates.

Sources: Government of India (2001b; 2009c), World Bank (2009c).

modern Indian state made normative choices, which they wrote into the 1950 constitution (it was intended that the state would act to build a nation in which caste divisions would be softened, people would be lifted out of poverty and men and women would be on more equal terms), the persistence of inequality is still an obstacle in the way of building a more inclusive national community. Although the Indian middle class is much discussed in the international press and there are many who would describe themselves using this label, the vast majority of the population do not fall into this category.

Partly as a reaction against these inequalities, party politics in India has changed. Political parties have proliferated, and the once dominant Congress Party has declined. In Chapter 5 we show how aspects of India's diversity, especially region, religion and caste have been connected to important changes in the Indian party system. The rise of Hindu nationalism has had an important impact on the nature of Indian society. But diversity of outlook remains. Despite the increasing acceptability of Hindu nationalist ideas and calls for a uniformity of outlook, because of the vagaries of coalition politics, lower-status groups and regional interests have gained more of a voice in the politics of contemporary India. These voices have been reflected through the media – increasingly internationalized and available to rural communities through satellite technology. The regionalization of the media, and the increasing diversity of civil society after the decline of Congress dominance, has resulted in a more disaggregated (and realistic) portrayal of India and its people.

Culture plays an important role in bringing people together in India. Much cultural activity is regional but there are cultural forms that reach a wider or a regionally diverse audience. English is not just an official link language; it allows a middle-class audience across India to access global literature, television and print media and, as noted above, Hinglish is gaining wider currency. There is a much larger audience for sport, especially cricket, and some films also travel beyond the region they were made in. Patriotism is often debated in Hindi films and advertisements often make references to national values. As we discuss in Chapter 6, there are many different ways in which Indians understand nationalism and the 'Indian nation'. Congress's conception of India's unity in diversity has been challenged by Hindu nationalists, arguing that India be defined as a community with a common Hindu culture. Both the Congress and Bharatiya Janata Party (BJP) conceptions have been challenged by those arguing for autonomy, or even independence, for their regions.

Many (although not all) of these demands for autonomy and calls for the creation of new states within India have been prompted by charges of underdevelopment of regions. As we discuss in Chapter 7, the Indian economy has experienced strong GDP growth since the 1980s but poverty continues to be the lot of a large number. India's software companies are celebrated as a success story. Cultural attention has focused on outsourced call centres, vividly portrayed in Chetan Bhagat's *One Night at a Call Centre* (2005). Indian manufacturing is much more competitive. Companies like Tata have an international profile courtesy of takeover bids and products like the Nano. However, the majority of jobs are provided by agriculture and this sector is lagging behind services and manufacturing. Indeed there are signs of a crisis in agriculture. State governments have more responsibilities for economic policy, and growing regional divergence is a feature of the Indian economy. The move away from the Nehruvian conception of national development through a strong central government poses new challenges. Inequalities between certain states of the federation are increasing, and this will impact on attempts to build a more inclusive Indian identity.

India's growing economic strength has changed India's standing on the world stage. Indian foreign policy, as we discuss in Chapter 8, has become more assertive. Rapid economic growth, skilful Indian diplomacy and the acquisition of nuclear weapons have encouraged many to regard India as a leading power in world politics. As we caution, however, it is important to note that there are significant continuities in its foreign policy, not least poor relations with Pakistan that are partly a result of disputes over conceptions of the Indian nation.

1

The Making of Modern India

Key historical developments are vital to help explain the character of contemporary India. Extreme examples of religious conflict, such as the shocking violence in Gujarat in 2002, have to be understood in the context of history. Interpretations of Indian history have been hugely controversial. In the nineteenth century James Mill divided Indian history into successive periods of Hindu civilization, Muslim civilization and British civilization. This simplified division exaggerates the importance of religion as the organizing principle of politics. It also implies that Hinduism and Islam in India were coherent and separate traditions. In fact these faiths have co-existed and intermingled, and contain many different traditions. In reality, although there were several periods of Indian history where conflict between religions occurred, for much of the time members of different religions co-existed peacefully, and the conflicts that did occur were often contingent 'result(ing) from chance political events or the clashing of festivals' (Bayly, 1985: 203). Hinduism includes so many different traditions, deities and scriptures that some scholars prefer to talk of the Hindu *religions* (Thapar, 1985).

Religious conflict is not inevitable. Indian history shows that members of different religious groups have successfully co-existed, both before and after partition. We have adopted a chronological narrative, in which certain themes that relate to later chapters, such as the diversity of India, relations between religious groups and governing structures, are prioritized. India's history is replete with examples of institutional solutions used to manage India's myriad diversities. Our review of India's more recent history reveals and how (and why) the Indian elites sought to articulate, and project, the identity of the

7

Indian nation. Finally, the ongoing conflict between India and Pakistan needs to be contextualized with an understanding of the politics of the late colonial period.

Ancient and Mughal India

India's civilization dates back to the Harappan period of 2000 BC; the remains of which are located in modern Pakistan. The Indian subcontinent has been at the crossroads of waves of migration, and also a target of many conquerors. Alexander the Great crossed into India in 327 BC and reached as far as the mouth of the Indus River in 325 BC. The patterns of conquest and migration partially account for the extreme religious, linguistic and racial diversity of the subcontinent, but its large size and natural divisions of territory have also played a role. India is home to followers of all of the world's major religions – Hindus, Muslims, Sikhs, Buddhists, Christians, Jews, Jains and Parsis. Present-day India recognizes 22 languages (plus English) in its constitution. Many others are not recognized, and hundreds of dialects are also used.

India has never been unified under one centralized authority, although the Mauryan Empire under Ashoka (268–231 BC) and the Mughals (1526–1707) came close to doing so. Even the British Raj (1858–1947) did not manage to bring all of India under its direct control. Two-fifths of the territory was controlled by Indian princes – Hindu Maharajas and Muslim Nawabs – at the time of independence in 1947. The rulers of the largest empires recognized the challenge of India's imposing size, and were unable to achieve absolute supremacy. Often lesser rulers were left in control of small kingdoms. Rivers, hills and mountain ranges defined the borders of these small kingdoms and helped preserve their autonomy and also the diversity of their territories.

The Mughals were originally from Persia and they managed to unify most of India. Under Aurangzeb only the very south remained outside their kingdom. The Mughals did much to spread Islam in northern India. The Mughal Empire experienced many vicissitudes. Neither Babur, who ruled from 1526, nor his son Humayan ruled effectively over the territory. It was Babur's grandson Akbar who consolidated Mughal rule. Akbar ruled from 1556 until 1605 and devised the system of administration and taxation that so influenced the British rule of the subcontinent three centuries later. His reign is

Illustration 1.1   The Taj Mahal

The Taj Mahal was a mausoleum built by the Mughal Emperor Shah Jahan for his late wife, Mumtaz. It is situated in Agra, in the state of Uttar Pradesh. Completed in the mid-seventeenth century it became a World Heritage site in 1983 and is a major tourist attraction in India.

widely regarded as the high point of the Mughal dynasty: he is frequently referred to as 'Akbar the great'. Akbar systematized the administration and introduced Persian as the language of governance (although this did not usurp the regional languages of India that remained in daily use).

Akbar promoted a policy of religious toleration and co-option within the royal circle, for example the mother of the Emperor Jehanghir was a Hindu Rajput. Akbar himself attempted a synthesis of religions – called *Din-e-Illahi* – although this did not extend beyond court circles. In addition, Akbar abolished the *jizya* tax, traditionally imposed on non-Muslim subjects in Muslim states of the era. Under Akbar the territorial reach of the Mughals was extended. During his reign he conquered the areas that are now known as Gujarat, Bengal, Kashmir, Orissa, Balochistan and parts of Afghanistan. This territorial acquisition required a reorganization of the empire, and in 1580 the provinces (called *subahs*) were reorganized as the basis of the system of administration. The Emperor retained control by moving the *subedars* (provincial governors) between provinces. This ensured that they did not create a power base that could be used to challenge the Emperor. The Emperor generally did not let sons succeed to the positions occupied by their fathers. This ban on inheritance prevented the rise of regional dynasties that might challenge the Emperor but had the undesirable effect of encouraging extravagance, as the spoils of office were lost after the death of the *subedar*. The movement of *subedars* was not a uniform policy. Some, primarily non-Muslim kings, were permitted to retain control of their territories. However, this inconsistent devolution of power weakened the cohesiveness of the empire (an extended version of this history can be found in Adeney, 2007). Despite this, the Mughals were economically successful. Indian trade with Europe, especially in textiles, expanded during this period, the Mughals gaining silver in return.

Aurangzeb, the great grandson of Akbar, was another notable Mughal Emperor, reigning between 1658 and 1707. Aurangzeb's image in India is one of an intolerant persecutor of Hindus. A pious Sunni, he was also intolerant of other sects of Islam. His confrontational and intolerant policies led to chaos within his empire. He was challenged by the Marathas under Shivaji, and the Sikhs in the Punjab. The end of the effective period of Mughal rule is usually taken to be 1707, the year of Aurangzeb's death. The challengers to the centre asserted themselves even more strongly under his weak successors. The most successful of these challengers was the East India Company.

The East India Company

What was to become the British Empire in India began with a trading venture. In 1600 the East India Company (EIC) was granted a trading monopoly with India by Queen Elizabeth I. The Company established several permanent trading posts on the coast of India. As Company power developed, three of these trading posts became the administrative centres of the Presidencies of Bengal (Fort William), Madras (Fort St George) and Bombay.

In this period the EIC was not the only foreign power vying for Indian trade. The Portuguese, Dutch and French were all heavily involved within India. Yet the EIC managed to consolidate its territorial gains through being granted the right (after military conquest) to tax the inhabitants of the Bengal Presidency. The control of land is vital to understanding power and wealth in India, and Bengal was a prosperous region. The taxation of the inhabitants ensured that the EIC was self-financing and could maintain an army using Indian resources. This army allowed the EIC to extend its territory by military means and promote itself as a useful ally for Indian princes. As Judith Brown has noted, '[w]herever possible the Company entered into subsidiary alliances with amenable regimes providing "protection" in return for alliances and payment for Company troops, as a cheap means of defending the borders of its territory' (1994: 49). If the prince defaulted on the payments, this was often an excuse for the Company to annex the territory. There was no coherent plan to acquire territory, but it would be a mistake to take at face value the statement made by Robert James, Secretary of the EIC in 1767: 'we don't want conquest and power; it is commercial interest only we look for' (quoted in Bayly, 1989: 91).

After allegations of high-level corruption in 1773, the EIC was slowly deprived of its powers by the Westminster Parliament. A Board of Control was established and the Governor of Bengal became Governor-General of India with control over the foreign policy of the other Presidencies. In 1833 a further step towards centralization brought the Presidencies of Bombay and Madras under the control of the Presidency of Bengal. Between the years of 1842 and 1846 the kingdoms of Punjab and Sind were brought under the control of the Company. Despite the increasing centralization, regional diversity remained a feature of Company administration. In addition, various systems of land tenure and taxation were used in different parts of Company-controlled territory.

In 1857 multiple grievances led to an uprising in north India that is generally referred to as the Indian Mutiny. The use of the term 'Mutiny' is contested. Many Indian nationalists prefer to call it the first war of independence, arguing that the term mutiny implies the legitimacy of British rule. But to call it the first war of independence would also be misleading. It was concentrated in limited areas and did not seek the independence of all of India. The causes of the uprising are disputed. The proximate cause was the introduction of a new rifle with greased rifle cartridges. The cartridges were greased with pig and cow fat. Having to bite the cartridges before inserting them into the rifles was highly offensive to Muslims and Hindus, who respectively regard the pig as unclean and the cow as sacred. Another source of discontent in the army was the annexation of the kingdom of Oudh by the EIC in 1856. This annexation fomented opposition to the British within the army, and it quickly spread. The EIC managed to suppress the uprising with the assistance of soldiers from the Punjab and western India. The ethnic composition of the army was altered from this point onwards with heavy recruitment among the Sikhs and Gurkhas who had not joined the uprising. The system was justified by the British theory of martial races, and a preference for heavy recruitment among certain groups continued after independence (Cohen, 1990). Gurkhas, recruited from Nepal, continue to serve in the Indian army.

The uprising and its violent suppression confirmed the dominance of the British in the subcontinent. The Mughal Emperor, already a token figure, was sent into exile and no other substantial power challenged the British in India. The British may have won a military victory but the uprising prompted a number of changes in the governance of the subcontinent. First, the princes were heavily reassured as the consolidation of territory ended. The British gave up the doctrine of lapse whereby territory could be annexed if the ruler died without leaving a male heir. The princes proved to be loyal allies of the British until 1947 (Copland, 1997). Secondly, the British were careful to disown any ambitions to change India's religious character by official means. Thirdly, the Westminster Parliament, already in a controlling position, abolished the EIC and assumed direct control of Company-controlled territory in India in 1858. This marked a shift from the Company Raj (rule) to what is commonly known as the British Raj. In 1876 the nature of British dominion was restated when the British monarch, Victoria, became the Empress of India. Finally, the British recognized that over-centralization contributed to detached and unresponsive government. Soon after, the process began of co-opting Indians into the governance of their country.

The British Raj

Queen Victoria's Royal Proclamation in 1858 announced direct rule by the British but also promised Indians a role in their own government. For the first time Indians were nominated onto the Governor-General's executive council. In 1861 the Indian Councils Act attempted to establish closer contact between the government and the governed, and reinstated and expanded the legislative element in the Madras and Bombay Councils. Indian representation was increased as half the membership of the expanded councils was to comprise people who did not hold official office. Although these non-officials were nominated by interest groups rather than elected, a step in the direction of representative (if not elected) government had been taken at the provincial level. The number of provincial legislative councils was expanded (previously comprising only Madras, Bengal and Bombay) by the provision to establish lieutenant governorships with legislative councils in the North-Western Provinces (1886), Punjab (1897), as well as Burma (Keith, 1936: 182).

Local representation in the districts was developed from 1882. This ensured that Indians acquired experience of governing their country, albeit in a very limited way. Financial expediency also encouraged the reforms as 'the cost of administering India was rising rapidly. In order to extend taxation it was necessary to increase local representation, which meant that Indians had to be allowed into government' (Bayly, 1989: 135). The Finance Minister of the Government of India's opinion on his Government's 1882 resolution concerning Local Self Government was that '[w]e shall not subvert the British Empire by allowing the Bengali Baboo to discuss his own schools and drains. Rather shall we afford him a safety valve if we can turn his attention to such innocent subjects' (quoted in Bayly, 1989: 135). The slow incorporation of Indian politicians into government helped divide the nationalist movement between those who wished to hold power in devolved institutions and those who saw this as a distraction from the larger task of ending colonial rule completely. The British strategy was therefore to secure central control by devolving power, much as Akbar had done.

The granting of self-government to the provinces proved to be an inexorable process, with every reform conceding a little more to educated Indians who were pressing for a say in their government. Indian politicians were able to cite precedents established in the other colonies, specifically Canada and Australia. The Indian Councils Act of 1892 further increased the size of the Governor-General's and provincial legislative councils as well as extending their area of competence. For the first time the principle of indirect election was recognized at the provincial level, even if it was based on nominations from select interest groups. However, the British retained control via an 'official majority' nominated by the provincial governor.

The formation of the Indian National Congress in 1885 (INC, also frequently referred to simply as 'Congress') facilitated Indian involvement in politics. The INC was not a political party in the sense that we would use the term today. It was created to articulate the concerns of an emerging Indian elite. Its members were not democratically elected and it was in no way representative of the people of India in terms of social and economic status. The majority of its members had attended public schools in Britain and practised at the Bar. They sought the expansion of the elective principle, and reform of the civil service and judiciary. However, over the next twenty years Congress evolved into a more democratic and inclusive entity. In this it was helped by further British reforms.

Although it evolved into a more inclusive entity along class, regional and caste lines, and specifically eschewed claims that it was exclusivist, Congress failed to shake the perception that it was a primarily Hindu organization. In part this perception arose because Muslim leaders had been disadvantaged by the British decision to cease using Persian as the language of government and higher courts from 1835. As a result, Muslims began to lag economically and socially behind the demographically dominant Hindus. Hindus in northern India, compared to Muslims, gained a disproportionate share of government education and employment by virtue of their earlier embracing of the available opportunities. For example, Muslims were hardly present among the small but influential group of university graduates in the 1880s (Brown, 1994: 126). This meant that the elite who set up the INC naturally included fewer Muslims.

Around the time of the formation of the INC, Sir Syed Ahmad Khan set up a movement to increase Muslim participation in educational institutions. He was a founder of the Aligarh Muslim University in the north of India. Many of the subsequent leaders of the Muslim community were educated at this university. He argued vociferously against Muslims joining the Congress, claiming that it was a Hindu organization. While the majority of its members were indeed Hindus, it needs to be remembered that Congress represented a well-educated elite segment which included very few Muslims. Sir Syed's call created a self-fulfilling prophecy (Robinson, 1993; Zavos, 2000). Congress was never able to create a truly multi-religious organization. In addition, the British encouraged the polarization of Indian society. Part of the British response to the activism of the INC was to depict Muslims as a loyal minority. The population of the British-controlled parts of India in 1941 was 296 million people. Muslims comprised 27 per cent of this amount. In the whole of India, including the population of the princely states, Muslims comprised 23 per cent.

The British partitioning of the province of Bengal is often said to be an example of the divide-and-rule policies of the British in the early twentieth century. A contemporaneous account of the British dominions argued that 'so long as we can keep the Hindoo races divided in sentiment, so long is our supremacy assured to us' (Mortimer-Franklyn, 1887: 206). In 1906 Bengal was divided between eastern Bengal and Assam and a province consisting of western Bengal, Bihar and Orissa. One province had a Muslim majority; the other had a Hindu majority. The INC vehemently opposed the creation of the new provinces because it divided a group that shared the Bengali language along religious lines. It also placed Bengali Hindus at a perceived disadvantage within the new province in terms of job opportunities. Keay comments that 'only the tidiest of minds would have tackled such a thorny project, only the most arrogant of autocrats would have persisted with it' (2000: 464). There were good administrative reasons to divide the province – it had a population of 70 million. Yet the British were aware of the political advantages of dividing the province along religious lines. Many educated Bengali-speaking Hindus were concerned about the creation of a Muslim majority province in which they would be marginalized along religious lines. However, they were also concerned about their status as a linguistic minority in a province merged with Orissa (Oriya-speaking) and Bihar (Hindi-speaking): 'Hindus generally saw in Curzon's scheme a partisan desire to create a Muslim majority province where none had previously existed' (Schwartzberg, 1978: 217). The Muslim League was formed in 1906, partly in reaction against this vocal Hindu sentiment which they interpreted as being anti-Muslim, but also in reaction to the loss of prestige and jobs of elite Muslims in the United Provinces in the mid-late nineteenth century (Robinson, 1993). The partition of Bengal was reversed in 1911.

Looking at the all-India situation, the Muslim League feared that Muslims would be dominated by Hindus in a democratic system in which there was no institutionalized power-sharing. The British encouraged Muslim fears of Hindu domination and entertained the Muslim demand for separate electorates. The INC rejected this demand because it did not accept that there was a separate Muslim nation within India. Nehru acknowledged that Islam originated outside of India but he argued that this religious tradition had been absorbed into Indian society and become part of a composite culture. The INC argued that all Muslims were Indians and that the main political issue was ending British rule. Separate electorates, it was

Box 1.1   1885–1947

1885   Formation of the Indian National Congress. First session held in Bombay.
1906   Formation of the Muslim League in Dhaka.
1909   Local elections held under separate electorates.
1914   First World War begins.
1916   Lucknow Pact between Congress and the League to pressure British into further constitutional reform.
1918   First World War ends.
1919   Government of India Act widens Indian participation at the provincial level.
1920   Non-cooperation/Khilafat campaign launched.
1922   Gandhi called off non-cooperation/Khilafat campaign following violence.
1928   Nehru Report on proposals for constitutional change – alienated Muslim League through rejecting separate electorates.
1929   Jinnah's 14 points – riposte to the Nehru Report's recommendations, advocates more guarantees for Muslims at the centre and in the provinces.
1930   Simon Commission. Boycotted by Congress and section of the Muslim League for not including Indian representatives. Start of civil disobedience campaign.
1931–3 Three separate Round Table Conferences held in London.
1935   Government of India Act.

▶

argued, were intended to divide the Indian population. Congress leaders claimed that Congress represented all Indians regardless of their religious backgrounds, and therefore minority protection was unnecessary. As became clear with the events that led to partition, many Muslims did not accept this and argued that they were a separate nation. Seeing politics in terms of the advantage of a particular group was pejoratively labelled 'communalism' whereby a politician was seen as being guilty of promoting sectional interest at the expense of a wider public interest. This charge was frequently made, and refuted, between politicians in late colonial India.

The divisions were played out in the limited provincial representation afforded by the 1909 Indian Councils Act. This provided for elections – the first to be held under a nationwide system of separate electorates (although only a tiny proportion could vote). The 'concession' of separate electorates in 1909 was 'nothing less than the pulling

▶

1937	Elections held under 1935 Act. Congress only takes up office in the provinces after securing agreement from the Viceroy over the extent of their provincial control.
1939	Viceroy commits India to participation in the Second World War without consultation – Congress resigns its ministries in protest.
1940	Lahore Resolution. Jinnah calls for the 'independent and autonomous states' to be grouped together (often called the Pakistan Resolution, the word Pakistan did not feature in his address).
1942	Cripps Mission offers Dominion Status at the end of the war but limits Indian participation in government during the war. For the first time the British recognize that an independent India may not be a united one by conceding the right of provinces to secede. Congress rejects the proposal and launches the Quit India campaign. Its leaders are arrested and imprisoned.
1945	End of Second World War. Congress leaders released. Simla negotiations on the composition of a new executive council between the League and Congress fail.
1946	Cabinet Mission Delegation to India. Congress is initially favourable, but Nehru announces that the Congress will not be bound by British proposals after independence. Muslim League then rejects the Plan.
1947	Prime Minister Attlee announces that India will be partitioned in June 1948. Mountbatten replaces Wavell as Viceroy. Partition bought forward to August 1947.

back of sixty-two millions of people from joining the ranks of the seditious opposition', quoted from Lady Minto's Journal in Banerjee (1949a: 209). British constitutional reforms encouraged the politicization of religion. This did *not* mean that differences between the two political organizations, the INC and the Muslim League, were irreconcilable. During this period the Muslim League and the Congress Party held concurrent sessions in the same place and many Muslims were members of both organizations, including Mohammad Ali Jinnah – who ultimately called for 'independent and separate states' for Muslims in 1940. That differences were not irreconcilable can be illustrated by the fact that in 1916 the Congress and League reached agreement on the future constitutional form of India in the 'Lucknow Pact'. This unanimity, and disaffection engendered by the First World War, contributed to the announcement in 1917 made by Secretary of State Montagu declaring that the 'progressive realisation of responsible government would be the goal of British rule in India'. This announcement was a major step forward in the constitutional development of the subcontinent.

The 1919 Government of India Act that followed the declaration of 1917 conceded more power to Indian elected representatives. Some responsibilities were devolved to the provinces, though not all of these were to be controlled by Indians. The Governor of the province possessed the power to determine which powers were to be 'transferred' to Indian control, and which ones were to be 'reserved' in the Governor's hands. Only 10 per cent of the adult male population had the vote (Brown, 1994: 205). These concessions were considered insufficient by most Congress members and the pace of events disconcerted British attempts to mollify Indian opinion by offering mild constitutional reforms that had little effect on the lives of ordinary people. Political conditions were changing. Inflation and taxation had increased substantially during the First World War, a war in which 60,000 Indians died. The war-related discontent created an atmosphere in which a more radical approach seemed viable. It was at this uncertain moment that M.K. Gandhi came to national prominence. His inspirational leadership helped transform the movement and put the British on the defensive.

Gandhi's impact on the INC was quickly felt. At its session in 1920 it moved towards a policy of non-cooperation with the British. In 1921 the constitution of the INC was changed. Among other things it called for the achievement of *Swaraj* (self-rule) by all peaceful and legitimate means (Chandra *et al.*, 1989: 186). Gandhi's tactics and rhetorical skills helped the INC to develop as a mass movement. His outlook was more inclusive. At the same time, Congress reorganized its provincial organization around linguistic criteria. It created 20 provincial organizations, when the British provinces numbered nine (not including Burma). Its reorganization along linguistic lines made the movement more accessible to non-English speakers and a more effective campaigning organization, able to establish itself all over the country, in both urban and rural areas. As Congress gained additional members in the 1920s and 1930s it was better placed to engage in large-scale acts of civil disobedience and promote Gandhi's idea of *Satyagraha*. The Congress became a mass organization in a way that the Muslim League did not.

However, not all of Congress agreed with Gandhi's policy of non-cooperation. Motilal Nehru, father of the first Prime Minister of India, called for working through institutions rather than boycotting

> **Box 1.2   Gandhi's impact on the Indian National Congress**
>
> Mohandas Karamchand Gandhi (1869–1948) followed the path of many other elite Indians by training and qualifying as a barrister in London. He established his leadership qualities during a sustained campaign for Indian rights in South Africa. On his entry to Indian politics in 1919 he quickly established himself as a Congress leader. He was often referred to by the honorific title Mahatma (great soul). He initiated numerous campaigns that used unusual tactics which undermined the credibility of the British Raj. He promoted the ideas of *Swadeshi* (buying local produce) and Satyagraha (peaceful resistance). Gandhi's strength was his ability to reach out to the masses and he played an important role in transforming Congress from an elite middle-class organization into a mass movement. A deeply religious man, he was particularly concerned to uplift those considered outside of the caste system and therefore 'untouchable'. As part of his attempts at social reform Gandhi referred to those suffering the stigma of 'untouchability' as 'Harijans', or the children of God. In 1930, in an evocative campaign to protest against the salt tax, he marched almost 250 miles to the sea to make his own salt – thus disobeying the law. Gandhi also adopted the technique of fasting as a means to achieve political outcomes. Controversially, he used this tactic to block the creation of separate electorates which had been proposed as a way of providing better representation for those from 'untouchable' backgrounds. He was less successful when he fasted in an attempt to stop the violence that surrounded partition. Gandhi's influence over Congress waned as independence drew nearer and Congress began to prepare for different kinds of politics. His assassination in 1948, by a Hindu nationalist who perceived him to be too pro-Muslim, shocked newly independent India.

them. 'The Swarajists', as they were known, decided to contest the elections and Motilal was one of those elected. This group gradually won over the Gandhian faction and the split was healed in the late 1920s. However, the divisions between the Congress and the Muslim League were not healed as easily. Although these two organizations had agreed in 1916 on a constitutional structure for India, the decision taken by Gandhi to call off the *Satyagraha* movement in 1922 had embittered relations. Gandhi had linked the peaceful protest against the Raj to the movement in support of the Turkish Khilafat, supported by many Muslims. Calling off the protest was therefore perceived as an affront to Muslims.

There was an opportunity to heal the divisions in the wake of the British Government's decision to convene a commission, under the

Gandhi's unique political style discomforted the British and increased the popularity of the Congress cause.

Illustration 1.2   A statue of the Mahatma

chairmanship of Sir John Simon, to report on future Indian constitutional development. The Simon Commission did not include any Indians and it could recommend to 'turn back the clock' on the reforms so far conceded. One wing of the Muslim League decided to cooperate with the commission. However, the non-Indian composition of the commission alienated the Congress and other wings of the Muslim League. An All Parties Conference was convened in 1928, to design an Indian constitution. The signs were favourable. The 1927 session of the Congress had accepted many of the constitutional proposals of the Muslim League. The 1928 Nehru Report, named after its prime author, Motilal Nehru, did not. It rejected the right of a religious community to veto provisions if they were detrimental to their basic rights. It also rejected the demand for the Muslim community to receive one-third representation in the central assembly. The disparities between the 1927 and 1928 positions are hard to explain. One explanation is that the All Parties Conference also included the Hindu nationalist party – the Hindu Mahasabha – who disputed that Jinnah could deliver the concessions he promised. They therefore argued against granting concessions, to which, in any case, they were opposed on ideological grounds. The second explanation is that Motilal Nehru was convinced that too many provisions to secure minority representation actually worked against the interests of the minorities. The refusal of the Congress-dominated All Parties Conference to accept the demands made by Jinnah led to the reunification of the Muslim League. Jinnah produced what became known as the Fourteen Points in 1929. Essentially he demanded extensive power-sharing and representation for the Muslim community in decision-making institutions. This position was incompatible with the proposals set out in the Nehru Report. The two movements moved apart even further when Congress began a struggle for *Purna Swaraj* (complete independence) in 1930.

Despite these differences, the later partition of the subcontinent was not inevitable. The League and Congress cooperated during the 1937 elections. Other parties successfully transcended the politics of religion, including the Red Shirts in the North West Frontier Province (NWFP) and the Unionist Party in the Punjab. But major differences between the League and the Congress persisted; revealed in their submissions to the Round Table Conference, of which three were held between 1930 and 1932 (although Congress only attended the one in 1931). These conferences, at which the British Government, Indian political parties and the Indian princes were represented, ultimately led to the creation of the 1935 Government of India Act. This did not mean that the 1935 Act was welcomed. As Attlee complained, 'I could not see that there had been any enthusiasm whatever for this Bill in India. There was, as a matter of fact, rejection by all the live movements in India', cited in Banerjee (1949b: 256).

Although both Congress and the League disliked many elements of the Act, in 1937 both contested the first set of elections held under the new system. These elections were held with a restricted electorate of 35 million in which middle and richer peasants were disproportionately represented. The Congress performed well. It secured 716 out of 1,585 seats and ultimately controlled eight out of eleven provinces. It did not perform as well in the seats reserved for Muslims, securing only 5.4 per cent of these seats, because the low number of Congress

Muslims meant that they were able to field candidates in only 12 per cent of Muslim seats (Brown, 1994: 308). Congress initially refused to take office in the provinces on the grounds that the Governor had the power to intervene in the administration of the province, but relented when the issue was clarified to its satisfaction. The success of the Congress in these elections had important consequences. First, it provided the Congress with experience of working parliamentary forms of government. It also led to the further expansion of the party's membership. However, these new members were not the 'masses' targeted by Gandhi. Many of the new members were wealthy aspirants eager to capitalize on the new success of the party (Manor, 1990). This development was to have far-reaching implications after independence. Finally, Congress realized it did not need an alliance with the Muslim League in areas such as the United Provinces. Congress had not expected to be as successful as it was. This alienated the Muslim League, with fateful consequences that are discussed below.

The outbreak of the Second World War upset British plans for orderly constitutional change and political stability. It was also during this period that divisions deepened between Congress and the Muslim League. The British declared war against Germany in 1939 and the British Viceroy, Linlithgow, confirmed India's participation in the war without consulting Indian political leaders. Congress members resigned from ministerial offices in protest. The absence of Congress participation in government undercut the legitimacy of the British colonial regime and encouraged the British to look for other political allies. The Muslim League was a potential source of support. The League had its own reasons for closer relations with the British. It had performed poorly in the 1937 elections, being shunned by voters in Muslim majority areas like Punjab and the NWFP who preferred to vote for regional parties such as the Red Shirts in the NWFP and the multi-religious Unionist Party in the Punjab. Overall the performance of the League was unimpressive; it was elected in under a quarter of those seats designated as 'Muslim seats'. It was further disappointed when Congress leaders reneged on an agreement to include the League in a coalition government in the United Provinces. The League accused Congress of engaging in 'anti-Muslim' activities. Another point of contention was the singing of the song 'Bande Mataram' by Congress members. This song, discussed in more detail in Chapter 6, is still controversial because of its anti-Muslim association. As was the case at the time of the uprising of 1857, what was important was that 'whether or not the[se allegations] were justified,

---

Box 1.3   The career of Jinnah

Mohammad Ali Jinnah (1876–1948) started his political career in India as a member of Congress. He joined the Muslim League only in 1913, shortly before the Lucknow Pact in 1916 signed up to by both organizations, but remained a member of Congress. At that time he was an exponent of Hindu–Muslim unity. Jinnah resigned from the Congress in 1920 after disagreeing with the policy of non-cooperation with the British and the 'fusion of religion and politics' under Gandhi (Jalal, 1985: 8). In 1929 he articulated a response to the Nehru Report's rejection of many of the Muslim demands previously accepted by Congress. In 1934 he became President of the Muslim League. Jinnah is most famous for the 1940 'Pakistan' Resolution when he called for independent and autonomous Muslim states to be grouped together. A notoriously inflexible negotiator, his motivations have been the subject of much debate. The 'orthodox' historians of partition have seen him as determined to create Pakistan, of which he would be leader. Revisionist historians have seen him as more concerned to protect Muslims within a Hindu-dominated state once the British departed, and have argued that he would have settled for less than independence – see Roy for an excellent overview of the debates (1993). Jinnah became Governor-General of Pakistan after its creation in 1947, but died of tuberculosis in 1948.

---

they were believed' (Talbot, 1990: xvii). The non-inclusion of the Muslim League in Congress governments in the provinces in 1937 led directly to the 1940 Lahore Declaration.

The Declaration was significant because Jinnah stated that there were two nations in India, calling for independent states which would reflect this. Curiously Jinnah did not mention the word Pakistan, even though the term was in circulation by this time having been coined as a name for a Muslim homeland in 1933 by a student at Cambridge. Jinnah's demand for Pakistan, at the time of the Lahore Declaration and for a long time afterwards, was loosely articulated. This ambiguity has been debated at length among historians. Some argue that the call for an independent Pakistan was in reality a bargaining chip to secure better representation for Muslims in a united India (Jalal, 1985). Others consider Jinnah to be determined to secure a separate state (Inder Singh, 1990). Viceroy Linlithgow encouraged the Muslim League to articulate its own agenda in order to undermine Congress's claim to be the only Indian organization whose demands had to be satisfied.

Congress struggled to advance its agenda during the war years. Its leaders spent much time in prison. Economic conditions were also difficult. The British conduct of the war exacerbated the famines in Bengal in 1943–44 in which 3.5 million people died. The economy suffered. Both rural and urban populations were hard hit by inflation (Bose and Jalal, 1998: 157). The power that individuals can have over constitutional fortunes was forcefully demonstrated by Winston Churchill's refusal to consider further reform in India. It was only after the Japanese successes in Burma and under pressure from the American president that Churchill sent Sir Stafford Cripps, a senior cabinet minister, to India to negotiate with Congress in order to obtain their support for the war. Most historians take the view that Cripps was set up to fail by Churchill. Despite this, the Cripps mission *was* important because for the first time the British Government accepted that India might not remain united – by offering the right of secession to *provinces* (rather than religious groups). Congress rejected the plan because they were denied the right to direct India's defence, and in response, launched the Quit India movement in August 1942. Massive numbers were arrested and jailed, including the Congress leadership. This meant that the day-to-day leadership of Congress and organization of the *Satyagraha* fell to lower-level leaders.

The end of the war in 1945 provided not only the conditions to release the Congress leaders but also an opportunity for future constitutional reform. The move to independence was facilitated by the election of the British Labour Government in 1945. The former Prime Minister, Churchill, had been an implacable opponent of Indian constitutional reform and independence. However, even in these more favourable conditions, the constitutional plans faltered primarily because of the difficulty of accommodating the demands of the Muslim League and the Congress. In 1946 a high-level British delegation, known as the Cabinet Mission, was sent to India. Both Congress and the League accepted their plan. Crucially, however, the plans did not include the composition of the executive council. This proved to be the stumbling block. The Muslim League had always claimed to be the sole representative of Indian Muslims. Regional parties such as the Red Shirts in NWFP and the Unionist Party in Punjab disputed this, and their electoral success in 1937 in those provinces bolstered their claim. The Muslim League's support was primarily concentrated in the areas in which Muslims were a *minority* of the population. Muslims in Muslim minority provinces (such as the United Provinces) felt more insecure and were more receptive to

Box 1.4   Jawaharlal Nehru

In common with many of the major protagonists surrounding the independence and partition of India, Jawaharlal Nehru (1889–1964) hailed from a privileged background and was a lawyer by profession. His father, Motilal Nehru, was a very successful lawyer and a prominent member of the Congress movement. Both Motilal and Jawaharlal made their admiration of Gandhi known in the early 1920s. An erudite writer and orator, Jawaharlal soon became one of the leading lights of the Congress and was elected as President in 1936. The personal bond between Gandhi and Jawaharlal was strong but their political views diverged. Nehru was a modernizer, much enamoured of western culture and science, and a socialist. While languishing in British jails for his part in the independence struggle, Nehru penned several works, the most famous of which was *The Discovery of India*. The book, published in 1946, evokes an attractive portrait of India with its diverse landscapes and different religious traditions. Nehru claims that India has a deep unity based on a shared civilization. He argues that Indian society is essentially tolerant and that it has a composite culture which has absorbed elements of the cultures that various incomers brought to India: '. . . every outside element that has come to India and been absorbed by India, has given something to India and taken much from her; it has contributed to its own and to India's strength' (Nehru, 1946: 146). *The Discovery of India* offers a lucid argument in favour of civic nationalism. Jawaharlal was also an advocate of centralized economic planning, the commitment to which had major ramifications for India's economic development after independence. Jawaharlal Nehru became India's first Prime Minister in 1947, a position he held until his death in office in 1964.

the message of the Muslim League than those in Muslim majority provinces (such as NWFP). The Muslim League's claim to be the sole representative was also challenged by the Congress Party who claimed that they represented the interests of *all* Indians, regardless of their religion. Congress demanded the right to nominate a Muslim to the executive cabinet. Jinnah resisted the right of either the regional parties or the Congress to nominate a Muslim. The point became moot when Nehru at a press conference stated that the British constitutional provisions would not bind the Congress in any future settlement. Historians are divided over whether Nehru or Jinnah bears responsibility for the partition. With the exception of the composition of the executive council, the constitutional set-up proposed by the Cabinet Mission Plan was closer to the plans that the Muslim League had advocated than it was to those of Congress (Adeney, 2002). However, other historians claim that Jinnah would have used the confederal institutions of the Cabinet Mission Plan as a stepping stone to create an independent Pakistan (Inder Singh, 1990).

The breakdown of the negotiations surrounding the Cabinet Mission Plan led to Jinnah proclaiming a Direct Action Day. Thousands of Hindus and Muslims died in attacks in Calcutta and revenge attacks in Noakhali (Khosla, 1949). It precipitated a wave of violence that continued up to partition. In the subcontinent large-scale communal violence between religious communities was rare, especially on this scale. In February 1947, Attlee, under pressure from Louis Mountbatten (who made it a condition of accepting the viceroyalty), announced that India would gain independence in August 1948. Mountbatten therefore arrived in the subcontinent as the Viceroy who would give India independence. The previous Viceroy, Lord Wavell, had been unable to reconcile the two sides. Mountbatten was seen to be an ideal candidate for the position because he was a member of the British royal family and therefore would be able to sway the princes into negotiating with the Indian political parties. He also had good personal relations with Nehru, having met him in Singapore while Supreme Allied Commander in South East Asia. The 'special relationship' between the two men was to lead to allegations of British interference in the partition award between India and Pakistan after independence. Soon after Mountbatten arrived he decided that uncertainty about the political future of India was inflaming tensions and contributing to the violent clashes. On 3 June he unilaterally announced that the date for independence would be brought forward one year, to August 1947 – only two and a half months later! Punjab and Bengal were to be partitioned between India and Pakistan – a solution Jinnah had rejected as a 'moth eaten Pakistan' in 1942.

The actual line of partition was drawn up in six weeks and can be seen in Map 1.1. A British civil servant, Sir Cyril Radcliffe, who had no previous knowledge of India (seen by some a necessary qualification to ensure impartiality), was appointed to determine the boundary line. Radcliffe worked from out-of-date maps and old and politicized census returns. As well as contracting a nasty stomach bug during his six-week stay in the country, Radcliffe did not visit the areas in question. Although the representatives from both the Indian National Congress and the Muslim League 'aided' him in his deliberations, he was the ultimate arbiter between their often conflicting demands. It

Map 1.1   India in 1947

was therefore entirely predictable that the final boundaries satisfied neither India nor Pakistan. Some areas with Hindu majorities went to Pakistan (including districts of Assam and the Chittagong Hill Tracts in eastern India), while some areas originally with Muslim majorities went to India (controversially including most of the district of Gurdaspur – providing a convenient land route into Kashmir for India).

The provinces of Punjab and Bengal were to be divided between the states of India and Pakistan, as voted for by the provincial assemblies in those states. Mountbatten made it clear to the princely states that they had to opt to join either India or Pakistan. Independence was not an option. However, two of the larger states, Kashmir and Hyderabad, opted to go it alone. Hyderabad, a state with a Hindu majority and a

Muslim ruler, was eventually incorporated into the Indian Union by force, as was a smaller state, Junagadh. Kashmir was more of a problem, as will be discussed later. The role of Mountbatten, the outgoing Viceroy of the British Raj in India and future Governor-General of India, in the process of dividing India has been a subject of controversy. It is now widely accepted that Mountbatten, after seeing an earlier version of Radcliffe's report, intervened to ensure that certain key districts were allocated to India, and one of these inter-ventions was to have far-reaching implications. As Lucy Chester notes, 'Pakistani critics interpreted Radcliffe's decision to grant most of Gurdaspur District to India as an attempt to provide India with a land link to Kashmir' (2002). The process of partition was extremely violent. Estimates vary, but approximately one million people were killed, and ten million crossed the border between the newly created countries. Tales of rape, abduction and premeditated violence were widespread, and fuelled revenge attacks in their turn. The slaughter of refugees on trains was one of the most emotive events – with trains pulling into Delhi or Lahore filled with dead refugees. These attacks contributed to an increased level of violence that the new states had not anticipated and were ill-prepared to deal with.

Forming the New Republic of India

To prepare the way for self-rule it was decided to convene a Constituent Assembly to design a new constitution. Delegates were selected by election and in 1946 Congress won an impressive victory in these elections. The Constituent Assembly also served as the *de facto* parliament for the transition government. After the creation of Pakistan, most Muslim members of the Assembly migrated to Pakistan and the Congress Party share jumped from 69 per cent to 82 per cent of the seats in the Indian Constituent Assembly. Congress controlled the chairmanship of the majority of committees (Austin, 1966: 10 and 18). Congress was confronted with different problems from those of the British Raj – it had to demonstrate its democratic legitimacy and justify the institutions of government afresh. Congress assumed power after independence in 1947 with a distinctive set of assumptions that set them apart from the departing colonial regime. The leading objective of the colonial administration was political stability and any pretensions to be a reforming government were swept aside by the pace of political events of the 1940s (Thornton,

1985: 238). The war against Japan and containing the nationalist movement had consumed the energy of the British rulers of India. In contrast, the INC offered a much more exciting prospect.

There were significant voices among the Indian nationalist elite calling for reform. Not least of these was Nehru. The INC stood for the modernization of India. Nehru held to the Fabian belief that the state could and should intervene to promote social change. Reform included addressing the weaknesses in Indian society that had undermined unity during the nationalist struggle. Thus reform of the caste system was high on the agenda. The problem of untouchability would have to be resolved by state action. The unequal status of women also had to be addressed. The communal violence of the 1940s was another problem that Congress leaders were anxious to deal with. The economy needed to be modernized, and India's widespread poverty cried out for a solution. The failings of the British were not to be repeated and there was a consensus that the state should provide suitable conditions for economic growth and industrialization. It is certainly true that not all of the Congress elite were as progressive as Nehru. It is also the case that the party resisted certain reforms as time passed. However, the ideals that were incorporated into the new state were in stark contrast to the idea of minimal government that dominated the colonial regime.

The nationalist elite also possessed a very different vision of the Indian nation than the British. Admittedly the vision was disputed. Gandhi had an idiosyncratic notion of India as a nation comprising village republics. The new Home Minister Patel favoured a more conservative version of the nation which gave due accord to the Hindu majority community. However, Nehru eventually won the argument in favour of a citizenship based on the territorial principle, whereby citizenship was given to those born inside a country. There were to be no ethnic or religious exclusions. At the same time Nehru favoured a national identity that celebrated India's diverse cultural experience and did not privilege the majority religious community (Adeney and Lall, 2005). This official composite national identity was written into the new national institutions. The nation had to be built and inscribed into the public imagination. The INC had been strongly critical of what they considered to be a 'divide-and-rule' strategy adopted by the British. Congress leaders were shocked by the communal violence that climaxed during the months before and after partition. It was hoped violence of this kind could be avoided in independent India. One way of doing this would be the creation of secular

Illustration 1.3   Raj Ghat

Raj Ghat in Delhi marks the spot where Gandhi was cremated after his assassination by a Hindu nationalist in 1948. Gandhi's funeral was held in Delhi. His funeral was attended by hundreds of thousands of mourners and portions of his ashes were sent to all the provinces of India.

state institutions. A broad consensus in favour of a religiously neutral secular state emerged among senior leaders. This form of secularism did not mean a separation of state and religion, or an anti-religious stance. It was defined as promoting neutrality between religions in the interests of equal tolerance. The details (and controversies) of institutionalizing the relationship between the state and religion were closely debated in the Constituent Assembly (Chiriyankandath, 2000), as will be further discussed in Chapter 6. Nehru was particularly keen to attack the 'poison' of communalism and did not hesitate to enlist the institutions of the state in this cause.

While the process of constitutional design was under way, the 'unfinished business' of partition had to be addressed. The majority of the princely states had acceded to either India or Pakistan depending on whose territory they were encircled by. But there were two notable exceptions: Hyderabad and Kashmir. The Muslim ruler of Hyderabad, landlocked within Indian territory, acceded to Pakistan. Yet his state had a Hindu majority population. India imposed an economic blockade and eventually invaded in September 1948.

Kashmir posed more of a problem. It was a Muslim majority state bordering both India and Pakistan (see Map 1.1). Its ruler was a Hindu Maharaja. Kashmir was the K in PaKistan. Punjab was the P in NWFP, Afghani was the A, I was Balochistan (Irani) and S was Sind. As such it was ideologically important for Pakistan to gain the territory of Kashmir. India also had an ideological commitment to the territory of the state. The accession of Kashmir to Pakistan would have confirmed for Pakistan the fact that India was a Hindustan (land of Hindus). Congress therefore did not accept the justification of Kashmir acceding to Pakistan on the grounds that it was a Muslim majority state. On a personal level, Kashmir was the ancestral home of the Nehru family. Nehru was personally attached to the state, and was captured by its beauty even though he was born and brought up in Allahabad in the United Provinces.

The Maharaja of the state entertained the notion of remaining independent. However, in 1947 Pakhtun tribesmen invaded Kashmir, supported by Pakistan. The Maharaja panicked and requested Indian military assistance. India refused to send such assistance until the Maharaja acceded to India. He did so, but on the condition that a plebiscite be held later to ascertain the wishes of his people. As will be discussed in Chapter 8, this plebiscite was never held.

India since 1947

Unlike its neighbour, Pakistan, India's Constituent Assembly created a constitution within three years. The assembly opted for a federal parliamentary system of government, which we discuss in more detail in Chapter 3. The recent experience of partition and the centralizing preferences of Congress leaders meant it was a heavily centralized federal system. Within five years of independence India held nationwide elections. Organizing an election among an electorate of 173 million people was no mean task and it was recognized as the largest democratic election the world had ever seen. It was conducted in a society in which a large percentage of the population were illiterate. Congress won an overall majority of the seats – 364 out of 489. Yet, even with its heritage of winning India's independence, Congress did not secure a majority of the votes. No political party has ever managed to do so in India but this has not undermined the legitimacy of the system.

One-party dominance (of Congress) continued at the national level in India until 1977. Under Congress, India introduced a centralized planning system with heavy emphasis on creating public sector industries (discussed in more detail in Chapter 7). Despite its dominance at the centre (in terms of seats), Congress was defeated at the state level in several key states in 1967 and its organization was severely weakened by splits in the late 1960s. Although Indira Gandhi (Nehru's daughter) won the election in 1971, she controversially deployed personality politics at the expense of the Congress as an organization. In 1975, to avoid being debarred from office for breaking the law on election expenses, she declared an Emergency. In the 1977 election, held after the two-year Emergency, the electorate declared its dissatisfaction with the abrogation of democracy and the newly formed opposition Janata Party won the election. But the first non-Congress government was weak. Indira Gandhi was returned to power in 1980 and her personal dominance of politics intensified. Indira's manipulation of politics was nowhere more notable than in the Punjab (as discussed in Chapter 5). The ramifications of her encouragement of the Sikh preacher Bhindranwale (in an attempt to undermine Congress's political rivals the Akali Dal) were widespread. Events got out of control, leading to the June 1984 siege and then the storming of the Sikh's Golden Temple in Amritsar in an attempt to dislodge Bhindranwale and his followers. The outrage following this operation led to the assassination of Indira Gandhi by her Sikh bodyguards a few months later and the accession of her son, Rajiv Gandhi, to the leadership of Congress and to the prime ministership. Rajiv led Congress to a landslide electoral victory in 1984 but the trend of Congress decline, seen at the state level since 1967, reasserted itself. This was confirmed in 1989 with the election of the National Front coalition.

Indian politics has been in a state of flux since the early 1990s. A key watershed was a process of economic reform put underway in 1991. Ironically this liberalization, which weakened controls on the economy introduced by earlier Congress governments, was driven forward by a minority Congress government between 1991 and 1996. This liberalization has had important repercussions for Indian politics and society. In addition, since 1996 coalition governments at the centre have become the norm. A collection of centre-left and regional parties formed the United Front (1996–8), which was followed by the National Democratic Alliance (NDA). The Hindu nationalist Bharatiya Janata Party (BJP) was the leading party in the

NDA, which formed two administrations (1998–99, 1999–2004). Despite showing signs of decline, Congress was unexpectedly resurgent in both 2004 and 2009, having learnt the lessons of coalition politics.

Differing and competing legacies

The politics of the late colonial period left an extensive legacy for the Indian state after 1947. We concentrate on three elements of this legacy. First, some claim that the British bequeathed a democratic tradition on India. Myron Weiner identified the representative institutions of the colonial period as a vital training school for India's emerging political class (1957). According to this view the experience gained in various elected bodies created an atmosphere conducive for the practice of democratic politics after 1947. There are reasons to doubt this legacy. The extent to which the British promoted democracy was highly limited. Elected bodies were based on a very limited electorate. The 1935 Government of India extended the vote to only those who met educational, tax and property qualifications. Only 28.5 per cent of the adult population were permitted to exercise their franchise in 1946 (Austin, 1966: 10). The British also used a variety of illiberal methods to coerce opposition politicians, such as press censorship and the detention of INC activists. It was left to the INC to complete the transition to a formal democratic system. Some critics have argued that the Congress elite were not especially sympathetic to the cause of democracy (Washbrook, 1997). Nevertheless it was the INC that wrote universal suffrage into the new constitution. The 1935 Government of India Act was significantly modified in the Constituent Assembly by the inclusion of a range of liberal rights and freedoms that are widely considered to be the essential conditions of democracy. The norms and traditions of the Congress movement have also been credited with creating a liberal political culture conducive to the success of representative democracy in India (Varshney, 1998). This colonial legacy is considered irrelevant by writers who argue that social structures and economic change determine democratic development. Others argue that India is only a formal democracy (Bose and Jalal, 1998: 206–7). Elections may occur but little follows from them. We take an alternative position and argue that India's democratic political system is to be taken seriously. A careful comparison of India, Pakistan and Sri Lanka shows that effective political parties were important factors enabling, or retarding, democratic development in the region (Adeney and Wyatt, 2004). Unlike other states in the region, India was well served by political parties that built links between the state and society.

A second legacy of colonial politics was apparent in the structures of government. The residue of the British parliamentary style and the preference for weak federal institutions is clearly discernible (Khilnani, 1997). The structures of government outlined in the 1935 Government of India Act were carried over into the post-independence constitutional framework. The four most notable features were: the federal system, the parliamentary system, the emergency powers of the central government, and the viceregal system. As Washbrook has observed, 68 per cent of the clauses of the Indian constitution were taken directly from the 1935 Government of India Act (1997: 37). The fact that this continuity existed does not mean that the British legacy was absolute. Federal antecedents existed in the subcontinent before, and during, the Mughal era. It is important to mention the fact that, as Bose and Jalal remind us, the Congress Party relied heavily on the bureaucracy (1998: 204). Without this important and strong institution, the ability of Congress to govern would have been undermined, as was seen in the neighbouring state of Pakistan. The structure and traditions of the British elite Indian Civil Service were largely absorbed into the new Indian Administrative Service.

The third legacy was the politicization of groups in Indian politics. The British claimed that India was profoundly divided as individuals owed their primary loyalty to groups. The most famous of the British tactics of 'divide and rule' was the decision to treat India as being divided into separate religious groups. The claim that these groups could not manage their 'antagonistic' relations within representative institutions was used by the British as an excuse to limit self-government. The system of separate electorates introduced in 1909 and expanded in 1919 and 1935 encouraged (although it did not create) mobilization by religious and other groups. The heightening of tensions between Hindus and Muslims described earlier in this chapter did not disappear with independence. Some political leaders have continued to exacerbate this tension and civil disharmony remains a problem in contemporary India. The introduction of a census in 1872 also contributed to the politicization of groups. The decennial census delimited caste, language, tribe and religion at the national and provincial level. Caste associations formed to press the claims of their 'community' and they demanded recognition in the census. Caste associations also lobbied the colonial government for social reform and a distribution of government jobs for their own group. When the suffrage was extended, the ambitions of the caste associations were projected into politics and larger caste groups were well placed to negotiate with political parties (Wyatt, 2010). Where communal tension was high, the census returns were used as evidence that a particular religious group was under threat or over-advantaged. This was seen markedly in the northern Indian provinces, where the proportions of Hindu and Muslims in particular were used to argue for specific institutional protections such as reserved seats and separate electorates (Adeney, 2002).

Conclusion

Contemporary India bears the imprint of the historical events we have reviewed in this chapter. There are common problems and arguments that remain relevant to understanding India. In closing we highlight three of them.

First, this history supports our claim that nation building is a fundamental issue in Indian politics. The INC fought a long political battle in the first half of the twentieth century. It stated a strong claim that India was a nation, even though its territory was not united. Indian politics up to 1947 can be seen in a three-cornered struggle. Most obviously Congress sought to undermine the legitimacy of the colonial regime and discredit the British view that India was not a nation. Congress was also involved in a struggle to achieve supremacy over other political forces in India. We have focused on the Muslim League but Congress was also challenged by a number of regional parties, caste leaders, Hindu nationalists, local notables and rulers of princely states. Several of these groups had their own opinion about how the Indian nation should be constituted, as discussed below. Congress argued for one united nation that included many diverse groups. Others were lukewarm towards Indian nationalism and argued that specific issues, such as caste equality, required urgent attention in advance of political independence. We have said relatively little about caste so far, and we say much more in later chapters, but it is important to note that it was a live issue before independence. The outcome of the 1946 elections and the subsequent departure of the Muslim League for Pakistan left Congress as the dominant political force in independent India. Accordingly, the Congress version of the Indian nation was written into the constitution and the official ideology of independent India.

Secondly, it is important to re-emphasize the divisive legacy of communal politics in the late colonial period. The Hindu nationalist movement was active from the 1920s onwards. They argued that India was essentially a Hindu country and that the structures of society and government should be designed to reflect that. At the heart of the Hindu nationalist movement was an organization formed on paramilitary lines to defend Hindus from the threat of physical attack. This organization was called the Rashtriya Swayamsevak Sangh (RSS) and they alleged that Muslims had aggressive intentions towards Hindu interests. Hindu nationalists started from a different premise to the Muslim League but they also wanted to define nations in terms of religious identity. The formation of Pakistan in 1947 confirmed the logic of religious nationalism for Hindu nationalists, even though they bitterly opposed the division of what they regarded as the sacred territory of Hindu India. A long-standing feature of Hindu nationalist propaganda has been stereotypical allegations against the Muslim minority. It is suggested that Muslims are a subversive and aggressive minority. The extreme violence of partition in 1947 and the incipient interreligious violence since the 1920s are taken by some as historical confirmation of Hindu nationalist stereotypes. Relations between religious groups were more harmonious after 1947 but tensions between Hindus and Muslims did not disappear completely. By the late 1980s the Hindu nationalist movement had developed into a formidable political force, with consequences that are addressed in later chapters.

A third theme of enduring importance is the tension between centre and periphery in Indian politics. This was an issue long before 1947. Both the Mughals and the British recognized the utility of devolving power. Congress was aware of this issue but tended to give priority to the centre. Giving the centre certain key powers allowed for some important issues to be resolved in an all-India fashion. Central planning was seen as a way of securing India's prosperity. Significantly it was to be *national* planning intended to promote equity between different regions and spread the benefits of economic development among different social groups. These centrist tendencies were resented by regional political movements.

In the rest of the book we give an account of contemporary India. As we have said, politics does not encompass all of Indian society and culture. However, it is clear that building the Indian nation has been a challenging task. Issues of religion, region and caste have had to be negotiated as India moved forwards after 1947. The historical antecedents discussed in this chapter have had a lasting influence on contemporary India.

2

The Diversity of India

India is physically and socially diverse. This is not surprising given the scale of the country. It is the seventh largest country in the world, not including Antarctica, in terms of land area. It covers over three million square kilometres – almost all of which is land mass. In comparison, the former colonial power, the United Kingdom, has only 7 per cent of India's land mass, and India's main rival, Pakistan, only 24 per cent. While large in comparison to most countries in Europe, India is only about one third the size of the US. But even in relation to the US, India is huge when it comes to population size, which passed the billion mark around the turn of the century and was projected to be 1.176 billion by 2010 (Government of India, 2001b). The only country with a larger population is China (2009 estimates are 1,339 million). Experts disagree as to the precise date, but by all estimates India is set to become the country with the largest population in the world in the next few decades. India is also one of the most linguistically and religiously diverse countries in the world, and is also divided by region and caste. The diversity, large size and geographical spread of its population structures the challenges that face India. India's human geography is also diverse, with notable differences in religious, linguistic and ethnic identities.

India shares land borders with several states; Bangladesh, Bhutan, Burma, China, Nepal and Pakistan. Many of these land borders are extremely long; India shares 4000 km of border with Bangladesh, nearly 3400 km with China, and approximately 3000 km with Pakistan, with whom it has fought three wars since independence. India also has approximately 11,000 km of coastline, and is separated from the state of Sri Lanka by a very narrow strip of shallow sea.

India's geography overlaps with the other states of the subcontinent: Bangladesh, Bhutan, Nepal, Pakistan and Sri Lanka. For the most part we only discuss India's geography but we do acknowledge the shared geography of the region. We show how cross-boundary issues contribute to shared environmental problems and resource disputes. The challenges arising from India's diversity are multiple. They include challenges of international security, environmental change, the maintenance of internal governance and the promotion of human development (Bradnock and Williams, 2002). This chapter will discuss the different manifestations of diversity in India and the ways in which they have each set the challenges for contemporary India. We begin with India's physical diversity and then move on to discuss India's social diversity in the second part of the chapter.

The Geography of India

To give a sense of India's physical diversity we move southwards in our account. So we begin with the Himalayas, move onto the Indo-Gangetic plain and finish on the Peninsula. There is, of course, much local diversity in the geographical zones we outline but the broad classification provides a useful orientation to India's fascinating physical environment. The Himalayan mountain range does much to define India's geography, as the range forms a barrier between the Tibetan plateau and the Indian subcontinent to the south. The drifting subcontinent collided with the Asian continent between 25 million and 70 million years ago, forming the Himalayas.

The Himalayas are still growing and are the source of many rivers including the Brahmaputra and the Indus. India's highest point, the mountain of Kanchenjunga, lies in the Himalayas. At 8598 metres it is the world's third highest peak. The Himalayan region is not densely populated owing to the harsh climate and a lack of arable land, although a few valleys, such as the Kashmir valley, do support important concentrations of population. The Himalayas run from the northernmost district of Ladakh in Kashmir, southwards through the states of Himachal Pradesh and Uttaranchal. India's border with China runs through this segment of the western Himalayas, until India meets Nepal. India's border with China resumes in the Himalayan range on the eastern edge of Nepal. In this area the state of Sikkim, annexed by India in 1975, provides a trading route to Tibet. The kingdom of Bhutan lies adjacent to Sikkim and is entirely landlocked. To the south of Bhutan the Indian state of Assam, through which flows the Brahmaputra, which rises in the eastern Himalayas, can be found. To

Illustration 2.1   The banks of the River Ganges

Many Hindus aspire to bathe in the River Ganges at least once in their lifetime, and take their loved ones to the banks of the river to be cremated.

the east of Assam are the hilly north-eastern states of India which are adjacent to China and Burma. These states are geographically isolated from the rest of India. The lie of the hills and dense forest contribute to the isolation. Road and rail links have to take a convoluted route and pass through a narrow piece of territory, the so-called 'chicken neck' that lies between Bhutan and Bangladesh. Again the terrain does not support a dense population.

To the south of the Himalayas lies the extensive Indo-Gangetic plain. The river Ganges, originating in the Himalayas, flows southeastwards through the states of Uttaranchal, Uttar Pradesh, Bihar and West Bengal before entering the Bay of Bengal. The river is vitally important for the large population that populates the plain. The alluvial deposits washed from the mountains and carried downstream by the river provide fertile soil essential for the agricultural economy of the plain. The ecology of the Indo-Gangetic plain has enabled it to support a higher population density than most other parts of rural India. Rainfall is sufficient for reasonable cropping in many areas and the Ganges provides water for some irrigation as well. The Ganges is also important in spiritual terms. The Ganges runs through the Hindu holy city of Varanasi, formerly known as Benares, as can be seen in Illustration 2.1. The river is mentioned in several sacred Hindu texts.

The Indo-Gangetic plain is bounded by several mountain ranges. These ranges are not as substantial as the Himalayas but they still separate regions from each other. The Aravalli hills run from the south west to the north east, beginning in Gujarat and ending near Delhi. To the west of the Aravalli hills in the state of Rajasthan lies the arid Thar Desert. Further north the Aravalli hills indicate the beginning of the Punjab sub-region, an area with a concentration of population supported by a strong agricultural economy. The Punjab (Punjab literally means the land of the five rivers) straddles the border with Pakistan. India and Pakistan have more or less successfully shared the waters from rivers like the Indus which cross the political border, and are so vital in this heavily irrigated and productive region, although tensions arise from time to time. To the south of the Indo-Gangetic plain lie the Vindhya and Satpura ranges which divide northern India from peninsular India and the main part of the Deccan plateau.

The Deccan plateau dominates the geography of peninsular India and it crosses several of India's largest states including Maharashtra, Andhra Pradesh and Karnataka. To the west the plateau is bounded by the Western Ghats, a range of hills and mountains that run north–south just inland from the coast. The narrow coastal plains benefit from being in the shadow of this range because generous amounts of rainfall are precipitated as clouds are driven by winds from the south west. A number of rivers rise in the Western Ghats and flow eastwards across the Deccan plateau. The Kaveri, Kistna, and Godavari are notable rivers, and agriculture has flourished in the deltas formed on the coastal plains where the rivers join the sea. The soil quality and levels of rainfall are distinctly variable across the Deccan plateau. The black cotton soil in the area immediately east of Bombay is highly fertile, well watered by rainfall, and supports the crop it is named after (Farmer, 1983). Other parts of the Deccan are noted for poor soil and a lack of rainfall. The Ghats cast a rain-shadow over some areas and the risk of drought is high in the centre of the plateau. A desperate lack of water rules out the possibility of agriculture in some of these areas and as much as 20 per cent of the region is described as wasteland. Across much of the Deccan plateau agriculture is only possible because of irrigation (Robinson, 1972). The availability, or lack, of water determines the possibilities for agriculture. Crops like cotton, rice and wheat require more water and are confined to areas with higher rainfall or good irrigation. Other crops such as millet or gram require less rainfall but are less profitable for farmers. The cooler climate of hilly areas in various parts of India opens other possibilities, like the cultivation of tea and coffee. Human interventions have reduced some of the environmental restrictions on agriculture. The construction of tanks and canals, some of the latter dating back over a thousand years, enabled more intensive agriculture to take place. More recently artificial fertilizers, genetically modified (GM) crops and tube well irrigation have allowed new crops to be introduced. However, the environmental limits have not been removed, as the over-ambitious cultivation of water-hungry crops has shown. The overuse of tube wells to draw underground water has depleted the water table in many areas and put the livelihoods of some farmers in jeopardy. The introduction of many water-hungry GM crops has also contributed to the farmers' plight, in addition to which many GM strains do not re-seed, requiring the farmer to buy new seeds each season.

Natural Resources

India has a moderate allocation of natural resources. As noted in the previous section, attempts have been made to maximize the gains from India's water resources. The partition of India in 1947 divided not only people, but it also split infrastructure that was never intended to be divided, including irrigation systems. The river systems in the Punjab were reorganized under the terms of the Indus Water Treaty in 1960, an agreement brokered by the World Bank. The management of river systems that flow through India and Bangladesh have been more troubled.

India has also initiated numerous dam-based irrigation and hydro-electric projects. The most controversial of these are the dams of the river Narmada in central India. Arundhati Roy, the prize-winning author of *The God of Small Things* (1997), has been very vocal in her support of this movement, and participated in the (unsuccessful) direct action against their creation. The damming of the river, as with other dams in the region, was extremely controversial because their construction (which is ongoing) will result in the flooding and subsequent destruction of over 245 villages (Narmada Valley Development Authority, n.d). The grievances of the families who have been, or will be displaced, continue to this day, and are further discussed in Chapter 5.

With such a large and rising population and a fast-growing economy, the demand for other raw resources is great. India has some of these raw materials, including iron ore, manganese, bauxite and mica. India is the third largest coal producer in the world, and also its third largest consumer (after China and the US). It retains most of its reserves for domestic use, and had to import coking coal for industrial use. Although India has reserves of oil, and there are hopes of further finds from ongoing exploration, it has to import the majority of its oil. India has a policy of subsidizing oil products, which is a difficult policy to maintain with a trend of rising prices for crude. As this commodity has to be imported at international prices, this policy puts a strain on public finances (Vaswani, 2007). This pressure will only increase as India's vast energy needs grow and international prices continue to rise. India has reserves of natural gas but these are insufficient to meet its energy needs, and it is in this context that the proposed gas pipelines, either from Central Asia (which would have to run through Afghanistan and Pakistan) or from Iran (which would have to run through Pakistan), are so vital and help explain India's renewed interest in Afghanistan, a subject to which we return in Chapter 8.

The People

There are many ways of classifying the people of India. In this chapter we discuss the religious and linguistic profiles of India. The social hierarchy of caste is an alternative form of classification. In this chapter we show how caste is linked to the Hindu religion but say much more about caste in Chapter 4. Another alternative, derived from economic status, is class, again discussed in Chapter 4. In that chapter we also consider how gender structures the population of India. A minority of the Indian population are the *adivasis* (indigenous people) who live somewhat apart from the rest of Indian society in that their social system is separate from the caste system and they have their own religious traditions. The state classifies many of this minority as 'Scheduled Tribes' and the 2001 census recorded 8.2 per cent of the populations in this category. We say more about the adivasis later in the chapter. The location in which people live offers another way of describing India's population, for example, the differences between cities and countryside. Important regional differences also shape the way that people think about themselves. A strong, but by no means the only, influence over these regional differences is language, and we draw out some of these links towards the end of this chapter. We begin our discussion of the people of India by looking at the size of India's population.

India will have the world's largest population within a few decades if its population continues to grow at its present rate. India's population live in diverse and unequal circumstances. The fertility rate of over 2.7 children per woman is higher than is needed for sustaining the population; furthermore it is regionally skewed. Most of the states in the south of the country, such as Kerala, Tamil Nadu and Karnataka, have undergone a transition to lower population growth rates. Northern states such as Uttar Pradesh and Bihar continue to have high fertility rates. These states are also the poorest in India (when measured in terms of GDP per capita) and the link between large family sizes and low levels of female education that has been observed elsewhere in the world also holds true in India. In the southern states of India, the fertility rate has dropped – not coincidentally these are the states in which female literacy is highest. In the 1970s the Indian state launched a drive to reduce the population through the use of sterilization. This policy was vigorously pursued by Indira Gandhi's son, Sanjay, targeting some of the most vulnerable sections of society; those less likely to protest effectively. Officials were given quotas of men and women to sterilize and often resorted to compulsory sterilization when there were not enough volunteers. This policy failed to address other developmental needs such as 'improved female education, nutrition and health' (Gwatkin, 1979: 52). Overall, it had a detrimental effect on future campaigns to curb family size in the north of the country.

Slow economic growth between the 1940s and 1970s limited the resources available for public welfare services. India has excellent medical facilities for those who can afford to pay. Wealthy middle-class families opt for fee-paying private schools. India has an extensive system of higher education (though of variable quality). The Indian Institutes of Technology (IITs) are extremely successful – and the demand for places is high. But, for the majority of the population, access to even basic education, sanitation or medical facilities is uneven. Facilities are often under-resourced and under-staffed. Many different governments have promised to improve access to these services for the poor, but much remains to be done.

In recent years, India's economy has been growing at a healthy rate of close to 8 per cent (see Table 2.1). Following the global credit crunch, growth slowed, but in the first quarter of 2010 India returned to 8 per cent growth. India's growing prosperity is not evenly distributed. Extreme poverty remains the lot of roughly a third of the population. India's central planning, embraced by Nehru in the 1950s, was bureaucratic and vulnerable to corrupt practice. The trickledown effect that neo-liberal economists in India assumed would occur after economic liberalization in 1991 has had a limited impact. As we discuss in Chapter 7, the proportion of the population living in poverty has fallen. However, the absolute number living in poverty is sobering and income inequality has increased (ADB, 2008: 128).

An interesting feature of contemporary India is its diaspora. The economy of the British Empire encouraged the migration of Indians overseas. A system of indentured labour was used to move workers to areas of labour shortage inside the British Empire. Sugar and tea plantations required substantial labour input and low wages made it difficult to recruit local workers. Agents would recruit labour in poorer parts of India, arrange for their transportation and give them a contract of several years' duration. Demand for labour was high in Malaya (now Malaysia and Singapore), Ceylon (now Sri Lanka), East Africa, Fiji and the West Indies. The labourers who survived the hazards of this system, which was often not far removed from slavery, often settled in the areas where they were employed. Other colonial migrants included members of trading families who sought out business opportunities overseas. Since the 1940s migration has periodically been encouraged as a solution to labour shortages in the UK. The wealthy oil economies in the Gulf region have attracted Indian workers since the 1970s. More recently, Indians have been drawn into a global economy for skilled labour, most notably in the Information Technology (IT) industry but also in business and medicine. Annually richer families send 160,000 of their children to be educated abroad, destinations of choice being the United States of America, the United Kingdom and Australia (Baty, 2009). Taken together, a sizeable diaspora has been created. The Indian diaspora has changed its character in the last few decades. Not only has it grown but it also includes a very wealthy and influential segment. Indian entrepreneurs have made their mark in the UK and the US. Several notable Silicon Valley companies have been formed by graduates of the IITs. The links between India and its diaspora are varied. Until very recently the Indian state did not regard Non-Resident Indians (NRIs) warmly.

Table 2.1   Per capita GNI
growth since 2000

2000–01	1.8
2001–02	3.7
2002–03	2.0
2003–04	7.0
2004–05	5.6
2005–06	8.0
2006–07	8.2
2007–08	7.6
2008–09	4.9

Source: Growth rates calculated by
Kunal Sen. Based on data from the
Reserve Bank of India
(http://www.rbi.org.in/home.aspx).

Policy has changed since the 1991 economic reforms. Various schemes have been devised to encourage NRI investments (Adeney and Lall, 2005). The BJP coalition devised the Person of Indian Origin (PIO) category in 1999 and in late 2005 the category of Overseas Citizenship of India (OCI) was introduced. Although this does not confer dual citizenship or voting rights, it does relax restrictions on entry to the country and confer other educational and economic advantages (Ministry of Home Affairs, 2009). In 2008 the World Bank estimated that India would receive $30 billion from its diaspora, more than China (*The Economist*, 2009c). The descendents of the earliest migrants tend to have the loosest ties to India. More recent migrants are most likely to return periodically to India. The Hindu nationalist movement has targeted the Hindu diaspora for support. Members of India's diaspora have access to the corridors of power, and have set up powerful lobbying groups in the US and UK. We give examples of their activity in Chapter 8.

India or Bharat? India's Cities and Villages

India is still a country that lives in its villages. We discuss the rate of urbanization in Chapter 4 but note here that the 2001 census recorded the rural population at 72 per cent of the total, a slight drop from 1991. Villages vary greatly, as one would expect from so many villages and many different regions, so we can only offer tentative generalizations. Agriculture is at the core of the rural economy. Unequal ownership of land is a common feature of village life. Sharma describes a typical north Indian village which illustrates this: two-thirds of the families in a village did not own any land at all; a further 20 per cent owned small plots of land; and 90 per cent of the land was owned by 15 per cent of the households (S. Sharma, 1999: 162–4). The shortage of land and the difficult position of marginal farmers mean that the number of households without any land has been increasing in villages across India. Employment for those without land tends to be poorly paid and seasonal. Wealthier families live in some comfort, in spacious brick-built houses, and poorer families tend to have houses of traditional construction with thatched roofs. The quality of services available to rural households tends to be poor. Electricity supply is often erratic with long periods without power. Not all villages have a connection to the electricity grid. The roads linking villages to nearby towns are of uneven quality – not all roads are in good repair or have an all-weather surface. The quality and availability of medical services also tends to be poor, obliging villagers to travel to the nearby town. A village may have a primary school but it is not always open. Overall, the quality of services has improved in recent decades, as is evidenced by increased life expectancy, which increased from 42 years in 1960, to 65 years in 2007 (World Bank, 2009a) and higher levels of literacy, but the rural population is anxious to see improvements in the quality of life. There are strong pressures to migrate in search of work.

India's urban population was measured in the 2001 census as 284 million or 28 per cent of the population. Towns and cities are of great economic importance. They have experienced rapid economic growth and there is concentration of wealth in urban areas; recent studies estimate that between 50 per cent and 55 per cent of India's gross national product is generated in urban areas (Mathur, 2002: 1). India has many leading cities including New Delhi, Mumbai, Kolkata, Chennai and Bangalore. The economies of these metropolitan cities are extremely buoyant but the wealth of the cities is not evenly distributed and living conditions vary substantially. Bangalore, India's equivalent of 'Silicon Valley' has a thriving economy that has benefited from public sector investment in technology, software companies and services such as outsourced call centres. The cities of Chennai and Hyderabad have also gained from investments in software and foreign direct investment. The newfound prosperity of these cities cannot obscure the

Illustration 2.2   The slums of Mumbai

It is estimated that over half of Mumbai's population live in slums, such as the one pictured above. Over a million of Mumbai's inhabitants live in one slum, Dharavi, as portrayed in the film *Slumdog Millionaire* (Boyle and Tandan, 2008).

problems of urban development. Investment in water supply, drains, sewers, roads and public transport has tended to be insufficient. Slums are a common feature of Indian cities, even in those such as Bangalore with a thriving economy. A recent report estimated that 'India's cities need at least 25m more homes' (*The Economist*, 2009b). More public services are provided in cities but the poor struggle to access them as city developers often overlook informal developments. The 2001 census provides a figure of 42.6 million people living in slums. Slum dwellers usually live in a legal grey zone. City managers are reluctant to evict them but equally reluctant to regularize the status of their dwellings. Many of the residents of these informal settlements are extremely vulnerable, both because of their uncertain status and the difficulty of finding secure, well-paid employment.

The city of Mumbai, known as Bombay until it was renamed in 1995, illustrates the urban mix of prosperity and poverty. Property prices in Mumbai are high; prices per square metre are one of the highest in the world and the cost of accommodation has risen

Box 2.1   India versus Bharat

Some see a divide between city and countryside in Indian society and politics and express this divide using the phrase 'Bharat versus India'. The issue was raised, though not for the first time, in the 1980s by an emerging farmers' movement arguing for a better deal for farmers. The movement used the slogan 'Bharat versus India' to sum up their political claims. The Hindi term for India, 'Bharat', is used to refer to the countryside. The cities are represented by the term 'India'. The leaders of the farmers' movement argued that the countryside was being exploited by a combination of merchants, the city population and their allies in government (Corbridge *et al.*, 2005: 25). The divide can also be seen from the perspective of some in the city. A strong interpretation of India versus Bharat from the perspective of the city has a normative agenda whereby cities are seen as progressive and modern. The city is taken to be an indication of the future direction of the country. The assumption here is that the countryside is slow-moving and traditional. This interpretation is satirized in Aravind Adiga's novel *White Tiger* (2008), which ironically contrasts the 'lightness' of the modern economy of the big cities and the 'darkness' of the rest of India. A softer interpretation of the phrase 'India versus Bharat' is that differences in prosperity and quality of life between city and countryside need to be reduced. The United Progressive Alliance (UPA) Government since 2004 has reflected this sentiment and spoken of the need to reduce rural poverty. It has leaned towards the countryside by giving debt relief to farmers and introducing a scheme to increase rural employment.

markedly in other Indian cities as well (*The Economist*, 2007). The high accommodation prices prevent even reasonably prosperous middle-class families from purchasing this accommodation. According to the estimate of *The Economist* in 2007, half of Mumbai's population, including many of the middle class, live in slums. Madhura Swaminathan has profiled the social conditions experienced by the poor in Mumbai which gives a sense of the general problems faced by the poor living in the larger Indian cities. The city-level statistics reveal rates of employment and literacy that are higher than most other parts of India. However, these advances are negated by very poor living conditions experienced by the majority of the population that live in the slums of Mumbai. The slums are located in very unpleasant locations which are often polluted and susceptible to flooding (which brings further pollution). Other environmental hazards include proximity to power pylons.

The accommodation is poorly built and crowded. A majority of households in Mumbai live in only one room. Access to toilets and washing facilities is poor. Some slums have no public toilet facilities at all, which leaves no alternative to open-air defecation. As well as being highly unpleasant for all who live and work in the neighbourhood, this increases the risk of spreading disease (Swaminathan, 2003: 87–94).

The experience of the famous Mumbai slum, Dharavi, provides another example. It occupies a minuscule 2.2 square km and has a population of over a million. The population is incredibly diverse, with migrants from all corners of India having made it their home. Dharavi is home to many Muslims, lower caste and Dalit migrants. It has a lively economy. Industries in and around the slum provide cooked food for hotels and bakeries and Dharavi is well known for its leather goods and pottery. State agencies do not penetrate the slum very effectively. So industry is unregulated (an 80-hour working week is not uncommon), census figures are unreliable, voter lists are incomplete and not all residents can get the ration card that should give them access to affordable food supplies. Yet determined action by residents has enabled them to get electricity connections, better water supplies, public toilets, and the covering of most open drains. Longer-term residents have earned a legal right to tenure and are able to build permanent houses if they can afford to do so and persuade neighbours to join them. Dharavi is still a crowded and challenging neighbourhood to live in but its residents have brought a certain order to it (Fuchs, 2005: 105–6, 116).

Adivasis

The adivasis are a numerically substantial minority. There is much debate about the definition and enumeration of this group. The Government of India has, as its own category, the Scheduled Tribes (ST), which is a list of 'tribal' people of India who are eligible to benefit from affirmative action policies. The ST list of more than 700 groups also forms a category when data are gathered for the census. Many writers and activists prefer the term adivasi, which has a broader meaning than the ST list (which does not include all groups that claim to be adivasis). The claim that the adivasis are the indigenous people of India is politically useful as it locates them in global discussions of the rights of indigenous populations. For this reason the government disputes the claim that the adivasis are the indigenous people of India (Xaxa, 2003: 378–9). The term 'tribal' is not universally accepted either. Leaders of some groups reject the term, either preferring the term 'hill people' or seeing themselves as being part of a distinct ethnic group (Omvedt, 1993: 252). The terms 'tribal' and 'Scheduled Tribe' also connote stereotypes that can be traced back to the colonial period. The tribes are frequently said to live remotely, usually in the forests and jungles of India. This remoteness is equated with a pre-modern economy untainted by the harmful aspects of development. A common image is one of a simple people living equally, in a state of innocence and at a distance from mainstream society. These stereotypes suggested the need for protection from outside influences and this was by and large the British policy, which included the use of protected areas to shelter adivasis from the depredations of incomers. The 1950 constitution continued many aspects of this paternalist policy but added a new dimension by giving the Indian state a responsibility for the development of tribal peoples (Corbridge, 2000: 68). Hence the category of Scheduled Tribes was created to identify those eligible for 'uplift' by the state.

The stereotypes do reflect, however unclearly, some important aspects of the social position of the adivasis. Groups of people with distinct ethnic identities do claim special affinities with remote localities. Some regard the forest as being their birthright, making economic and cultural use of the land. Their ethnic identity is usually reinforced by a distinct language and culture. Adivasi religious practices are often distinct from Hindu traditions, and adivasis do not usually participate in the caste segmentation that divides mainstream society. There is enormous diversity among the adivasi population of India, with many different languages and divergent customs in use. Two concentrations of the Scheduled Tribes stand out. More than half of the population live in the parts of central India covered by the states of Chhattisgarh, Jharkhand, Madhya Pradesh, Maharashtra and Orissa. In many of the states of the north east, STs are a majority. A number of groups, namely the Bhils, Bodos, Gonds, Minas, Mundas, Oraons and Santhals have a population of over a million (Xaxa, 2003: 380–1). Some groups are very small, such as the Todas in the Nilgiris with a population of just 1560 in 2001. Adivasi groups may form a minority in more than one state. So, the Santhals are well established in Jharkhand, Orissa and West Bengal. In addition, they were among the indentured labourers brought to the tea gardens of Assam, and an identifiable Santhal population continues to live there.

That said, the adivasis have experienced great change in modern India. Their economic position is not uniform. Forested areas have been used as a resource for national development. Dams, mineral extraction and logging have brought environmental devastation to areas in which many adivasis live (Gadgil and Guha, 1992: 193–7). Adivasis have lost land to incomers and many have been displaced by the large projects of the state and private sector alike. At the same time some adivasis, albeit a minority, have experienced prosperity with the spread of education and economic development. The idea that adivasis live in 'a splendid or primitive isolation' cannot be supported by the experience of areas like Jharkhand where development has 'brought factories, roads and outsiders' (Corbridge, 2000: 74). A background assumption in discussions of the adivasis is that they live at a distance, cultural and/or physical, from the mainstream of Indian society. It is difficult to make a strong generalization about the issue of separateness. It is unlikely that many groups have completely avoided interactions with others. Over time, contact with Indian society has intensified for the reasons given above. Social distinctions within adivasi communities have sharpened as well with the formation of new class groups, and social distinctions akin to the kinship arrangements of caste groups have not been absent either. Adivasis have migrated and have a growing urban profile. Some adivasis have converted to Christianity, and the provision of education by missionaries contributed to the growth of a middle class among the adivasis. The impact of surrounding society has been much discussed with some evidence of convergence between adivasi religions and Hinduism being observed. Some adivasis have reverted to their earlier religious practices and dissociated themselves from Hinduism (Xaxa, 2003: 400–03).

India's Diversity

India is renowned for its diversity – and a variety of identities demarcate the population of India. These identities are based around language, religion, region, gender, race and tribe. India's people speak many different languages and follow many different religious traditions, cuisines and cultures. Differences in skin colour and facial features can be discerned across many regions of India. However, migration patterns over the millennia have contributed to diversity even within regions and states, and the origins of the different communities in India occasionally become a political issue. Assertion by the so-called 'sons of the soil' against 'outsiders' might be related to the diversity within a particular region (as in the case of Assam) or it might be tied to a discourse about the racial authenticity of the original inhabitants of a region. So, for example, it is claimed that the original Dravidian inhabitants of south India were oppressed following an 'Aryan' invasion from north India. The notion of an 'Aryan' invasion is deeply contested but it remains a powerful, though controversial, political idea.

The salience of different identities has varied over time and according to political circumstances. Yet compared to many other countries in the world which are very ethnically diverse, India has been remarkably stable, and has also remained democratic, with the exception of the Emergency (1975–7). Although conflicts have occurred between the state and members of different groups, as well as between different states, given the large size of its population, India is much more stable than the common perception. The differences discussed in this chapter can become the basis of social identities. In other words they influence the way that individuals think about the collective group(s) of which they are a member. Indeed most of these social markers can be used as a basis for constructing an ethnic identity.

Religion

The majority of the population of India are Hindus. As discussed in Chapter 1, India was partitioned in 1947 by the British ostensibly on the basis of religion. After the creation of Pakistan, the proportion of Hindus as a percentage of the population increased dramatically, from 66 per cent to 85 per cent of the population. However, sizeable religious minorities remained, as can be seen in Table 2.2.

Hinduism originated in India. While over 80 per cent of the population are Hindu, they are not homogeneous. The Hindu religion is plural. This is hinted at in the term 'Hindu', which was derived from the Arabic term used to refer to the people living on the other side of the Indus River. Of course, most religions are divided into different traditions (for example Christianity into Catholic and Protestant, Islam between Sunni and Shia). But unlike Christianity and Islam, Hinduism is not usually monotheistic and there is no single religious text which is a universal reference point. Many Hindus, but not all, give central importance to a body of text known as the Veda. These texts set out ritual practices and are the source of *mantra*, verses used

Table 2.2 A comparison of religious groups in India, 1951 and 2001

Religious group	Absolute numbers 1951	Percentage of population 1951	Absolute numbers 2001	Percentage of population 2001	Difference
Hindus	304,441,631	84.94	827,578,868	80.46	– 4.48
Muslims	35,803,227	9.99	138,188,240	13.43	+ 3.44
Christians	8,161,293	2.28	24,080,016	2.34	+ 0.06
Sikhs	6,297,191	1.76	19,215,730	1.87	+ 0.11
Buddhists	240,743	0.07	7,955,207	0.77	+ 0.7
Jains	1,620,170	0.45	4,225,053	0.41	– 0.04
Others	1,847,627	0.52	7,367,214	0.72	+ 0.2
Total	358,411,882	100	1,028,610,328	100	0

Sources: adapted from 1951 and 2001 Census of India (Government of India, 1953; Government of India, 2001b).

in worship. Three other notable texts, which are very popular, are the *Mahabharata*, the *Ramayana* and the *Puranas*. Hinduism is a theistic religion and many different gods are worshipped. Some gods, including Siva, Vishnu and Ganesh, are worshipped in many locations across India. Other deities have a following in a small area. A god may be particular to a village or known in one region. Many argue that the individual gods are different representations of a single transcending God (Flood, 1996: 5–14, 35–8 and 103–8). There is no equivalent of a church hierarchy for Hinduism. Larger temples visited by Hindus will be served by a resident Brahman priesthood. These priests lead acts of worship and also preside over life-cycle rituals, such as weddings and funerals. A number of very senior leaders, *shankaracharya*, have the title and are widely respected, but there is no supreme leader or institutional forum in which they cooperate. Instead, each shankaracharya will be associated with a particular *mutt*, or monastery (Fuller, 2003).

There are numerous traditions within Hinduism. The most prominent traditions are Saivism and Vaishnavism. Siva is the deity at the centre of Saivism. Vishnu and his incarnations are central to Vaishnavism. Both traditions have a broad following across India and have a Brahmanic orientation. In other words, the traditions are rooted in the ritual language of Sanskrit and upheld by Brahman priesthoods. The large temples tend to be associated with one or another of these traditions. There are also smaller traditions with local deities in which devotion is expressed in regional languages. These traditions are popular, and are especially attractive to lower-caste worshippers (Flood, 1996: 171–8). We discuss nationalist ideologies in more detail in Chapter 6 but it is worth noting here that Hindu nationalists have considered the extreme pluralism of Hindu religious practice to be a source of weakness. They have tried to promote unity among Hindus and make the Hindu religion more homogenous. To this end they encourage senior Hindu religious leaders to meet and cooperate. They hope to gain the support of these leaders and create something approximating a religious hierarchy. Hindu nationalist organizations have tried to give certain elements of Hinduism more of a pan-Indian appeal by encouraging Hindus to worship in a similar way. So, for example, Hindu nationalists in south India have popularized a festival in which images of the god Ganesh are immersed in water. The festival was already popular in western India. A great deal of attention has been paid to Ram, an incarnation of Vishnu, who is the central figure of the

Temple architecture in India varies enormously between regions. A distinctive feature of many south Indian temples is the *gopuram*, a tower that is often highly decorated. The Meenakshi temple has four main entrances on its outside walls and a gopuram towers over each one.

Illustration 2.3   Shree Meenakshi Temple, Madurai

Ramayana epic. However, even Ram is worshipped in different fashions. The popular festival of light, Diwali, which celebrates the return of Ram and Sita to Ayodhya following their exile to the south of India (events depicted in the *Ramayana*), is celebrated differently across the country and has taken on different significance in different areas.

The social hierarchy of caste is closely linked to Hindu religious practice. A key element of Hinduism is the notion of *dharma* or moral order of society. Individuals have a duty to fulfil their social obligations, which include correct behaviour according to status of the caste group to which they belong (Flood, 1996: 11–12). The *varna* classification, discussed in more detail in Chapter 4, can be used to put a caste group into one of four occupational groups – *Brahman* (priestly), *Kshatriya* (warrior), *Vaisya* (merchant) and *Sudra* (artisan).

Illustration 2.4   Preparing Diwali candles

The candles are washed and then left to dry in the sun, before being filled with oil (from the Coke bottle in the picture), ready for lighting. The candles symbolize the candles lit to welcome Ram and Sita back to Ayodhya after their exile.

These categories are only notionally related to occupation. Caste status is inherited and ritually determined. One cannot change caste status by changing occupations. The varna categories are referred to in Hindu sacred texts such as the *Rig Veda* and the *Manusmrti*. The standing of a caste group is estimated according to the ritual purity of that group. Higher-status groups are considered to be more pure and in danger of polluting that purity if they come into the wrong kind of contact with a caste group considered to be less pure. As Ludden notes, 'it is the distinctions, not the similarities among countless caste groups (jatis) that form the primary basis of Hindu social identity' (1996: 6). The ultimate logic of the idea of ritual purity is that some are considered so impure that they are deemed 'untouchable' and said to be outside the caste system. At the top of the ritual hierarchy are Brahman priestly castes. Another key divide in the caste system is between the so-called twice-born castes, which include Brahmans, Kshatriyas and Vaisyas, compared to the Sudras. Members of the twice-born castes are said to have progressed to a special stage in the process of rebirth and reincarnation. Male members of twice-born castes are entitled to wear a sacred thread over their shoulder and around their upper body to signify their status. These upper-caste groups are a minority, constituting about 11 per cent of the Indian population (Varshney, 2000: 9).

The institution of caste is a controversial one given the unequal outcomes and discrimination it produces, which we discuss in Chapter 4. Caste has also become intertwined with party politics, as we show in Chapter 5. Since the early nineteenth century a number of Hindu reform movements have emerged. The caste system has commonly featured in proposals for religious change. Gandhi argued for the retention of the caste system after it had been purged of the practice of untouchability. A number of Dalit critics have also taken up the issue. Dr Ambedkar strongly attacked Hindu beliefs and practices, arguing that they upheld caste discrimination. He followed this up by converting to Buddhism at the end of his life. Many of Ambedkar's followers did likewise and this has contributed to a revival of the Buddhist tradition in India (and partially explains the sharp increase in the number of Buddhists shown in the census figures in Table 2.1). Dalit critics have also focused on the plural nature of Hindu traditions in India. They have returned to the much discussed question of how extensive the Hindu tradition actually is. This question was initially raised by British census enumerators and strongly contested by nationalist politicians keen to unify Indian society and keep to a minimum the number of officially recognized divisions. More recently, some Dalit activists expressed the view that the religious traditions of the lower castes are quite separate from the Brahmanic religions favoured by the upper castes and should not be called Hindu at all (Ilaiah, 1996).

The other religions may be small in terms of their proportion of the population, but their absolute numbers are huge. As can be seen from Table 2.2, in 2001 there were approximately 139 million Muslims within India. This is the third largest Muslim population in the world, after the 204 million Muslims in Indonesia and 164 million Muslims in Pakistan. Yet in Indian terms they are a small minority. Hasan notes that India contains 'a bewildering diversity of Muslim communities' (1997: 7). The Muslims of India are primarily Sunni but approximately 18 per cent are Shia (Mukerjee, 2005). Unlike in neighbouring Pakistan, violent sectarian conflict between Shias and Sunnis is rare. However, conflicts between Shias and Sunnis exist; Hasan notes that in parts of Lucknow, a town with a large number of Muslims in

Illustration 2.5   The view from Jama Masjid, Delhi

The Jama Masjid in Delhi is situated in Old Delhi. It is India's largest
mosque. It was commissioned by the Mughal Emperor Shah Jahan (who
also commissioned the Taj Mahal in Agra, and the Red Fort in Delhi).

Uttar Pradesh, conflict between the two sects is often greater than
between Hindus and Muslims (1997: 8).

As well as differences between sects of Islam, differences exist
within sects. Sunni Islam in India is divided most prominently between
the Deobandi and Barelvi schools and also between the Tablighi
Jamaat and the Jamaat-i-Islami, founded by Maulana Maududi (Hasan,
1997: 7 and 196–210). Shias are also divided. The two best known
traditions are the Twelvers and Ismailis. Sufi-ism is the final prominent
sect, an offshoot from Sunni Islam, known for their mysticism. The
differences between, as well as within, the different traditions/sects are
too complex to enumerate here, but it is important to note that to talk
of a Muslim 'community' in India, ignores not only the regional and
linguistic diversity, but also attitudes of belief. It is too simplistic to
assume that Islam in India is a religion simply transmitted by an invading power. Much of Indian Islam is syncretic in nature, having been
adapted locally and drawing on other elements of Indian culture.

As Ludden notes, 'Islam is as old in India as in Turkey [and] older
than American Christianity and European Protestantism . . . [it has]

very deep roots indeed' (Ludden, 1996: 5). Muslims are primarily concentrated in the north of the country, in the states of Uttar Pradesh, Bihar, Jammu and Kashmir, Assam and Bengal. But there is a sizeable population in the south of the country; especially in the state of Kerala. Islam has diverse roots in India. Arab traders brought their religion to the Malabar Coast in Kerala in the seventh and eighth centuries, and trading routes disseminated the religion more widely. The invasion of northern India from central Asia from the eleventh century spread Islam in that area. The political dominance of the newly arrived rulers brought Islam to prominence. The central Asian invaders and migrants who came to the Indian subcontinent when much of the territory of India was ruled by the Delhi Sultanate and the Mughal Empire were accorded high status. 'Muslims who claim foreign descent . . . claim a superior status for themselves as *ashraf* or "noble"' (Sikkand, 2004: 110). This status differs from non-Ashraf Muslims who are said to have converted to Islam. There were a variety of incentives to do so, including ingratiation on the part of those seeking political favour. In addition, the egalitarian theology of Islam appealed to some with low status in the Hindu caste system. As we shall see below, religious conversion has often been used by those suffering the stigma of untouchability within Hindu society. However, as noted above, status differences are also observed among Muslims in India, and '[c]aste exists as a basis of social relations, although it differs from the Hindu caste system in details' (Hasan, 1997: 8).

Just as Hinduism in India is regionally differentiated, so is Islam. Muslims in India are not united as a political force; many Muslim leaders left for Pakistan, and the prominent Muslim politicians such as Maulana Kalam Azad who remained were usually associated with the ruling Congress Party. These politicians, often subscribing to the one nation theory, were not interested in representing Muslims as a separate community, but rather as Indians. In the final stages of drafting the Indian constitution, reserved seats for Muslims were removed. We discuss the issue of reserved seats further in Chapter 6.

Muslims in India have generally had a lower educational, economic and social status. Muslim votes have become more important for certain political parties in a few regions of India since the party system has fractionalized (as discussed in Chapter 5). Political parties such as the Samajwadi Party (SP) in Uttar Pradesh, the Telugu Desam Party (TDP) in Andhra Pradesh and the Rashtriya

Janata Dal (RJD) in Bihar all articulate programmes designed to attract Muslim voters.

The Christian population is equally diverse. The earliest Christian community to establish itself in India was a branch of the Syrian tradition which has been present in India for at least fifteen centuries. Some claim that the visit of St Thomas to India in AD 46 led to the conversions which established this community. The Syrian tradition is well established in what is now the state of Kerala. The activity of Portuguese missionaries in the sixteenth and seventeenth centuries laid the foundations of the Roman Catholic Church in India, and Christians comprise 30 per cent of the population of what is now the state of Goa (the Portuguese colony was forcibly integrated into the Indian state under Nehru in 1961). The two existing Christian traditions in India were joined by a third as Protestant missionaries began working in India during the eighteenth century. This missionary activity intensified during the nineteenth century, although the 1858 Act which proclaimed India to be part of the British Empire contained references to discouraging the activities of the missionaries. The Protestant Church became established as a result of the 'mass movement' conversions of the late nineteenth and early twentieth centuries. Indian Christians were reckoned in 2001 to number 24 million or 2.3 per cent of the population. The largest proportion of the Christian population in India is concentrated in the four southern states of Kerala, Tamil Nadu, Karnataka and Andhra Pradesh. It is only in some of the small north-eastern states that Christians actually form a majority of the population (Mizoram, Nagaland and Meghalaya).

Caste has also had an influence on Indian Christians (Wyatt, 1998). Most of the mass movement converts were Dalits who found Christianity attractive because they suffered the stigma of untouchability within Hindu society. However, a change of religion did not completely remove the burden of untouchability. Converts to Christianity often maintained their caste traditions, including patterns of marriage and social contact. Hindu society continued caste discrimination against Dalit converts, as Ursula Sharma notes: 'where the low and untouchable castes were concerned, their conversion to Christianity changed the attitudes of high castes to them not one whit' (1999: 78–9). Discrimination also blighted social interaction within many churches. It was not unknown for separate communion rails and graveyards to be reserved for Dalit Christians and Christians from upper-caste backgrounds. Until very recently, few Dalit Christians were ordained as priests. Relations between Hindus and Christians were generally good, however, in the mid 1990s there was a sharp increase in attacks on Christians, the most infamous of which was the burning to death of the missionary Graham Staines and his two sons in their car in the state of Orissa in 1999 (Zavos, 2001). These attacks in Orissa have continued – in 2008 Christians were subject to severe reprisals after the killing of a prominent Hindu leader (for which a Maoist group claimed responsibility). The increase in violence can be directly attributed to the rise of Hindu nationalism – Christians are viewed as 'foreign' to India, it is argued that their allegiance lies outside India. As noted, similar arguments are applied to Muslims, whether or not they were the descendants of converts or the descendants of migrants/invaders. Conversion has always been controversial in Indian politics, and despite Article 25 of the Indian constitution guaranteeing 'the right freely to profess, practise and propagate religion', laws banning religious conversion by 'allurements or force' have been passed in many states, including Orissa, Madhya Pradesh and Arunachal Pradesh. In 1977 the Indian Supreme Court, ruling on the constitutionality of these laws, made a distinction between propagation of religion and conversion to that religion. It observed that '[w]e have no doubt that . . . what the Article grants is not the right to convert another person to one's own religion, but to transmit or spread one's religion by an exposition of its tenets' (Aruna, 2002). These issues continue to be controversial.

The Sikh population is slightly smaller than the Christian population, comprising fewer than 2 per cent of the population, but they are also much more territorially concentrated. The Sikh religion was inspired from the ideas of Guru Nanak in the fifteenth century. Sikhism is monotheistic. The five religious symbols of Sikhism (the five K's) are: the *Kesh* (uncut hair), *Kanga* (a wooden comb), *Kara* (a steel bracelet), *Kirpan* (sword) and *Kachera* (short trousers).

Sikhs are concentrated in the state of Punjab; the Sikh 'homeland' where the Golden Temple is located. The Golden Temple is the most holy site of Sikhism due to the residence of the Sikh holy book, the *Guru Granth Sahib* (also known as the eleventh Guru) within it. At the time of partition in 1947 the Punjab was divided, and many Sikh holy sites, including the birthplace of Guru Nanak, ended up on the 'wrong' side of the border. Many Sikhs migrated from the areas in the Punjab which were awarded to Pakistan. Some moved to the capital of India, New Delhi, where there remains a sizeable Sikh community. Sikhs (and Punjabis of other religions) were traditionally viewed as a martial race by the British Raj, and today they are well represented in the Indian army (although their proportion has declined since the 1970s, a contributing factor in the conflict in the Punjab in the 1980s).

Many Hindus view Sikhs as lapsed Hindus or as a sect of Hinduism. This includes the BJP and the other members of the family of Hindu nationalist organizations, the Sangh Parivar. The Indian constitution, Article 25 (1b), states that 'the reference to Hindus shall be construed as including a reference to persons professing the Sikh, Jaina or Buddhist religion'. It 'therefore adopted the Hindu Nationalist framework of viewing Sikhs, Jains, and Buddhists as "Indian" and part of the "Hindu" family' (Adeney, 2007: 97).

The Buddhist religion is also indigenous to India. It arose from the ideas and practice of Siddhartha Guatama who became known as the Buddha (the awakened) in the sixth century BC in northern India. Buddhism rejects the caste distinctions of Hinduism. Buddhists comprise less than one per cent of India's population, although Buddhism has spread widely throughout the world. The Mauryan Emperor Ashoka, who reigned from 268 BC to 239 BC, converted to Buddhism after the bloody conquest of Kalinga, in the area which is now the state of Orissa in India. His missionaries spread the faith to Sri Lanka, and subsequently it spread to many other countries in Asia. Although it has not been as successful in India as it has in other countries in Asia, in recent years, Buddhism has gained converts from the Dalit community. Its most famous convert was the Dalit political leader, and one of the authors of the Indian constitution, Ambedkar, whose statues can be found all over India. The increase of Buddhists (see Table 2.2) from 1951 to 2001 in relative terms can be mainly attributed to this conversion and that of his followers (although the annexation of Tibet by China in 1950 and the subsequent self-imposed exile of the Dalai Lama and thousands of his followers in Dharamsala in Himachal Pradesh, India also increased the Buddhist population).

The relationship between Hinduism and adivasi religions is a complex one. Some regard the adivasis as being within the very plural Hindu religious tradition. Ghurye (1980) argued that the adivasis had been 'Hinduized', and he identified a number of festivals, rituals and deities that were shared between the adivasi and Hindu religions. It is also the case that religious practice has changed, with some adivasis adopting more mainstream Hindu customs. Hindu missionaries, keen to claim the adivasis as part of a Hindu majority, have encouraged this trend. Others, including many adivasis, see their religious practices as being quite separate (Adivasi, 2009).

Since the 1980s, religion has become more politicized, and large numbers of people have been killed in infamous incidents of violence. High-profile incidents include the violence against Sikhs in Delhi in 1984, attacks on Muslims after December 1992 and the assault on Muslims in Gujarat in 2002. It is important to note that these major incidents can all be connected to a particular political event (such as the assassination of Indira Gandhi in 1984 and the aftermath of the destruction of the Babri Masjid in 1992). These outbreaks of violence were not the result of innate incompatibility between peoples of different religions. Interreligious violence has been frequently instigated for political motives. Several explanations have been used to explain why or how religion has been put to political use. Brass argues that political parties gain from such violence because they can pose as protectors of their favoured community (2003). Varshney argues that civic associations which bring communities together pre-empt violence (2002). Wilkinson argues that political parties can prevent riots if there are electoral incentives for them to do so (2004). What these explanations have in common is an appreciation that religious conflict is not inevitable. Some political leaders use riots to position themselves as protectors of one particular community. It is alleged that Congress politicians benefit from the secular image of protecting the Muslim minority. In contrast, Hindu nationalists stand to gain if they can provoke a violent response from among Muslims because it confirms the stereotypical image of Muslims as a source of threat, an 'enemy within' (Mayaram, 1993).

An example of a high-profile attempt to mobilize political support from a religious issue was the campaign to build a Ram temple in the north Indian town of Ayodhya. Hindu nationalists argued that a sixteenth-century mosque, the Babri Masjid, had been constructed over the birthplace of the god Ram. Street campaigns, which included invitations to the public to buy bricks to be used in the actual construction, attracted a good deal of attention. The demand for a Ram temple was made very forcefully, with some promising direct action to demolish the mosque if the authorities did not act. The campaign made Muslims apprehensive, and a particularly sensitive point in the campaign came in September and October 1990 when a *rath yatra* (pilgrimage by chariot) was organized. The leader of the BJP, L. K. Advani, set out to take a 'pilgrimage' in a vehicle made to resemble a chariot. The planned route ran from Somnath in Gujarat to Ayodhya in Uttar Pradesh. The rath yatra was seen by many as provocative. Tensions were heightened in many localities and riots broke out along the route (Mayaram, 1993: 2530; Davis, 1996: 27–9). In spite of violence associated with incidents like these, India has still managed to avoid the most severe consequences of interreligious violence. It is difficult to maintain sustained mobilization along religious lines because cross-cutting cleavages within India's large and diverse population make other appeals for political loyalty highly plausible.

Language and Region

India's linguistic diversity is notable. Hindi is the most widely spoken language in India. However, the definitions of 'Hindi-speakers' have varied between the different censuses of India. According to some definitions Hindi speakers comprise approximately 30 per cent of the population; in others they comprise approximately 40 per cent (the different definitions vary according to how many 'dialects' the census enumerators decide to classify as 'Hindi' rather than as separate dialects/languages). The majority of the population speak one of numerous other languages as their mother tongue. Outside of the northern Hindi heartland regional languages thrive. Most of these languages are territorially concentrated in states – especially since the linguistic reorganization of states in the 1950s – although these linguistic groups are internally differentiated.

Figure 2.1 below shows the 22 languages recognized in the Eighth Schedule of the Indian Constitution. Inclusion in the Eighth Schedule confers certain rights on a language, including the right of its speakers to sit exams for civil service employment in their mother tongue.

As the chart (Figure 2.1) demonstrates, Hindi is not the mother tongue of the majority of the population. The government of newly independent India was driven by a number of imperatives when it came to the issue of language. English was the language of the departing colonial power and some argued that genuine independence required it to be removed from official use. On the other hand, English was spoken by many elite figures in politics, business and education. Furthermore, English functioned as a link language between the leading figures from different linguistic regions. One alternative, favoured by quite a few nationalist leaders, was to make Hindi, the language spoken by the largest number of people but not the majority, the new national language of India. It was recognized that this was not an easy choice but proponents of this idea felt that a

Figure 2.1   Linguistic population of India, 2001

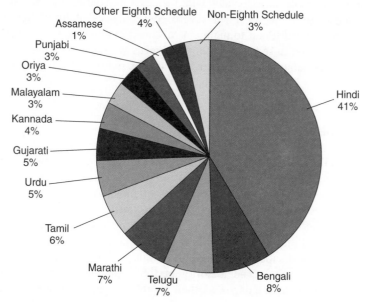

Source: Adapted from the 2001 Census of India (Government of India, 2001b).

mass drive to spread the use of Hindi would be a useful tool for nation building and the outcome would be highly efficient as communication across India would be greatly eased. The choice was an important one. The adoption of one language privileges speakers of that language over speakers of languages that are not selected for use in government business. These issues are the subject of discussion in Chapter 6. The choices of national and official languages are important for nurturing a shared national identity. The manner in which language issues were resolved says much about the process of nation building used by the Indian elite.

The links between language and regional identity are important. Language is an important medium for expressing cultural sentiments as well as being a cultural artefact in itself. Before 1947 a number of cultural movements had formed to promote the use of their language and argue for issues of special interest to their region. The administrative units of British India, including the provinces of the 1935 Act, did little to help the expression of coherent regional sentiments. For many it made sense for government business to be transacted in the local language. This implied the reorganization of the provincial/state level of government into linguistic units. We detail how this happened in the next chapter. The new states were not perfect reflections of regional sentiment (there are still linguistic minorities without a state of their own). No single Hindi-speaking state was formed either. That said, regional identities are much more coherently expressed in contemporary India. This is partly for party political reasons; we discuss the rise of regional parties in Chapter 5, but the formation of linguistic states was fundamentally important in the development of regional identity. The new states were official bodies prepared to support regional language and culture. Groups that were unrecognized were shown what might be possible if they lobbied for a separate state of their own.

Conclusion

The large and diverse land area of India ensured that it was difficult to unite the subcontinent under one government. Even when empires such as the Mughals or the British covered most of the territory of India, as discussed in Chapter 1, the extensive swathe of territory facilitated the introduction of structures of government with high levels of territorial autonomy. It would be extremely difficult to rule India without some devolution of power, and this devolution of power throughout history has ensured that different regional languages and cultures have survived and flourished. These are substantial challenges for political elites seeking to build a national community with an element of unity and shared purpose. However, India's diversity has not prevented a sense of 'Indianness' from emerging, although a consequence of India's regional diversity is that we have to use the term 'Indian culture' with great care. This is because culture shows great regional diversity. As we will discuss in detail in Chapter 6, for most Indians there is a shared sense of being Indian, although this sense of Indianness co-exists with other identities. It cannot be denied, however, that there are areas of India and sections of India's population for whom being 'Indian' is extremely problematic, often as a result of discrimination by the government, such as the areas of India that have experienced ethnic conflict. Often this reflects a strong sense of geographic or cultural isolation from the centres of power. There is a geographical aspect to contestation in Indian politics. Until the 1980s many saw the Hindi heartland in the north as dominating Indian politics. The decline of Congress and the rise of coalition politics altered this geography of power as non-Hindi speaking states became more influential in the central government. The 2004 election campaign raised the question of whether India was being dominated by the concerns of economic winners concentrated in the metropolitan cities. Others argue that extreme social inequality, such as that experienced by the Dalits, excludes some groups from a putative national community (Gorringe, 2008).

We need to be aware of cultural variety *within* the Indian states. There has been substantial migration within India so that minority groups exist which do not regard themselves as completely identified with the region where they now live. As would be expected, the extreme diversity has impacted on Indian politics and many identities have become politicized. In general however, as James Manor has persuasively argued, the cross-cutting nature of the cleavages in India has facilitated accommodation along many different lines (1996). This is because Indians have multiple identities. They have their religious identity, their linguistic identity and their caste identity (not to mention a gender identity and age identity). They also have a political and social and economic identity. This means that (for example) even if two individuals share a religious and a caste identity, a Hindu, Marathi speaker who is a Brahman is a rather different person from a Hindu, Tamil speaker who is a Brahman. These two individuals might share the same concerns about the status of their religious community, but be divided from each other over issues of language, state and region.

This multiplicity of identities has ensured that many Indians shift their 'preoccupations . . . prevent[ing] long running bitter conflict from developing along one fault-line in society' (Manor, 1996: 464). Thus diversity has contributed to, rather than hindered, the stability of the state. However, just because an individual has multiple identities does not mean that these identities are as important as each other or share the same weight. Which identity or identities are more prominent at one particular time is situational – often depending on the security of that identity. This security has often been promoted/or undermined by decisions taken by elites and choices of institutional structure, the subject of Chapters 3 and 6.

3

Governing Structures

Even six decades after independence, an outsider examining India's governing structures would be struck by their similarity to many British institutions. The similarity is not accidental. The British slowly developed parliamentary and federal institutions of government in the ways outlined in Chapter 1. These were not fully democratic or fully federal institutions but they were consistent with the logic of a parliamentary system. The elite that wrote the constitution gained their first experience of government in a system designed by British politicians and administrators convinced of the efficiency of their own institutions. Although the 1950 constitution has been amended 94 times since independence, its basic structure remains the same. What has changed more markedly, however, has been the society within which it operates. Contemporary India is a very different country than it was at the time of independence. These changes are discussed in more detail in the following chapters. Many of these changes have affected how the governing structures of India now operate; for example, the presidency, a largely ceremonial post, has grown in importance in recent years. The formal institutions have shown remarkable durability. The informal conventions that shape political behaviour have changed and contributed to a political system that operates rather differently than it did in the 1950s.

India's constitution is the longest in the world. As noted in Chapter 1, approximately two-thirds of the 1950 constitution was taken without amendment from the British-designed 1935 Government of India Act. India's sheer territorial size and diversity precluded a unitary state structure where all power resided in the central legislature. Instead, India is a federation, where powers are constitutionally divided between two levels of government: the centre and the states. India has a parliamentary system of government because the head of the government, the prime minister, is elected via the legislature and is not directly elected, as is the case where a president is the head of the government.

Executive

In India the head of state is the president who presides over formal state occasions and acts as a constitutional umpire. The president is indirectly elected by the two houses of the national legislature and the state assemblies. Important decisions are made by the prime minister and his or her cabinet who are collectively responsible to the legislature. The national legislature is divided between two houses. The lower house, known as the Lok Sabha, is the house in which the fate of a government is decided. A government continues only as long as it can survive a vote of confidence. The upper house, the Rajya Sabha, has considerably fewer powers. Many of the same conventions of parliamentary government in the UK also operate in India. By convention, if a government is defeated on a major policy issue it must resign. Similarly, if it loses a vote of no confidence, it must also resign, as the BJP-led coalition government did in 1999. Governments can call their own votes of confidence, as did Manmohan Singh's United Progressive Alliance (UPA) Government in 2008 after the left parties withdrew their support from the Government (over the issue of the nuclear treaty with the US). This served to legitimize the deal, and also strengthened the Government.

Prime Minister and Council of Ministers

India has a cabinet government and follows much of the Westminster tradition in this part of the executive. The president of India asks the leader of the parliamentary party, which can command a majority in the lower house of the legislature, to form the government. Until the late 1980s this was an obvious choice; with the exception of 1977, Congress won a majority of seats in the Lok Sabha. But since 1989 no single party has won a majority. All governments have been formed as coalitions and/or have been minority governments, supported from outside by parties not prepared to join the governing coalition. The 2004–9 UPA administration was a minority coalition government able to secure support from other parties. The UPA coalition secured a notable victory in the 2009 general election and was able to form a coalition government with a clear majority. By convention the prime minister is a member of the Lok Sabha. But this is a convention only. In 2004 Manmohan Singh was selected as Prime Minister even though he was a member of the Rajya Sabha. This followed Sonia Gandhi's significant decision not to take the post of prime minister even though she secured election as an MP and was leader of the Congress parliamentary party. This was because members of the previous ruling coalition, the Bharatiya Janata Party, were successfully making political capital out of the charge that a non-Indian would become a prime minister (despite holding Indian citizenship by virtue of her marriage to Rajiv Gandhi, Sonia is Italian born). Dr Singh is a noteworthy prime minister in many ways. As a Sikh, he is the first non-Hindu prime minister of India. He was Leader of the Opposition in the Rajya Sabha during the BJP years. India's first woman prime minister, Indira Gandhi, was initially a member of the Rajya Sabha. Narasimha Rao was not a member of either house at the time of his elevation to the most powerful position in Indian politics in 1991. Both subsequently contested seats for the Lok Sabha which they won. However, departing from convention, Manmohan Singh decided not to contest for a Lok Sabha seat, as his only attempt at securing one, from Delhi South in 1999, was not successful.

The powers of the prime minister resemble those of the prime minister of the UK. The prime minister is *primus inter pares*; he or she has the power to select members of the Council of Ministers, although these are formally appointed by the president. Ministers are responsible for making policy and directing government departments. Jawaharlal Nehru, India's first and astonishingly hard-working prime minister, was also foreign minister for the entirety of his premiership. Prime Minister Manmohan Singh is also in charge of the Ministries of Planning, Culture, Personnel, Public Grievances and Pensions, as well as the Department of Atomic Energy. Early in his first stint as Prime Minister he was also in charge of the large portfolio of Ministry of External Affairs. The prime minister chairs the Council of Ministers. She or he is also Chairman of the Planning Commission, a powerful body, determining the nature and scope of the five-year plans.

The size of the Council of Ministers has varied under different prime ministers, who can create new positions. At the time of writing there are 33 cabinet ministers, including the prime minister, and 45 additional Ministers of State. Under the Ninety-First Constitution Amendment in 2003 a limit was placed on the number of ministers which 'should not exceed 15 percent of the total number of members'

Illustration 3.1   India Gate

The political centre of India's capital city lies in New Delhi. The British moved their capital to Delhi (from Calcutta) in 1911. A British architect, Edwin Lutyens, oversaw the remodelling of the city to produce a capital adjacent to the existing city, which became known as Old Delhi. In 1931 the new city was finished, though of course New Delhi has continued to expand. India Gate is an important monument in the layout of the new city. This war memorial has been adapted to commemorate combatants who have died since the 1914–18 war. Much of the imperial architecture remains. The demolition of some smaller buildings raises concerns about the survival of 'Lutyens's Delhi'.

Table 3.1 Prime Ministers of India

Tenure	Prime Minister	Party	Elections won, comments
Aug 1947– May 1964	Jawaharlal Nehru[1]	Congress	1952, 1957, 1962, died in office
May–Jun 1964	Gulzari Lal Nanda	Congress	
Jun 1964– Jan 1966	Lal Bahadur Shastri	Congress	Died in office
Jan 1966	Gulzari Lal Nanda	Congress	
Jan 1966– Mar 1977	Indira Gandhi[2]	Congress	1967, 1971
Mar 1977– Jul 1979	Morarji Desai	Janata	1977
Jul 1979– Jan 1980	Charan Singh	Janata	
Jan 1980– Oct 1984	Indira Gandhi	Congress (I)	1980, assassinated in office
Oct 1984– Dec 1989	Rajiv Gandhi	Congress (I)	1984, assassinated in 1991
Dec 1989– Nov 1990	Vishwanath Pratap Singh	Janata Dal (S)	1989
Nov 1990– Jun 1991	Chandra Shekhar	Janata Party	
Jun 1991– May 1996	P V Narasimha Rao	Congress (I)	1991
May 1996	Atal Bihari Vajpayee[3]	BJP	1996
Jun 1996– Apr 1997	H. D. Deve Gowda	Janata Dal	1996
Apr 1997– Mar 1998	Inder Kumar Gujral	Janata Dal	
Mar 1998– May 2004	Atal Behari Vajpayee	BJP	1998, 1999
May 2004–	Dr Manmohan Singh[4]	INC	2009

Notes:
1 Nehru became Prime Minister after independence in 1947 but elections were not held until the winter of 1951/1952.
2 Indira Gandhi invoked the emergency provisions in the constitution and postponed elections between 1975 and 1977. The elections that were due in 1976 were not held until 1977.
3 As the leader of the largest party in the Lok Sabha, Vajpayee was invited to form the government but was unable to muster enough MPs to form a majority. He was forced to resign after 13 days.
4 Dr Singh emerged as Prime Minister after the elections.

of the House of the People. The realities of coalition politics have meant that there are more powerful groups to accommodate, not only of different political parties, but also factions within political parties. Members of the Council of Ministers are chosen either from the Lok Sabha or Rajya Sabha. Occasionally outsiders are co-opted, but within six months they must become a member of the legislature. As in the UK, the cabinet works under a convention of collective responsibility. However, the cabinet, a body not mentioned in the constitution, has the formal status of being the ultimate decision-making body in the executive.

Smaller cabinet committees deal with specific policy areas. Although Nehru was a formidable prime minister, with a wide-ranging scope of interests, strong cabinet government operated. The Prime Minister's Office (PMO) has increasingly become an important part of government. The PMO is staffed by senior civil servants as well as personal advisers. This institution has become more powerful and prominent, giving the prime minister greater control over policy issues which might otherwise be decided by the relevant minister. Parliament is frequently marginalized in the policy-making process. Nehru took parliamentary procedure seriously but not all subsequent prime ministers were so scrupulous. Indira Gandhi tended to avoid the Lok Sabha where possible (Frank, 2001: 296). State-level institutions also have a role. In particular, significant policy variations between states occur in the areas of welfare, agriculture and education. A few states took up the issue of land reform with vigour whereas most states took fairly minimal action. States are able to innovate and so some states have had an effective industrial policy that has attracted investors (Sinha, 2005). In the late 1970s the state of Maharashtra used an employment guarantee scheme to reduce rural unemployment, and this was later copied by the central government. States also have enhanced responsibility for economic matters following the 1991 economic reforms. This has decentralized decision making further.

President

Nominally, the constitution provides that the executive power of the Indian Union resides in the presidency, but in practice it is the prime minister who exercises executive power and the president does his or her bidding. The members of the Constituent Assembly had the British model of the head of state in mind when they codified the president's limited powers in the constitution. But it was not until 1976, during the Emergency of Indira Gandhi, that the president was constitutionally compelled to act on the advice of the prime minister (in the Forty-Second Amendment to the constitution). The president's signature is normally required for the passing of laws. However, in the case of finance bills the president is not allowed to withhold consent or return it to the legislature. Similarly, if the president returns a bill for consideration to the parliament, as long as the bill passes both houses, presidential assent is not required. In May 2006 President Abdul Kalam returned a bill to parliament relating to new regulations for MPs holding offices for profit. The UPA Government refused to shelve the bill and the president was not able to block it in August 2006 when the bill was passed again by both houses of parliament.

The president is not directly elected; this would challenge the power of the prime minister and possibly lead to deadlock. Instead she or he is indirectly elected for a five-year term, through an electoral college. This college consists of the Rajya Sabha, the Lok Sabha and the elected members of the state legislatures. The number of votes wielded by members of state legislatures is determined on the basis of the population of the states as enumerated in the 1971 census, while votes for the Lok and Rajya Sabhas are determined by a formula derived from the numbers of votes of the state legislatures. This electoral procedure, while complicated, ensures that the president is representative of the Union and the states. The president is elected by the single transferable vote electoral system which ensures that a president must receive more than 50 per cent of the electoral college vote to be elected. This is an important provision in such a diverse society, with divisions along many lines, not least between the (generally) Hindi-speaking north and non-Hindi-speaking south. The president may be impeached for violation of the constitution, but this has not yet occurred. The constitution also provides for a vice president, who is elected through a similar procedure to that for the president, although the state legislative assemblies are not included in this electoral college.

The president decides which party leader to ask to form a government. In contemporary India, in the absence of a single party able to get a majority, the political implications of this decision are considerable. It is conceivable that the first party asked to form a government might be able to tempt parties in a larger opposing coalition to defect. The decision of President Shankar Dayal Sharma to ask the BJP to form a government in 1996 was an example of a controversial decision. Another important power is the right to dissolve parliament and call fresh elections. Although such a dissolution would normally take place on the advice of the prime minister, in 1991 President R. Venkataraman took the decision to dissolve parliament only six days after Prime Minister Chandra Shekhar's resignation.

The final significant power of the president relates to emergency powers. There are three types of emergency powers in Part XVIII of the constitution. They comprise provisions in case of external aggression, war, internal disturbance or armed rebellion (Articles 352–5); provisions in case of the failure of constitutional machinery in states (Articles 356–9); and provisions in case of financial emergency (Article 360). The third provision has never been used. The first type of emergency, which admittedly covers a large number of eventualities, was declared during the Chinese invasion of India in 1962; in 1971 in response to the war between India and Pakistan; and in 1975 against the one and only internal 'armed rebellion' deemed a threat to the Indian state. In reality this was a politically motivated imposition in response to a campaign by opposition political leaders to make Prime Minister Indira Gandhi resign her seat, after she was convicted for committing an offence during her constituency campaign in the elections of 1971. The judgment of the Allahabad High Court in June 1975 that Indira Gandhi was guilty of an electoral offence required her resignation from the Lok Sabha, and barred her from elective office (and the prime ministership) for six years. The declaration of the Emergency gave her the opportunity to change the election law under which she had been convicted. Parliament, stripped of opposition leaders, who had been arrested, passed this law which was applied retrospectively.

The second type of emergency provision is commonly known as President's Rule and has been widely used. This provision in the constitution covers situations where the constitutional machinery in states and Union Territories has failed. This provision has been applied 120 times since independence. This power ostensibly rests with the president, who receives a report from the governor of the state advising that the state cannot be governed in accordance with the constitution. In practice, as with many of the president's other powers, this provision has been exercised on the advice of the prime minister. The vast majority of prime ministers have used and abused this provision to dismiss the elected assembly of the state in question, often for nakedly political reasons. With the exception of the caretaker prime minister Gulzari Lal Nanda, Deve Gowda is the only

Table 3.2   Presents of India

Year of commencement in office	President
1950	Dr Rajendra Prasad
1962	Dr Sarvepalli Radhakrishnan
1967	Dr Zakir Husain (died in office)
1969	Varahagiri Venkata Giri
1974	Dr Fakhruddin Ali Ahmed (died in office)
1977	Neelam Sanjiva Reddy
1982	Giani Zail Singh
1987	R. Venkataraman
1992	Dr Shankar Dayal Sharma
1997	K. R. Narayanan
2002	Dr A.P.J. Abdul Kalam
2007	Pratibha Devisingh Patil

prime minister not to have used this emergency power. The decision of Nehru to dismiss the assembly in Kerala in 1959 after the election of a communist state government was the first obviously political use of the powers, although this was the sixth time that it had been imposed. Indira Gandhi made exceptional use of this power; she deployed it 54 times during her several tenures as prime minister, almost half the total times the provisions have been used.

In 1994 the Supreme Court delivered the Bommai judgment that significantly changed the way in which President's Rule is applied. The judgment required that a state government under threat of dismissal first be given the chance to prove its majority in the state legislature. President Narayanan was the first president to use the Bommai judgment. He rejected the United Front's October 1997 attempt to dismiss the state government of Uttar Pradesh. He returned the recommendation to the cabinet, and requested they reconsider it. The Government heeded the President's words of caution, as did the BJP Government in September 1998 when President Narayanan rejected the recommendation to dismiss the state government of Bihar. The constitutional precedent has been firmly established in

Illustration 3.2   Rashtrapati Bhawan

Lutyens' most famous design in New Delhi is the official home of the President of India, Rashtrapati Bhawan. During the British era this was known as Viceroy's House (Irving, 1982).

contemporary India. President Kalam assented to its use in Bihar in 2005 but he showed himself willing to oppose the executive on other matters (discussed above). Since 1998, President's Rule has been imposed 10 times, but most of those times were short-lived affairs when coalitions were being negotiated following elections. The only exceptions were in Bihar in 1999 and Nagaland in 2008. It was imposed in Bihar following a massacre of Dalits by high-caste landlords. On this occasion President Naryanan agreed to its imposition, but the decision to proclaim it was withdrawn after 26 days when it became clear that Congress would not support its imposition in the Rajya Sabha. In 2008 it was imposed in Nagaland against a BJP-backed government. This has been seen by some as the most recent case of a political imposition of President's Rule (Singh, 2008).

Since independence there have been three Muslim presidents, one Sikh president and one Dalit president. Dr A.P.J. Abdul Kalam was the third Muslim president of India, and was nominated by the BJP government. He is a scientist and although it may look curious that a BJP government would nominate a Muslim, Dr Kalam had impeccable credentials that 'proved' his loyalty to India. He was heavily involved in several scientific achievements that (in the eyes of many Indians at least) increased India's world standing. These included the launch of an Indian satellite into space, the development and operationalization of the Agni and Prithvi missiles and the weaponization of strategic missile systems. Most notably, he was involved with the Pokhran nuclear tests in May 1998 which made India a nuclear weapons state (prompting Pakistan's own tests later that month). The current President, Pratibha Devisingh Patil, is the first female president of India. She has a long record of legislative service, in state assemblies as well as the Lok and Rajya Sabhas. She previously served as Governor of Rajasthan, and was the compromise choice between the Congress and the left-wing parties in the UPA, although she has long standing links to the Congress. For this reason her election was opposed by the BJP.

Public Services

The bureaucracy was a key unit in the governing structure under the British Raj, and continued to be an important part of the executive after independence. The national government and state governments run separate bureaucracies which recruit members by competitive examination. However, there is a bridge that links the two separate areas of government. A distinctive element of the civil service in India are the All-India Services, an elite segment of the bureaucracy that serves at both the national and state levels, and can move between the two levels. This small cadre is recruited nationally and used to provide leadership in key areas of government activity. The British evolved this approach and described their elite bureaucrats as the 'steel frame' of India which provided control of key areas of government business such as tax collection and law and order. The British system was continued with minor changes and the elite Indian Civil Service (ICS) was converted into the Indian Administrative Service (IAS) after independence. Of a similar standing to the IAS are the specialist elements of the All-India Services: the Indian Police Service and the Indian Forest Service.

The IAS provides highly capable officials that hold senior posts in central government departments and public sector companies. When they finish their training, IAS members are assigned to the IAS cadre of an individual state. The majority of the IAS members work for state governments. A proportion of each state cadre are sent on deputation to the central government. Many IAS members spend part of their early career acting as District Collector or District Magistrate. In this post they supervise a wide range of government activity in their district. Somewhat unusually they often have responsibility for both administrative and judicial matters. The examinations for entry to the All-India services are fiercely competitive and these jobs are very prestigious. The All-India services highlight a number of issues relating to the nation-building theme that runs through this book. First, the language controversy discussed in Chapter 2 was relevant to the recruitment to these services. Using only Hindi as the official language of India was a real concern for people from non-Hindi-speaking states who perceived that they would be at a disadvantage in taking these examinations. The retention of both Hindi and English as official languages was thus an important means of maintaining national integration. Secondly, members of the IAS are drawn from all over the Union, and although there are no quotas to ensure this, the distribution of recruits from different regions is relatively equitable. Many members of the IAS are posted to different states than the one they were born in, and are expected to be proficient in many languages to aid the integration of the Union. Thirdly, the IAS is supposed to be a bulwark of the Indian Union, and its members head both the central and state government bureaucratic services. While it is denied that members of the IAS serving in the states are the eyes and ears of the centre, the retention of an All-India service strengthens the centre. The central government sets the conditions of service and, by virtue of these, the service members have some protection from arbitrary treatment by local politicians.

It is important to stress the elite nature of the All-India Services. They are a tiny, though vitally important, part of a large bureaucratic machine. At the time of writing, the IAS numbered only 4572 (Spary, 2009). The bureaucracy as a whole has been criticized for having too much power, misusing that power, and failing to achieve the objectives set for it. Bureaucrats have influence over how public monies are spent, who gets access to public services and how development projects are administered. At the level of local government, mid-level bureaucrats have more power than elected councillors. In some cases a bureaucrat can override or even dismiss local councils. Under the system of planned development established under Nehru, officials were given powers to regulate and control business so that economic development brought with it social gains. The development record of the Indian state is mixed (we discuss this further in Chapter 7), and the bureaucratic controls have been heavily criticized, often using the

Illustration 3.3 North Block

North and South Block in New Delhi lie close to Rashtrapati Bhawan. The blocks are situated opposite each other across Rajpath. Collectively they form the Secretariat and house many important government departments including the Ministry of Home Affairs, Ministry of Finance and the Ministry of External Affairs.

derisive term 'licence-permit raj'. Business found it difficult, though certainly not impossible, to operate. Economic growth was slow to accelerate and poverty levels did not fall as quickly as they did in other developing countries.

It is often alleged that bureaucrats abuse the power they have or are unresponsive to ordinary citizens. The discretionary powers given to civil servants created opportunities for corruption. Businesses wishing to evade the system of licensing sometimes opted to bribe officials. Ordinary citizens frustrated by delays paid bribes to get a telephone line or an electricity connection. Gauging the extent of this corruption is impossible so it is difficult to assess the significance of this criticism (Parry, 2000). However, the perception of a corrupt bureaucracy is difficult to shift (Luce, 2007: 62). After political parties they were the sector considered to be most affected by corruption in India. In the State of Democracy in South Asia (SDSA) survey, 38 per cent of respondents had no or little trust in the civil service, compared to 18 per cent that had a great deal of trust (2008: 249).

While recruitment to the national and state bureaucracies is governed by competitive examination, the process includes an element of affirmative action popularly known as 'reservation'. Quotas are reserved for various groups considered to be historically disadvantaged, although candidates still have to sit the exams. The strongest provisions are mentioned in the 1950 constitution. Caste groups suffering the stigma of untouchability and tribal groups also considered to be at a disadvantage are given constitutional entitlement to compensatory discrimination. These groups were identified and are listed in an appendix or 'schedule' to the constitution, hence the terms: Scheduled Caste (SC) and Scheduled Tribe (ST). In central government service, places are reserved roughly in proportion to the population of the SC/STs in the total population (thus 22.5 per cent of central government jobs are reserved for SC/STs). The 2001 census recorded the populations as 16.2 per cent for SCs and 8.2 per cent for STs. These quotas have been controversial, both in principle and their application. Among the higher castes resentments are expressed that their prospects are being limited and that the principle of merit in recruitment is overlooked. The implementation of reservations has been criticized. Many reserved jobs remain unfilled and the upward mobility of those candidates who are recruited often appears to be blocked. Entrants from SC and ST backgrounds are over-represented at the lowest level of the civil service.

The politics of affirmative action is a central part of government and politics in contemporary India. Since the early 1990s the use of the reservation policy tool has been extended to bring more benefits to lower-caste groups and others listed in the Other Backward Class (OBC) category (an issue we discuss in more detail in Chapter 4). The Supreme Court has stipulated that not more than 50 per cent of jobs should be reserved. The use of affirmative action by the state governments includes some interesting variations as each state government sets policy. Where the lower castes are politically influential, OBC benefits offered are generous and more fully implemented. In some cases the Supreme Court ruling has been defied and the majority of state government jobs reserved. Some state governments have used the policy to improve gender equity and a quota within a quota operates so that jobs are reserved for women. Reservations are very controversial (we say more about this in Chapter 4) and are deeply opposed by most upper-caste voters.

The IAS is an important institution that still commands respect. It provides an aspirational career path and the entrance exams are highly competitive. This is in spite of competition for talent from the corporate sector in India and abroad. There have been suggestions for reforming the IAS but it has been resilient and India's politicians find it a useful tool for policy formation and control of the larger bureaucracy. The functioning of the bureaucracy as a whole has been strongly criticized but the Indian state has achieved some of its development objectives. In the states of the Indian Union where the political will is strong significant advances have been made and the achievements of the bureaucracy have been recognized.

State governments are responsible for most routine law enforcement in India. As with the other state government departments, the senior ranks are recruited and trained by the central government and posted to the states. The Indian Police Service (IPS) functions in a similar way to the IAS, with a small number of officers assigned to each state. Law enforcement in a federal system is a complex task and the central government runs a large number of agencies that deal with special policing and security tasks, including border security, protecting VIPs, narcotics, and counter-terrorism. The IPS supplies senior officers to these agencies. The police have a decidedly mixed reputation. Ever since the days of the Raj the police have enabled the Indian state to deploy substantial coercive power. Incumbent politicians rely heavily on the police for maintaining public order and gathering information. Yet the general public are more reluctant to trust the police. In the 2005 SDSA survey, 47 per cent of respondents had little or no trust in the police, while only 17 per cent had a great deal (2008: 249). This supports the general view that the police are widely perceived to be corrupt, brutal and not to be trusted. Transparency International noted that 28 per cent of respondents reported paying a bribe to the police in the last twelve months (2009b). Part of the corruption stems from poor working conditions and low pay received by rank-and-file police. Political interference weakens the independence of the police. Senior politicians influence transfers and access to prestigious posts. This has resulted in officers 'canvassing obliging politicians' for better assignments (Raghavan, 2003: 130).

As a 2006 Supreme Court judgment noted, the public perception is that 'many of the deficiencies in the functioning of the police had arisen largely due to an overdose of unhealthy and petty political interference at various levels starting from transfer and posting of policemen of different ranks, misuse of police for partisan purposes and political patronage quite often extended to corrupt police personnel' (Supreme Court of India, 2006: 5). The Supreme Court ruled in the *Prakash Singh vs. Union of India* case that both the centre and the state levels of government should 'comply with a set of seven directives laying down practical mechanisms to kick-start police reform' (Commonwealth Human Rights Initiative, nd). The aim of this reform was to ensure the independence of the police, to allow them to operate without fear of political interference or punishment (such as being transferred to undesirable postings or over-frequent transfers which interfere with family life). These guidelines included the establishment of a State Security Commission to ensure that the state government does not exercise pressure on state police and that the police act in accordance with the laws of the land; the creation of a Police Establishment Board in each state to determine postings, promotions and transfers; a minimum tenure of two years for mid- and high-ranking officers, and the establishment of a Police Complaints Authority. However, by 2008, as the Commonwealth Human Rights Initiative noted, limited progress had been made and the Supreme Court set up a Monitoring Committee to assess levels of compliance. As of that date only a few small north-eastern states were compliant (Commonwealth Human Rights Initiative, 2008).

In certain states of India the police have acted in a partisan manner in a way that seriously undermines the impartiality of the Indian state and hinders national integration. This was seen dramatically in Gujarat in 2002 when police were reported to have said 'We have no orders to save you' to the Muslims being persecuted, raped and killed (Human Rights Watch, 2002). In the end the army was called in to redress what has now been widely recognized as the political interference of the Gujarat state government in the policing (or lack of) of the situation (Raghavan, 2003: 126).

Legislature

The national legislature is a bicameral one, a feature common to most federal systems. The Lok Sabha is formally known as the House of the People in the constitution. Constitutionally, the Council of States is the upper house; commonly known as the Rajya Sabha. This is the

Illustration 3.4   Parliament

India has a bicameral legislature. Both houses of parliament use the same building, *Sansad Bhawan.*

house that represents the states of the Union. In 2009 the Lok Sabha had 545 members. These included 58 elected women (plus one nominated Anglo-Indian woman) and 47 representatives elected from seats reserved for STs and 84 elected from seats reserved for SCs. These seats are provided in the constitution to ensure effective representation of these castes and tribes, but also to rectify historical injustices (McMillan, 2005). Political parties campaign in these seats but must nominate as their candidate a member of either an SC or an ST (depending on whether it is reserved as an SC or a ST seat). A similar proposal has been made with regard to gender. In 2009 only 11 per cent of Lok Sabha MPs were women; the highest percentage elected. In the 1990s different governments sought to pass a bill providing that a third of the Lok Sabha and Vidhan Sabha (state legislatures) seats be reserved for women. Although there are very few female MPs, women have held a number of important positions. As well as India's first female prime minister, Indira Gandhi, these include: Uma Bharti (a prominent Hindu nationalist and former Chief Minister of Madhya Pradesh), Sheila Dikshit (Chief Minister of Delhi), Sonia Gandhi (Congress President), Jayalalithaa Jayaram (former Chief Minister of Tamil Nadu), Mayawati (Chief Minister of Uttar Pradesh), and Sushma Swaraj (BJP member and Deputy Leader of the Opposition in the Lok Sabha after the 2009 elections). In June 2009 the Lok Sabha elected its first female Speaker – Meira Kumar – also a Dalit. Bills to provide a quota of women legislators have constantly been rejected by political parties representing lower-caste groups. They demand reservations within reservations (i.e., that a certain percentage of the women's seats should be reserved for women of lower castes). The UPA government introduced the bill into the Rajya Sabha in May 2008 (so that the dissolution of the Lok Sabha in 2009 would not lead to the automatic 'lapse' of the bill – as the Rajya Sabha is a permanent body). In March 2010 the Rajya Sabha passed the bill in spite of vociferous opposition from some smaller parties. In order to become law it will have to be passed by the Lok Sabha and as an amendment to the constitution it will have to be ratified by half of the state assemblies as well. However Government support for the Bill is strong and the BJP has indicated its support for the measure.

Members of the Lok Sabha are elected through direct election from single member constituencies (with the exception of the two nominees from the Anglo-Indian community). That India has only 543 elected MPs means that most elected representatives face a daunting task representing effectively all their constituents. The average number of electors in each constituency was 1,314,506 in 2009. In comparison, constituency sizes for Members of Congress in the US averaged 650,000 and in the United Kingdom averaged 70,000 electors for each MP. Thus the UPA's 2005 proposal to increase the number of representatives in the Lok Sabha has benefits other than permitting women's reservations. The states and Union Territories of India have representation that approximates their population, with two qualifications. The re-districting of constituencies to recognize changing distributions of population has been distorted to assist India's family planning policy. Re-districting occurs (infrequently) but it is confined to individual states. Secondly, the smaller states of the Union as well as the six smaller Union Territories have one seat regardless of how small they are. So the Union Territory of Lakshadweep had approximately 46,000 electors in 2009 and one MP, compared to Pondicherry with over 762,000 electors. The Union Territory of Delhi has seven seats. This is not a serious distortion given that there are only 13 MPs representing the Union Territories.

As discussed in Chapter 2, the southern states have undergone a transition to lower population growth rates. This is in sharp contrast to many of the northern states including Uttar Pradesh and Bihar. In the 1970s the southern states were concerned that they should not be penalized in their representation at the centre because of the lower population growth rates. Their demands resulted in a 1976 constitutional amendment which froze the proportion of seats allocated to each state until 2001. As the differences in population growth rates had not disappeared by 2001, a further constitutional amendment was passed, continuing the freeze until 2026. The cycle continues, and in 2026 any change in representation to reflect the population figures will have major political ramifications; which makes it unlikely to happen (McMillan, 2001).

Elections to the lower houses of India's legislature are held under simple plurality rules; a candidate needs a plurality rather than a majority of votes to be elected. In other words the candidate with the largest number of votes in each constituency is elected, even though usually they will not have won a majority of votes. Under normal conditions elections must be held for the Lok Sabha every five years, but within that period, unlike the US which has fixed-term elections, the prime minister can choose when she or he assumes will be the most fortuitous time to 'go to the country'. Prime Minister Vajpayee did not have to hold an election until September 2004 but chose to hold elections in spring 2004 because he perceived that the BJP was popular in the polls and would win. He was wrong (as were many academic pundits on India). In contrast, Manmohan Singh chose to hold on for as long as possible, until spring 2009. The only time when elections were not held within five years was during the Emergency called by Indira Gandhi in 1975. During the Emergency, the constitutional niceties of which are discussed above, opposition leaders were arrested and imprisoned, and freedom of the press was seriously curtailed. This reduced parliament to a talking shop, a rubber stamp for the whims of the executive.

The Lok Sabha is the most powerful chamber of parliament, where financial legislation originates. It is a debating chamber, and also one which scrutinizes legislation. It does not sit in permanent session, although there are no set times for sessions. However, there is normally a monsoon session, a budget session and a winter session each year, and it breaks for Easter and Christmas/New Year. The number of days within any one year that it sits varies widely. In 2005 it sat for 85 days in total, in 2008, only 46.

The Rajya Sabha is also elected, albeit indirectly, by the state legislatures, which are directly elected. As an upper chamber in a federation, its purpose is to represent the states. The chamber is capped at 250 members, including 12 members nominated by the president to represent 'persons having special knowledge or practical experience in respect of . . . [l]iterature, science, art and social service' (Article

80 (3)). In 2008 the Rajya Sabha had 233 members elected from the states and 12 members nominated; a total of 245. Unlike some other federations where the units of the federation possess equal representation (in the US all states have two seats in the Senate regardless of population size), in India the larger states possess a larger number of seats than the smaller ones. Thus, Uttar Pradesh is allocated 34 while all the north-eastern states, with the exception of Assam, have only one seat each. But, proportionally, the smaller units possess more representation in the Rajya Sabha than they do in the Lok Sabha. One third of its representatives are elected, in a similar manner to the US Senate, every two years. This means that it is a permanent body, albeit one which has a partial change in membership every two years.

The powers of the Rajya Sabha are greater than those of the British House of Lords but less than the US Senate. Although they cannot initiate financial legislation, nor block a money bill, all other bills can originate in the Rajya Sabha (although the vast majority originate in the Lok Sabha). The consent of the Rajya Sabha is required for the passing of all legislation with the exception of money bills. Thus, the BJP Government had to withdraw its imposition of President's Rule in Bihar in 1999 because of anticipated opposition in the upper house. If the Lok Sabha and the Rajya Sabha disagree, then the president may call a joint session of parliament where decisions are made by a simple majority. As the Lok Sabha has over twice the members of the Rajya Sabha, *de facto* power resides in the lower house. But the Rajya Sabha, as the chamber of the states, possesses the sole power, by a two-thirds majority, to amend important federal provisions, such as to empower parliament 'to legislate with respect to a matter in the State List in the national interest' (Article 249) and to 'provide for the creation of one or more all India services' (Article 312).

Both houses of parliament can initiate the constitution change process. Most changes require a majority in each house of parliament, if two-thirds of the members were present and voting, and if assented to by the president. However, there are exceptions, mainly relating to the relationship between the centre and the states. Changes in the executive power of the Union and the distribution of powers between the centre and the states, the representation of the states in parliament, and provisions relating to the election of the president require the consent of both houses (with two-thirds sitting) but also require half the states to ratify the legislation. As a result a constitutional amendment relating to the ability of states to collect a service tax is still awaiting ratification by the requisite number of states. An extraordinary bias to the centre exists whereby parliament can amend several articles of the constitution by a simple majority. The article that has been changed the most by a simple majority is that relating to the boundaries of the states of the Union, and indeed, their very existence (several states were abolished in the 1956 reorganization, including Hyderabad and Madhya Bharat). Article 3 provides that the legislature of the state has to be *consulted* before such changes are made, but there is no requirement that their consent has to be secured. By this provision the reorganization of states in 1956 was achieved, and subsequent changes, most recently in 2000, were effected.

The parliamentary system makes it difficult for the two houses to act as an independent legislature or a serious check on the executive. Unlike a presidential system, the government and the legislature have a shared destiny. A government comes into being because it has the confidence of the Lok Sabha and that very same position allows it to dominate the lower house. This is even more the case when the governing coalition has a majority. Government business is given priority and it is nearly impossible for independent legislation to make it to the statute books. Beyond this structural challenge a number of other factors restrict the power of the legislative arm of government. The committee structure is underdeveloped and legislation does not have to be referred to a sub-committee for scrutiny unless the government wishes to consult further. The government can legislate while parliament is in recess by means of a presidential ordinance (which places the onus on parliament to repeal a measure already in place). However, the role of parliament has changed somewhat as governments with a single party majority have disappeared. It is not unusual for government legislation to be defeated or heavily amended as it makes its way through the two houses of parliament. The role of the speaker has been enhanced, with greater need for a mediator between government and opposition (Hewitt and Rai, 2010).

The social composition of the Lok Sabha has changed in recent years. After independence MPs tended to come from upper-middle-class backgrounds and many were professionally qualified. The stereotypical Congress MP was a male, upper-caste lawyer. The gender composition of the house is still largely male (an issue we profile in Chapter 4) but the occupational background of MPs has changed, with many more farmers being elected. Politicians from lower-caste backgrounds are also much more common. One driver of this change has been the rise to prominence of the lower-caste parties based in the northern states of Bihar and Uttar Pradesh. Another trend, also largely driven by the politics of these two populous states, is the growing presence of politicians with criminal backgrounds in the Lok Sabha. In 2009 a non-governmental organization (NGO) identified 153 MPs with cases pending against them (26 per cent), with 76 of them facing serious charges (National Election Watch and Association for Democratic Reforms, 2009: 2). The lower-caste parties have also been criticized for lacking interest in policy and concentrating on providing patronage and government jobs for their supporters (Luce, 2007: 118–22). As Transparency International's barometer reveals, political parties are overwhelmingly perceived to be corrupt in India, with 58 per cent of the population considering political parties to be affected by corruption (2009a: 28). In addition, the State of Democracy in South Asia Survey found that 45 per cent of people did not have much, or had no trust at all in political parties (SDSA, 2008: 253).

However, the trend is not one of straightforward decline. There has been a general improvement in the educational qualifications of members of the lower house. The number holding college degrees increased from 58 per cent in the first Lok Sabha of 1952 (Hardgrave and Kochanek, 2000: 85) to 73 per cent of the current Lok Sabha (National Election Watch, 2009: 16). It is also difficult to defend the earlier status quo, whereby a majority of MPs in the Hindi-speaking states (66 per cent in 1952) came from minority upper-caste backgrounds (Jaffrelot, 2009: 6–7). Parliament still discusses important policy issues, as the continuing debate over reservations of seats for women demonstrates. The State of Democracy in South Asia Survey found that there were higher levels of trust in parliament than there were for political parties in India (SDSA, 2008: 252). However, the issue of criminalization cannot be ignored and the reputation of the Lok Sabha was not helped by the mid-2006 brawl on the floor of the house between members elected from Bihar.

Judiciary

As with the bureaucracy, the judiciary was an important part of the British state. The colonial legal system introduced important changes to the administration of justice in India and it also created work for the new Indian middle class. As we noted in Chapter 1, many nation-alists trained as lawyers, though some preferred not to participate in nationalist politics. The legal profession is still a respected profession. A free and fair legal system is essential for a democracy to be consolidated, as well as for the federal system to operate effectively. The highest court in the land is the Supreme Court, which is the court with ultimate jurisdiction concerning disputes between the centre and the states, as was the case with the Bommai judgment of 1994, discussed above. The Supreme Court has some important powers, for example it can declare an Act of parliament to be unconstitutional, as it did in 2003 when it overturned an electoral law that interfered with the obligation on candidates to declare their assets, educational qualifications and criminal charges. The Court sees itself as a protector of the spirit of the constitution and has fought doggedly to maintain this role. The Supreme Court rules on constitutional matters and can review amendments to the constitution. In 1980 a judgment reaffirmed the right of the court to protect the basic structure of the constitution (Rudolph and Rudolph, 1981). The Chief Justice is assisted by 25 other judges of the Supreme Court, all of whom are appointed by the president, often acting on the advice of the prime minister and after consultation with senior judges.

The courts have made some important contributions to upholding the democratic process but there have been numerous failures as well. The decision of the Supreme Court to uphold the State of Emergency and actions taken under it is described by Mehta as 'the worst in Indian judicial history' (2007: 73). Lower courts, from the High Courts down to district courts, have also acted in ways that undermine democracy's effectiveness. A few cases are dealt with promptly but for the most part the legal system operates very slowly. Victims face inordinate delays and some charged with offences spend years in prison before they have been tried. Mehta estimates that 'India's federal judicial system has a backlog of almost twenty million cases' (2007: 72). Although the Supreme Court still acts independently, other courts have been less robust, especially where the behaviour of politicians has been concerned and only very rarely have politicians been convicted in cases in which they are involved. Even in high-profile cases where politicians have been charged with corruption on a massive scale, cases take years to come to court. As noted above, many prominent politicians continue to hold office at the state and national levels, even though cases against them are pending.

The phenomenon of Public Interest Litigation (PIL) deserves mention here. Introduced after the Emergency, PIL is a means by which an individual or a group can seek legal redress over an issue that does not directly affect them. The rationale behind the change was that the more vulnerable sections of society, those unable to access the judicial system in practice, could have their interests protected. The Supreme Court is prepared to hear cases on a wide range of issues. To make it easy for ordinary people to litigate, submissions can come in the form of a simple letter. PIL cases have addressed important issues in areas of human rights, workers' rights and the environment, as well as high-profile political cases such as the *Jain Hawala* case in 1993. The Supreme Court intervened to make crimes of sexual harassment easier to address legally via the ruling in the *Visakha* case in 1997 (R. Sen, 2009: 72). However, PIL has also been criticized. It has added to the proliferation of cases in India's already overburdened legal system and produced ad hoc rulings. Middle-class litigants have used PIL to resolve issues and some outcomes have been ambiguous. As Williams and Mawdsley note, these though often with laudable aims such as seeking the reduction of air pollution in Delhi, have as often been 'at the expense of the poor' (2006: 666). Despite these criticisms, PILs are still highly significant. Mehta has concluded that PILs have 'given hundreds of poor people a route by which to approach the Court' (2007: 71). The Supreme Court has, in many cases, embroiled itself 'in the most divisive social issues', making policy recommendations (Peiris, 1991: 72 and 82). One such example was discussed in the previous section: the reform of the police. The device of PIL has enabled the Supreme Court to introduce important legal and policy changes.

Federal System

The federal system is an important part of India's democratic political system. The system does not devolve as much power as most other federal systems. Even with this bias towards the centre, the federal aspect of the Indian political system is important. India's federal constitution provides a formal basis for a more plural system of government in which power is dispersed between different levels of government. Political changes over time have changed the way the federal system works. The party system has a much more regional character. A good proportion of the parties in the Lok Sabha directly identify themselves with linguistically defined states of the federation. This has changed the working of the federation, the Lok Sabha, and also the executive, which is now controlled by a coalition of parties, including regional parties. Single party government has not been possible since 1989 and looks unlikely to return in the near future. This has affected the workings of the federation – political parties in the governing coalition at the centre as well as in the states have sought to use leverage to secure economic and political benefits for their states, as discussed below. The federal system has helped to accommodate some of India's diversity.

India's large territorial size and diversity meant that a federal structure was essential if India was to be governed effectively. Governing structures which were based around territorial autonomy had been used by many previous rulers, including the Mughals and the British. The 1950 constitution produced a centralized federation. Unlike the US and Switzerland, where previously independent states came together, the Indian federation was created by re-working an existing political system. For this reason, one of the authors of the constitution, Dr B. R. Ambedkar, deliberately styled the Indian federation as a Union. The constitution was designed after the violence of partition, a war with Pakistan and within the institutional constraints of the Government of India Act of 1935. The first prime minister, Jawaharlal Nehru, was determined that a federal structure would not detract from the centre's ability to direct economic planning.

The federation is therefore extremely centralized along financial lines. The centre dominates the collection of taxes and it has control over all income tax (except that on agricultural income), customs and excise, and corporation tax. The types of tax that states are allowed to impose do not produce as much revenue and are less buoyant. The states can raise sales taxes and commercial taxes, but have been reluctant to impose direct taxes and user charges on agriculture. In practice, states have relied heavily on sales taxes on alcohol, which gives the state an interest in promoting its sale. Despite their lower tax base, the states have an extended range of responsibilities for important public services which required substantial resources to fund. The states have traditionally relied on the centre to allocate them the resources to carry out their substantial responsibilities and to ensure social and developmental equity between the states. The Finance Commission determines the distribution of centrally collected revenue to the states in the forms of grants and loans. In addition, the Planning Commission, an extra constitutional body, diminishes the states' sphere of autonomy in economic matters by the allocation of discretionary grants. This is a controversial area as states governed by parties opposing the centre are naturally apprehensive that they will be overlooked in the allocation of grants.

A federal form of government divides sovereignty between the centre and its units; there are some powers that only the centre can legislate on, and some powers that only the states can legislate on. In India, there is also a concurrent list that both levels of government can legislate on, but the centre has precedence. There are 95 powers on the Union list, including defence, foreign affairs, interstate trade and commerce; 62 powers on the state list, including public order, police, public health, agriculture, and local government; and 47 powers on the concurrent list, including education, social security and population control. Residual power rests with the centre. This is in addition to the extraordinary emergency powers, discussed above, by which the president (for which, read the central government) can dismiss state governments and dissolve the assembly.

The initial consolidation of the federal system occurred with the integration of the princely states into the Union. This produced a federation with 27 states but a number of unresolved issues. The system was asymmetric as the British system granted different status to various provinces. The boundaries of the units had no obvious logic, most of whose boundaries were determined by historical accident rather than taking into account cultural factors. It was not uncommon for several different languages to be spoken in one of the new 27 states, and linguistic groups were also divided in ad hoc ways among different units. After independence, with the memories of the violence of partition in their minds, the elites of the Congress sought to draw back from their commitment to reorganize the provinces along linguistic lines. But many of its members, as well as those outside the party, were determined to hold the Congress to its commitment. In 1953 serious agitation started in favour of a Telugu-speaking state to be separated from the then named state of Madras. The centre refused, but, after the widely reported hunger strike death of Potti Sriramulu, was ultimately forced to concede the demand. This led to the establishment of the States Reorganization Commission (SRC), to determine the boundaries of the other states of the federation.

The SRC's instructions were not to focus on solely linguistic considerations; the national unity and integrity of India were to be paramount. Their report was released in 1955, redrawing the political map of India. However, several areas were not reorganized at the time: the provinces of Bombay (because of competing claims over the commercial capital of Bombay) and Punjab (because of concerns over creating a Sikh majority state). Both were reorganized in 1960

Note: The external boundaries shown on this map do not purport to be officially recognized boundaries of India.

Map 3.1   States of India, 2009

and 1966 respectively. The north east of the country, divided along multiple cleavages, was also no easy candidate for reorganization. From the 1970s this area has gradually undergone many reorganizations along tribal lines, but these have caused many reactions and counter-claims. In 2000 three new states, Jharkhand, Uttaranchal and Chhattisgarh, were created. Demands for the creation of more states abound – some along linguistic lines, others along tribal or administrative lines. In December 2009 the central government agreed to carve out a new state in the Telengana region of Andhra Pradesh, a decision which was in response to a hunger strike by the leader of the movement for a new state. The move took many by surprise because other political parties in Andhra Pradesh had not been consulted. These political leaders were uncomfortable with the decision and widespread protests both for and against the new state obliged the central government to pass the issue back to the political parties in the state (Kumar, 2010). The outcome of this episode is far from clear, but more states are likely to be created in the future.

The structure of the federation generally replicates that of the centre. There is a governor, appointed by the centre, who formally holds the executive power of the state in a way that replicates the president in Delhi. Then there is a chief minister who possesses similar powers as the prime minister does at the Union level, and a state cabinet, drawn primarily from the legislature. The chief minister is generally the leader of the majority party in the legislature, or one who can command a majority of support in a divided legislature. Most states only have one chamber, and the representatives to this chamber are called Members of the Legislative Assembly (MLAs). These chambers have often acted with less decorum than the Lok Sabha.

India's federation entered a new phase in the 1990s. First, coalition governments at the centre have relied heavily on regional parties. This meant that the politics within particular states played out on the centre stage, notably the tensions between the Dravida Munnetra Kazhagam (DMK) and All India Anna Dravida Munnetra Kazhagam (AIADMK) in the state of Tamil Nadu or the tensions between the Bahujan Samaj Party (BSP) and Samajwadi Party (SP) in Uttar Pradesh. It also meant that the states with a powerful political party in both the governing coalition at the centre and their state were more likely to benefit from central resource allocations, as seen by Chandrababu Naidu's successful demands (the TDP of Andhra Pradesh was a vital supporting member of the NDA between 1999 and 2004). Coalition politics has also changed the dynamics of President's Rule. Although the Bommai judgment has changed the parameters in which it can be imposed, in general, regional parties are less likely to call for the imposition of President's Rule as they are aware that it could be used against them by an alternative administration. This happened in 2002 when the regional and secular parties of the NDA coalition failed to call for the imposition of President's Rule in Gujarat after a massacre of up to 2000 Muslims, plus the displacement of approximately 150,000 more following the burning of a train carriage in which 58 Hindu pilgrims were killed (Human Rights Watch, 2002). A much better case warranting the imposition of

President's Rule is harder to imagine in recent times. However, there are exceptions; a leader of one of the parties in the governing coalition, Jayalalithaa, was vociferous in calling for the dismissal of the rival political party's government in Tamil Nadu in 1998, although this demand was not conceded.

Secondly, economic liberalization has increased the economic resources of certain states, while diminishing those of the centre. Those states with powerful regional parties as well as strong per capita income such as Punjab, Gujarat or Maharashtra have become even more powerful bargainers. At the same time, the states generally experienced a decline in the level of fiscal transfers from the centre. Therefore, although some states have been able to attract large amounts of foreign investment (Andhra Pradesh), others have not been successful (Bihar) and have thus been doubly disadvantaged. The Eighty-Eighth Amendment to the Constitution provided that both the states and the Union would be able to collect and appropriate a service tax, Value Added Tax (VAT). As services accounted for almost 50 per cent of the country's GDP in 2000, this is a significant resource. But this amendment requires ratification by half the states before it comes into force. Other small changes have been made, including the allocation of a higher percentage of the centre's tax revenue to the states, but this change has not been significant. The change in resource allocations may lead to tensions arising between states within the federation which are more economically successful, while others lag behind. Standards of living are much higher in some states (such as Karnataka) while they lag behind in others (such as Bihar). These differences were present before economic liberalization, but they have generally been exacerbated by it.

Local Government

Local government is an important layer of government because many states of India have huge populations and the capital of a state may be extremely distant from ordinary people's lives. This layer of government was very important during the British Raj; it was responsible for maintaining law and order and collecting taxes. Most of these powers were taken away from local government and controlled by the state government after independence. Since the 1990s some powers have been returned to local government. Urban local bodies (ULBs) are responsible for towns and cities. In rural areas a *panchayat* system was created out of village councils that had governed villages for hundreds of years. The term literally means a gathering of five wise elders. At independence, Mahatma Gandhi wanted to structure India's constitution around these village institutions, as well as devolving the economy to the village level. A much more modest scheme was devised with a panchayat system operating at three levels. Each district, which usually has a population of several million, has a panchayat council. Below that there is a panchayat for the subdivisions of a district. At the very lowest level is the village or *gram* panchayat which has responsibility for one larger village or several smaller ones. It is at the local level that people have most direct contact with government (and most commonly experience official corruption). Until 1994 the system of local government was very patchy. District panchayats were formed by indirect elections and it was not unknown for elections to urban bodies to be suspended. In most states only meagre powers and inadequate funds were provided for panchayats. Panchayats were often dominated by locally powerful landowners from upper-caste backgrounds.

It is only recently that panchayats have been recognized formally as part of the government of India. The Seventy-Third and Seventy-Fourth Amendments to the constitution in 1994 called for the devolution of resources to the district and village level, codified provisions for elections to these bodies to reduce the under-representation of women and SC/STs. A third of all elected council seats are reserved for women. The position of panchayat chairperson is also reserved in the same proportion. In addition, provisions are made to guarantee the election of SC/ST candidates. These changes were intended to increase the effectiveness of development efforts, and to increase participation but they have had mixed success and the devolution of power is not complete. Panchayats are expected to implement schemes funded by the central government but few state governments have created genuinely powerful local government and they routinely underfund local bodies. Powers have usually been held back with key decisions still being taken by the state administration. In Tamil Nadu, for example, urban local bodies do not control social housing or education. Changes to the system of representation have empowered women and lower castes to take part in the governance of their immediate area but they have faced resistance. Powerful groups attempt to put up proxy candidates to fill reserved posts in the hope that the proxy will govern on their behalf, and women have faced not only resistance but also intimidation as they enter politics (Mayaram,

Figure 3.1   The separation of powers

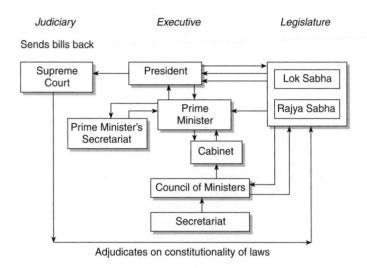

Adjudicates on constitutionality of laws

2002). Some Dalit candidates have even been murdered by higher-caste groups angry at the reservation of the panchayat president (Viswanathan, 2005). Nevertheless, most observers have treated these reforms as a positive development while noting how the system might be improved further (Crook and Manor, 1998: 83–4).

Conclusion

The institutions of the Indian state were designed to assist the task of building a national community, the 1950 constitution having outlined a set of institutions and state structures that were central to the nation-building project. The strong powers held by the Union government were important as the centre could protect the territorial integrity of India and contain threats to internal stability. The design of the executive gave the centre the means to impose its policies and ideas on the states. Devices like central planning, the central allocation of finance to the states and the elite IAS made the national government relevant to government throughout India. The large and unwieldy bureaucracy includes an important element of central influence in the form of the elite IAS. The affirmative action programmes that provide jobs were intended to promote social cohesion. Social and economic uplift was meant to give lower-status groups a more equal position in a national community. The judiciary is subject to state government influence but it still has to operate national and state laws. The institutions of the Indian state provide an official framework that helps to define a national community.

In contemporary India the centre has lost some of its power. Political and economic changes have given more power to the state governments in India's political system. We need to stress that this change is largely informal. The basic structure of the 1950 constitution remains intact and this includes institutional features, such as the system of taxation, which state governments and regional political parties find irksome. On paper the central government retains formidable powers but it is less able to use them. India's governing structures are certainly robust, but they have been flexible enough to adapt to change. They have accommodated new demands and rising forces in society. Some of the ambitions of the regional parties have been realized as the centre has been less assertive since the early 1990s. Demands made by the OBCs have also been accepted. Indian politics and government have changed over the six decades of independence – as have many of the social divisions within society. This is the subject of Chapter 4.

4

Social Change

India has undergone important social change since it gained independence from Britain in 1947. Some of these changes were in process already but the context changed significantly with the transition to democratic self-government. The colonial regime had been innately conservative and politically authoritarian. After independence the political system became much more democratic and there was an official presumption that the Indian state should encourage social reform. As a result of these reforms and gradual increases in prosperity, India in the early twentieth-first century is a very different place to live in. We focus on changes in the key areas of population growth, caste, class and gender. However, not all changes have been positive, and the changes just mentioned have empowered certain sections of the population more than others.

Demography

India's population grew exponentially in the twentieth century, despite coercive and voluntary population control programmes. The population growth since 1951 is remarkable (see Table 4.1). Population growth was much slower before 1947. An advance in one decade might be offset by the combined impact of disease and famine in the next. Since 1947 the Indian state has been able to prevent large-scale famine from occurring and progress has been made in controlling some life-threatening diseases. The infant mortality rate also improved (Dyson *et al.*, 2004: 1–3). The population of independent India has tripled in a little over fifty years. In 1999 India's population passed the one billion mark. However, the rate of population growth rate is slowing. One estimate identified a growth rate of 2.09 per cent

Table 4.1   India's population since 1951

Year	Population (millions)
1951	361
1961	439
1971	548
1981	683
1991	846
2001	1029
2010 (estimate)	1176

Source: Compiled from Government of India
(2001b).

between 1983 and 1994, 1.97 per cent between 1994 and 2000 and
1.69 per cent between 2000 and 2005 (Sundaram, 2007: 3122). This
growth rate varies between regions of India: as discussed in Chapter 3.
    India's political elite are very aware of the population issue. A
massive administrative effort is undertaken every 10 years to measure
India's population by a census. A wide range of data are collected,
much of them available online. The Indian state has taken various
measures to promote population control but the policies used have
been controversial. The policy gained greatest notoriety during the
Emergency period between 1975 and 1977 when forcible sterilizations
were carried out. Religious and cultural taboos have discouraged
many families from using birth control though this has changed with
increasing levels of literacy. A relationship exists between the level of
education of the mother and the number of children that she bears.
Many poorer families rely on children, especially sons, to provide
security for them in their old age – something that has not changed in
India in 60 years of independence. State policy on family planning
attracts much less attention in contemporary India but it is still a point
of contention. Some states have lower population growth rates than
others and this is a divisive issue, as we discussed in Chapter 3. Family
planning can still be advanced by coercive means and women are put
under pressure to carry the responsibility for birth control. This might
include sterilization with attendant health risks and in some cases
inter-uterine devices (IUDs) are used on women without their knowledge or consent (Swaminathan, 2002: 133–4).
    There has been a substantial movement of population from the
countryside to India's towns and cities. Every decade the census
shows the urban population growing faster than the countryside, but

interestingly the rate of growth has slowed, to 2.7 per cent 1991–2001, from 3.1 per cent in the previous decade. This confounds the image of runaway urban growth (Hust, 2005: 2–3). For some this raises the question of how the rate of urbanization can be accelerated so that pressure on the land can be eased. However, most of the population still live in rural areas. In 2001 the rural population was recorded at 72.2 per cent of the overall population though some argue that is an overestimate because the census uses a fairly narrow definition of what counts as a town. A few states, including Tamil Nadu with an urban population of 43.9 per cent, are ahead of the national trend, while some other states, including Assam (12.7 per cent) and Bihar (13.4 per cent), are still heavily rural (Dyson and Visaria, 2004).

Caste

Caste is an important organizing principle in Indian society. It is a complex form of social stratification in which people are accorded status on the basis of their relative ritual purity or impurity. Despite changes in Indian society since independence, and affirmative action measures, it remains important as a means of regulating social and economic interaction for the majority of Indians. The idea of purity is linked to Hindu religious traditions that consider some objects, such as dead bodies, excreta or the meat of animals, to be polluting. Caste status is largely hereditary. Individuals are born into a particular caste group. They usually marry within that group (a practice which anthropologists term 'endogamy'). Interactions between different caste groups are ordered by purity-based principles, with the 'purest' groups at the top of the social hierarchy. The building block of the caste system is the 'jati' or subcaste. Subcastes vary enormously in size. One jati may have a population of a few thousand whereas another might have several million members. Marriage usually takes place within one jati and this maintains the endogamous character of the system. Caste is a complicated social practice subject to many variations. For example, there are some groups that practise exogamy and find marriage partners from a select list of other subcastes. It is important to stress that the way in which caste works varies according to local custom and practice. This means that the caste 'system' is actually quite fragmented because it operates in a localized way. It is at the village, neighbourhood or district level that different caste groups interact and observe pollution rules and the varied customs

Illustration 4.1   Caste divisions

Untouchability encourages social separation. In this case the main part of the village is a few hundred metres down the road, the Dalit hamlet is the other way.

observed in these localities do not integrate in a straightforward way into a national caste system.

In Chapter 2 we outlined the system of varna classification in which the twice-born castes are placed at the top of the ritual hierarchy. A point we need to emphasize here is that the notion of ritual purity creates great inequality. Those included in the four varna categories are together referred to as 'caste Hindus' in contrast to the so-called 'Untouchables' who are said to be outside the caste system. The idea of untouchability stems from notions of ritual purity. Untouchability is an inherited status derived from an ancestral occupation considered so impure and defiling that physical or social contact would contaminate a caste Hindu. This notion has serious social consequences because it separates a large group of people from mainstream society. The political and ethical implications of caste are considerable and we discuss them further in this chapter and the next.

However, although the varna classification is a useful way of describing the links between caste and occupations, and highlights

the principle of ritual purity which is important in the social practice
of caste, it offers us a relatively simple ideal type. As noted, the
everyday practice of caste varies by location. Instead of four categories, we are faced with jati subcastes that have no automatic place
in the varna hierarchy. In some parts of India the Kshatriya and
Vaisya categories are completely absent and the only upper-caste
groups are Brahmans. It is also not clear that untouchability places a
group outside of the caste system. After all, untouchability would not
exist without the larger caste distinctions. Despite the fact that the
system of varna classification may be incomplete and misleading, it
remains an important part of social and political discourse. Members
of a jati frequently make claims about their status with reference to
the varna classification. Before 1947 it was not uncommon for
members of a lowly jati to claim that they were ancestors of a
formerly proud Kshatriya jati that had recently fallen on hard times.
They would therefore petition the British census enumerator to
recognize a claim for higher status. After independence details of
caste were removed from the census; however, advocates of a particular jati still make general claims to status on the basis of the varna
classification. The Indian state recognizes the distinction between the
lower and upper castes as a form of social disadvantage and, as we
discussed in Chapter 3, reserves jobs in public bodies for the Other
Backward Classes.

The hierarchical caste system has long been a controversial feature
of Indian society. In the pre-colonial period some Hindu religious
reformers argued against the inequalities of caste and for improvement in the status of those suffering the stigma of untouchability.
Caste inequality was also publicized by Christian missionaries.
British colonial administrators have been attacked for their preoccu-
pation with caste. The decennial census listed caste groups according
to precedence and this gave caste a degree of precision that the vague
ordering of pre-colonial society lacked. The census also encouraged
electoral competition between caste groups.

The broad consensus on caste among the nationalist elite at the
time of independence was that it was a backward social institution
that would be out of place in a modern and democratic India. This
view was widely shared among the intelligentsia and the upper-
middle class who articulated the view of 'official India'. This
contributed to a public discourse in which 'casteism' was considered
to be a social evil, and the politically correct response was to
denounce it. Nehru complained in his book *The Discovery of India*

Box 4.1   Yadav politics

The Yadav caste group epitomizes the changing character of caste in modern India. The Yadavs are widely regarded as having modest caste status and are officially listed in the Other Backward Class category. Yadavs are identified by the traditional occupation of cow herding – taken as evidence that Yadavs are descendants of the god Krishna. This link supports a claim to high caste status. The historical accounts propagated by Yadav caste associations claimed the group should be recognized as upper-caste Kshatriyas in the varna classification. The link to cow herding was taken to indicate that other pastoral castes were also Yadavs and these groups were encouraged to join under the same banner. The interests of the Yadavs are pushed forward by the All-India Yadav Mahasabha (AIYM), which is active in 17 states. Old marriage rules which identified smaller kinship groups that subdivided the Yadavs are not as widely observed (Michelutti, 2004: 48–58). These processes have created a group that is less internally divided, numerically large and better able to participate in politics. The Yadavs have also increased their influence as a middle-class segment has emerged from within their ranks. Yadavs were among the tenant farmers who gained from the limited land reform of the 1950s and the economic growth that followed the green revolution (Hasan, 1998: 87). The Yadavs are the most politically assertive caste group in modern Indian politics. So much so, that they have been described as a caste of politicians who learn their craft in the womb (Michelutti, 2004: 46). The Yadavs are represented by two influential political parties: the Samajwadi Party in the state of Uttar Pradesh, and the Rashtriya Janata Dal in Bihar. The leader of the latter party, Laloo Prasad Yadav, was not shy of identifying with his caste background. Forthright and witty, he was happy to be seen milking cows. As Chief Minister of Bihar he exposed the urban pretensions of Delhi-based critics who mocked his preference for keeping cows at his official residence. Charged with corruption, he was obliged to give up the post but his influence continued as the post transferred to his illiterate wife, Rabri Devi. Laloo Prasad Yadav was a supporter of the UPA and served as railway minister during its first administration. In the adjacent state of Uttar Pradesh, Mulayam Singh Yadav, the leader of the Samajwadi Party, claimed the legacy of the socialist movement. By stitching together an alliance of caste groups (of which the Yadavs are the strongest) and Muslims, he has become an influential figure in national politics. Mulayam was defence minister in the UF government between 1996 and 1998, and also served as Chief Minister of Uttar Pradesh three times between 1989 and 2007. In Bihar, Laloo Prasad Yadav holds together a similar alliance and was Chief Minister between 1990 and 1997.

that the caste system was 'reactionary', 'restrictive' and that it was incompatible with democracy (1946: 257). In 1952 another Congress politician, Chandrasekhar, stated that caste 'has outlived its utility and has now become a painful, undemocratic, and anti-national anachronism. The question therefore, is not whether the system is desirable but how to abolish it in the shortest possible time' (Chandrasekhar, 1972: xxi). In spite of these strongly worded sentiments, caste has persisted and is deeply intertwined with the contemporary Indian political system. Yet the social practice of caste has changed. This is partly because caste is a dynamic element in Indian society and it is partly because political developments have encouraged change in the ways that caste is understood and practised.

Caste has the potential to shape political identification. The format of democratic politics has encouraged this. Universal suffrage increases the power of the more numerous groups in society – therefore caste groups with a substantial population would be well placed to lobby the government and get benefits from elected politicians. This encouraged smaller subcaste groups to affiliate through a process of fusion to increase their influence. A notable case are the Yadavs, a federation of caste groups concentrated in north India that boasts a population numbered in millions.

The way in which caste is understood as an identity has begun to change in another way. Rather than caste being seen as a set of rules that determine behaviour, anthropologists have observed a process of 'substantialization'. So caste is said to be a shared sense of belonging or substance. In other words, caste becomes more a form of identity than merely a predetermined status. Observing the minutiae of caste rules becomes much less important and this breaks down the divisions that operate within a caste group. This enables a caste group to function on a much larger scale. This has been important as many people have moved from their villages, where the observation of caste distinctions can be closely monitored, into towns where the forms of social interaction are less clear. Through the relaxation of rules it is easier for a more mobile population to forge links with other members of the same caste group and acknowledge a wider group of people as fellow members of the same group (Gorringe, 2005). Another related change made by some caste groups has been the relaxation of strict rules on the selection of suitable marriage partners. Again this reshapes the basis on which a caste group functions, and introduces flexibility into caste interaction. However, caste remains vitally important in determining most marriages.

The practical implications of caste are extensive. Caste continues to frame social and economic life in contemporary India in spite of official efforts to diminish its importance. The continuing practice of untouchability denies millions of Indians their human rights (Human Rights Watch, 2007). Untouchability persists in a number of forms. The historical legacy of residential segregation can still be felt in villages which might have streets inhabited by members of a single caste or in the case of the Dalits, possibly a separate hamlet. Some temples are informally kept for the use of caste Hindus, thus excluding Dalits. Common services, like the village well or the local teashop, might also be exclusively used by caste Hindus. Dalits are often subject to intimidation if they attempt to break these restrictions. Patterns of untouchability are reproduced in the economy as Dalits are pushed towards menial jobs. These jobs include sweeping, cleaning, construction and agricultural labour. All of these jobs will be poorly paid. In the very worst cases Dalits are obliged to work as scavengers, removing human excrement from toilets or cleaning sewers manually. The work is unhygienic, unpleasant in the extreme and hazardous to human health. The practice was abolished in 1993 but the law has been poorly implemented and an estimated 1.3 million Dalits still carry out this work (Irwin, 2009: 13).

Caste discrimination affects other groups as well. The lower castes have a higher status than the Dalits but they are still aware of their subordinate position in society. In ritual terms the lower castes are made aware that they do not have the social standing accorded to the 'twice-born' upper castes. They are denied religious privileges and the hereditary Brahman priesthood that control the larger temples (and many smaller ones too) marks other groups out as religious inferiors. The lower castes make up approximately 50 per cent of the population. They are not a homogenous group. There is a division among the lower castes between the so-called 'backward castes' (43.7 per cent) and the dominant castes (6.3 per cent) (Varshney, 2000: 17). The dominant castes are economically privileged by virtue of being owners of large amounts of land. The majority of the backward castes were both ritually and economically disadvantaged but an important social change has been the emergence of a growing middle class among the backward castes. We say more about the backward castes and the official policies implemented under the OBC rubric below.

The nationalist urge for social reform was expressed in the 1950 constitution. Untouchability was abolished and discrimination on the basis of caste was declared unconstitutional. A series of laws, beginning with the 1956 Untouchability Offences Act, were introduced. The Scheduled Castes, as discussed in the previous chapter, were given reservations in legislatures and jobs. Compensatory discrimination also included scholarships and quotas for college and university places. Also, the Indian state, as first mentioned in Chapter 3, took some steps to improve the position of lower-caste groups. The scope of action on behalf of OBCs was not as extensive. State governments were expected to initiate action and so, in states with a powerful upper-caste elite, policies were less comprehensive.

These policies have contributed to changes in the ways in which caste is experienced in India. A minority among the lower and Scheduled Caste groups now have the potential for upward economic mobility. As well as political changes enabling some caste groups to assert themselves, economic changes have softened the sharp distinction between the upper castes and prosperous lower-caste farmers. Access to education and government jobs will further improve the class status of selected members of the lower castes. These affirmative action schemes enabled an educated elite to emerge within the lowest strata of Indian society, as well as making it more likely that younger members of the lower and Scheduled Castes are educated, articulate and less inclined to accept discriminatory behaviour. Access to well-paid government jobs has allowed a minority of the Scheduled Castes the opportunity to join the salaried middle classes. Legal changes make it less likely that untouchability is practised, and social interaction is not as controlled as it once was.

Assertion among the Subordinate Castes

A very substantial change in Indian society has been growing resistance to the hierarchy and indignities of the caste system. Those at the lower end of the system have resented their subordinate status and have taken actions to improve their status. Two vitally important trends are the growing political influence of the lower castes (or OBCs) and the increased assertiveness of the Dalits. Although caste inequality has not been eradicated, substantial change has occurred.

Before independence, political leaders from lower-caste backgrounds argued that they also suffered discrimination and disadvantage. The nationalist elite, largely from upper-caste backgrounds, were less convinced by these claims. However, because the lower castes were a much larger group than the Scheduled Castes it was felt that some concessions had to be offered. The Government of India approved the title 'Other Backward Classes' (OBC), which attempted to obscure the issue of caste (though in popular usage 'OBC' is a synonym for backward castes). It was left to state governments to implement policy in this area. Policies included affirmative action or 'reservation' of jobs and scholarships. The OBCs are potentially a very influential group, given their potential voting power and improved economic fortunes. Changes in agriculture, described in Chapter 7, have made some OBC farmers prosperous. As discussed later in the chapter, the rural middle classes are often from OBC backgrounds.

The backward castes in western and southern India were politically active before 1947. They resented upper-caste privileges and argued successfully for state action to redress the balance. This movement picked up momentum in northern India in the 1960s. In the late 1970s, politicians who were sympathetic to the OBCs argued that the central government should offer reservations in employment. This was confirmed by the Mandal Commission report published in 1980. The report recommended reserving 27 per cent of all central government jobs for OBC candidates. When it was proposed in 1989 that the government should implement the recommendation, it was greeted with fury by many from upper-caste and urban middle-class backgrounds. Violent protests followed, including self-immolations in front of the media. These opponents of the Mandal report felt that such a large quota on top of the 22.5 per cent reserved for Scheduled Castes and Scheduled Tribes threatened their own prospects. When the report was implemented in 1993 by a Congress government, it indicated the rising influence of the OBCs. Congress had opposed the Mandal recommendations in the 1980s but it was felt expedient to change policy given the numerical strength of the OBCs and the rise of other parties seeking the OBC vote. Political conflict over the issue of affirmative action erupted again when in April 2006 the UPA government proposed to set aside 27 per cent of places for OBCs in educational institutions under the direction of central government. These institutions include the Indian Institutes of Technology, the Indian Institutes of Management and the All India Institute of Medical Sciences. Entry to these prestigious institutions is highly competitive and there was bitter opposition to the policy. In 2008 the Supreme Court ruled that a 50 per cent quota for OBCs, SCs and STs in these institutions was constitutionally valid.

An overlapping development was the growing assertiveness of the Dalits. Dalit politicians have been active at the national level in India since the 1920s. Since the 1970s, Dalits have become increasingly assertive. The 1950 constitution promised greater equality but there is a well-known gap between the policies on untouchability and their implementation. One reaction to this gap between promise and fulfilment has been growing political militancy. Activists resent the colloquial names used to demean those suffering the social stigma of untouchability. A small group of radicals known as the Dalit Panthers helped crystallize these sentiments. They were inspired by Marxism, the ideas of Ambedkar and the Black Panthers in the United States. The group was most notable for its manifesto, published in 1973, that inspired other activists (Joshi, 1986). They considered the official term 'Scheduled Castes' to be misleading and made use of the term 'Dalit' instead. This term, literally meaning crushed or oppressed, reminds people that untouchability is still a social problem. Many other movements and organizations have since been formed which take an assertive approach to the issue of untouchability and caste discrimination. The term Dalit is also in wide use in the English-language press in contemporary India, displacing less empowering terms like untouchable and Harijan. Dalit activists see their task as being one of forcing the government to implement state policy. As we will see in the next chapter, the party system has been reshaped as lower castes and Dalits have organized themselves behind political parties that favour them.

In spite of the assertiveness of subordinate groups, caste remains an extremely important facet of Indian society. Economic change has only assisted certain groups and individuals and caste continues to define occupations for many, forming the basis around which business networks are formed (Bayly, 1998: 318–20). The system of reservations has yet to be extended to the private sector and in the corporate sector well-educated upper-caste individuals are at a huge advantage in recruitment. In smaller enterprises, family and kinship networks, heavily informed by caste, determine who is employed and in what capacity. Individuals from rural lower-caste backgrounds are hugely disadvantaged in this competitive environment (Thorat, 2005). In short, caste identity has an important influence on what might be described as class identity.

Class

We define class as a group with similar life chances, levels of property ownership and/or roughly equivalent employment status. This shared economic status might be reinforced by a tendency to live in the same neighbourhood, have similar life styles and media images that define different social groups. In other words, shared economic opportunities might become the basis of class identity (Scott and Steele, 2005: 29–30).

It is not always clear in India that people of similar economic standing feel a common identity. Other forms of identity based on caste, religion, language, and ethnicity produce forms of solidarity that push shared class interests into the background. Yet it is possible to identify different class groups in India and see how economic changes alter the way that groups of people relate to each other. An important aspect of social change in contemporary India is the extent to which class is becoming recognized as an important marker of identity (an issue we take up later in this section). A distinction can be made between capitalist classes who own property and do not exchange their labour for a salary or wages. We can contrast this with members of the middle classes who own some property but also have to sell their labour in order to make a living. A third group are those who have only their labour to sell.

The evolution of class stratification in India has been shaped by its distinctive economy, heavily influenced by agriculture; its history, profoundly shaped by British colonial rule; and the pre-existence of another form of social stratification: caste. As we saw in the previous section, caste does have an important influence on economic activity. Those with higher-caste status usually have better-paid occupations and those with lower-caste status often work in poorly paid occupations. In other words, class and caste status overlap to a very great extent. However, this is not absolute. One aspect of social change in contemporary India is limited upward mobility. Some individuals from lower-caste backgrounds have achieved middle-class status. In what follows we provide a concise account of class stratification referring to the capitalist classes, the middle classes and to the evolution of class in the Indian countryside.

Capitalist Classes

The capitalist classes are very diverse in India. The industrial bourgeoisie emerged at a fairly late stage in Indian history. The incipient industrial bourgeoisie complained that the colonial regime did not encourage Indian-owned industry and in many cases actively disadvantaged it with favourable terms for British businesses. As in most societies, the super-rich form a tiny minority of the Indian population.

The industrial bourgeoisie is very small but the prevalence of family-owned businesses (discussed in Chapter 7) means that it is relatively easier to identify than in advanced industrialized societies where ownership is much more fragmented among shareholders and financial institutions. The enormous wealth controlled by the owners of industry means that it has been an influential group politically since the 1930s.

A distinction is sometimes made between the national bourgeoisie that is now well-established with business concerns across India, and regional capitalists who have more geographically concentrated businesses. These regional business houses are often family-owned, some have emerged relatively recently and they are often well connected to state governments. For example, in Andhra Pradesh the Ramoji Group, which publishes the newspaper *Eenadu*, has interests in real estate, food processing and film-making (Baru, 2000: 217–18). Another segment of the capitalist classes are those who run small and medium-sized enterprises. They usually operate businesses away from the large metropolitan cities and engage in a huge range of activities including brick making, textile production, commodity trading, construction and food processing. An equivalent group, discussed below, are the owner-managers of large farms. This segment of capital looks to the local state for support and they tend to rely less on innovation but use their influence with the local state to bend labour regulations and keep wages low (Harriss-White and Gooptu, 2001).

The Indian middle classes are a large, internally differentiated group, but a subset of this group, the so-called new middle class, are beginning to forge a sense of identity. A very rough measure of the size of the middle classes can be taken from estimates of income and consumption. The National Council of Applied Economic Research (NCAER) conducted a survey in 2001–2 which estimated 52.8 million households had an income of over 90,000 rupees (over 1200 GBP) a year. The NCAER describes this as the Middle High Income category, claiming that the number of households in this category had grown by 260 per cent since 1989–90. In terms of purchasing ability, a family with an income of over 90,000 rupees had a reasonable chance, close to 50 per cent, of owning a motorcycle or a scooter, a colour television and a fridge. Assuming an average household size of 5.6, this suggests nearly 300 million people are located in the Middle High Income category (Bery, 2004; NCAER, 2005: 7) However, there are inequalities of income within this broad group, which are divided between town and countryside. Of the 52.8 million households in the Middle High Income band, 24 million lived in the countryside. Therefore, although a large number can be grouped together in an income band, they are associated with different economies.

Urban Middle Class

The Indian middle class that has been most closely scrutinized is the urban middle class. This is a group that was cultivated by British colonial administrators who promoted education in the medium of English. The British ambition was to create a class that would staff the lower levels of the colonial bureaucracy and adopt a sympathetic attitude to British ambitions (Misra, 1961). Class can be defined in more complex ways that introduces factors like cultural and political attitudes. Education and cultural tastes are important markers that set the urban middle class apart from other status groups. The expansion of education and especially higher education since the colonial period has contributed to the character and growing size of the middle class. Education in English is economically advantageous and a route to social mobility. There has been much talk of a 'new Indian middle class' whose facility with English gives it a particular identity, and distances it from prosperous groups who favour other Indian languages (Fernandes and Heller, 2006).

The urban middle class is politically important. Leela Fernandes argues that the middle class were enthusiastic supporters of the Congress project of economic modernization, scientific progress and planned development (2006: 20–3). At the same time the state helped sustain and enlarge the middle class by providing higher education and jobs that are so vital for a salaried middle class. The middle class has become even more prominent since the mid 1980s. Rajiv Gandhi styled himself as a leader attentive to the consumerist aspirations of the urban middle class. It is assumed, not always correctly, that the middle class are the main beneficiaries and supporters of the post-1991 economic reforms. The urban middle class are portrayed by external observers as the vanguard of a vibrant economy whose riches are only waiting to be tapped by multinational corporations entering India. There is no denying the political and cultural importance of the urban middle class but it has been presented as a distorted image. The English-speaking new middle class is much smaller than the 300 million members of the middle income group.

The politics of the middle class were brought into focus by the 2004 general election. The ruling NDA coalition argued for re-election on the basis of economic performance. The election campaign was preceded by the 'India Shining' advertising campaign. A series of press and television advertisements were used to push the idea that high rates of economic growth were making India more prosperous and at ease with itself. The images identified the Indian middle class as key beneficiaries. Interestingly the advertisements were heavily criticized and the NDA lost the election (Wyatt, 2005b). The middle class may be a strong political force but it has yet to achieve decisive electoral influence. Elections are still dominated by ordinary, and mainly rural, citizens.

Classifying the Countryside

Important distinctions need to be made between those who manage, those who manage and labour in their own fields, and those who spend most of their working life labouring on farms they do not own (Harriss, 1991: 72–7; Stern, 2003: 96–7. The rural upper class are commonly described as those who own enough property to be able to avoid labouring on their own farm. They may have a diverse portfolio of assets that keep them wealthy. In the 1950s this group evaded the initial round of land reforms and kept a large amount of land in family ownership. The number of large farms has declined since 1960, when 29 per cent of agricultural land was part of a large farm. The number of farms has increased and holdings subdivided as land has been inherited between several children or been sold off. Still there is marked concentration of landownership, with the last measure (in 2003) showing that 11.8 per cent of agricultural land was concentrated in just 0.8 per cent of farms (Government of India, 2007: 24). The owners of large landholdings use hired labour to run a farm or get income from renting out plots to tenant farmers. The upper class often make high returns by lending money to other villagers. The profits from rural activities might be invested in urban property and the education of their children. The rural upper class have high standards of living, being able to consume on a par with the wealthier segment of the urban middle class. While this class gains some political power from money and muscle, it is a numerically small group and has been supplanted by the emerging rural middle class.

The rural middle class own or let a large enough farm to have a fairly secure income. They have been evocatively described as 'bullock capitalists' because their farms are too small to benefit from heavy mechanization and some traditional techniques, such as an animal-drawn plough, serve them well (Rudolph and Rudolph, 1987: 50–3). Farmers in this category have been able to afford, often with government subsidy, the combination of irrigation, fertilizers and seeds needed to increase farm yields. Members of the family work on the farm but they also need to hire labourers at peak times. This class is very numerous and is often from the so-called backward caste background. In terms of income, the middle-class category overlaps with those who run small businesses in the countryside. The fortunes of this segment of rural society have been linked to political decisions since the late 1960s. Government policies on agricultural subsidies (including credit) and purchase prices have an impact on the incomes of the rural middle classes. The state and central governments can intervene in markets to ensure that farmers make a profit, for example buying and storing grain, to guarantee a remunerative price for farm products. Input subsidies, such as cheap fertilizers, reduce the cost of producing food. Farmers lobby hard for cheaper inputs and higher support prices. This lobby has been most effective in the north west, in states like the Punjab, where most government purchasing occurs. In other areas official purchasing is often below the price on the open market and is of little help to farmers. That said, the rural middle class are not without influence. They do get subsidies, and agricultural income taxes are rarely levied.

Important tensions divide the rural middle and upper classes. The rural middle classes were anxious to be heard by the state and were keen to displace the upper-class/upper-caste elite that dominated the Congress Party in north India after independence. Commentators do not agree on the importance of class as a factor in Indian politics and political economy. A related issue is the extent to which the state is independent of class forces. Pranab Bardhan has offered a concise and enduringly persuasive account of class-based politics in India. He argues that no one class group has achieved dominance in India. Instead politics has been shaped by tensions between what he terms the 'proprietary classes' consisting of 'industrial capitalists, rich farmers, and white collar workers and professionals' (1988: 215). Among analysts influenced by Marxist thinking there is a rough consensus on the importance of the rural middle class.

Below these strata is a larger group of landless, or nearly landless, labourers. Some peasant families own or rent a very small plot of land of perhaps one or two acres. These holdings are usually insufficient to produce a living for a whole family and are known as marginal hold-ings. The majority of farms, 71 per cent in 2003, are in this category (Government of India, 2007: 27). The owners of marginal holdings often work as labourers on larger farms or migrate in search of work. This is a vulnerable position to be in and rural families without land often live in poverty. Wages are paid on a daily basis and work is not always available. Middle-class families usually have the resources to survive a poor harvest but labourers who do not have savings are exposed to seasonal vagaries. Again caste and class overlap very substantially. It is very common for Dalit families to have to eke out a living in this way. Agriculture also supports a large number of arti-sans who do not work in the fields but whose self-employment is often precarious. Even this class has experienced social change. The increased availability of school places offers an opportunity for labouring families that can afford it, to keep their children in school. However, many children are not able to take advantage of these opportunities or are able to attend only infrequently because of work commitments. In some areas the labour market has tightened, with fewer workers available for arduous labouring work and more women being drawn into paid work. Economic growth in the countryside has increased the availability of off-farm work. This combination of factors forces labourers' wages up in some villages. Government schemes such as the 2005 National Rural Employment Guarantee Act (NREGA) (renamed the Mahatma Gandhi National Rural Employ-ment Guarantee Act in late 2009) to increase the availability of work have had some benefit. However, many of this class remain extremely poor, eking out a precarious existence.

There are important underlying tensions between different classes in India. In the countryside the landlords and the middle classes are keen to keep wages low and increase the profitability of their farms. They also want high prices for their products. The lower classes have an important claim for equity. The combination of low wages and rising food prices are a very real threat to their life chances. The Indian state recognized this tension and since the 1960s has made limited efforts to finesse the differences through the public distribution system (PDS). The PDS buys food at a price high enough to remunerate farmers and then, in theory at least, sells food at a lower price to the poor. However, the system relies on the inclination of the central and state governments to support the outlets selling subsidized food. The PDS is now being undermined (Karat, 2006). The Food Corporation of India is a key agency in this system but the central government has

Illustration 4.2   Public distribution system

Making subsidized food available helps alleviate poverty. It also makes for good politics. This poster advertises an inexpensive packet of spices and reminds customers of the political leader who backs the scheme.

been scaling back support for the organization. In addition, not all state governments implement a policy of selling subsidized food with vigour, creating very real problems of food insecurity.

Gender

India is in many ways a patriarchal society. Social structures, in the form of customary practices and commonly understood meanings, usually advantage men relative to women. However, Indian women are not simply subordinated to patriarchy. Many are extremely active agents that make a huge contribution to Indian society, the economy, culture and politics. Important social change has occurred in India since the mid-twentieth century. The spread of education, politically driven changes, social activism and new economic opportunities have opened up many opportunities for both men and women. Indian society is also not uniformly patriarchal – men do not dominate in all spheres of life and women are able to preserve a degree of autonomy.

Other factors, including class, caste, religion and ethnicity, shape gendered relations. Practice also varies by region. So, for example, in Kerala and Karnataka a few communities are organized on a matrilineal basis (Menon, 1998). Indian society is in many ways socially conservative. Parents exert close control over many areas of their children's lives. It is generally assumed that parents or relatives should take the responsibility for arranging marriages on behalf of their children. Relationships between single young people of the opposite sex are discouraged or monitored. Premarital sex is discouraged and homosexuality is generally considered taboo. There has been change in this area, with some members of the younger generation arguing for, and gaining, their personal autonomy. Marriage against caste customs and personal choice of partners is not unknown either. In July 2009 the long-standing criminalization of homosexuality was declared unconstitutional by the Delhi High Court.

The relative standing of Indian men and women is often determined by customary practices that set out gender-specific roles for members of each sex. It is usually assumed that women should bear the reproductive burden, which includes primary responsibility for caring for children. Women are much less able to take on full-time employment outside of the home. One area of controversy is the illegal practice of dowry whereby a daughter's parents make substantial gifts to the couple, or the groom's family, at the time of their marriage. In fact the practice varies greatly. Not all families expect or make such gifts – although it is more common than not. It is not always clear if the dowry is a gift designed to confirm the prestige of the families making and receiving the gifts or is a more prosaic transfer of capital intended to make the new household economically viable. The gifts vary. They might include jewellery, household utensils, cash payments or a transfer of business assets. The practice has been criticized by social activists because it places a burden of expectation on the bride. Women's groups have argued that women have suffered when families have attempted to extract further dowry. In the worst cases, tensions over dowries have been linked to the harassment or even murder of the bride (Waters, 1997: 23). As Sanghavi *et al.* note, dowry deaths are 'commonly executed by first dousing the woman with kerosene and then setting her alight (and are) . . . often disguised as accidents and suicides' (2009: 1282). Between 1995 and 2005, recorded dowry deaths increased by 46 per cent and in 2005 the National Crime Records Bureau recorded over 7,000 dowry-related deaths (Chu, 2007). Sanghavi *et al.* question the reliability of these statistics, noting that in 'urban areas, 26% and 22% of all deaths in women were caused by fire-related injuries in age groups of 15–24 and 25–34 years, respectively' (2009: 1284). Their estimates for fatal fire accidents are six times those reported by the National Crime Records Bureau. Many analysts argue that economic liberalization and increasing consumerism have exacerbated dowry-related violence among all sections of society.

The sex ratio is another area that has attracted a great deal of attention. The survival rates of females are noticeably lower than that of males in the Indian population. The 2001 census recorded an all India ratio of 933 females to every 1000 males, but for the under six age group that ratio decreased to 927 females for every 1000 males. As far as survival rates of children are concerned the relative neglect of female children is considered to be a contributing factor. Women's health issues are not given priority, meaning that women are more likely to experience ill-health and die early (Waters, 1997: 25). Data that are disaggregated by state and district show substantial variations in the sex ratio. The 2001 census shows that the state of Kerala possesses a larger female population, the ratio is 1058, whereas the lowest ratio of 861 was recorded in the northern state of Haryana. The sex ratio has not improved with the gradual strengthening of the Indian economy and improvements in other development indicators. In addition to the neglect of female children, a study in *The Lancet* found evidence that 'the deficit in the number of girls born as second children is more than twice as great in educated than in illiterate mothers' (Jha *et al.*, 2006: 216). The causes of the skewed sex ratio are complex and extremely difficult to study. A number of causes have been suggested. In the background there is a frequent preference for a male child. In Hindu custom (as in Sikhism) the religious rituals a son performs for his parents at the time of their death are important. More importantly, there are economic factors to consider. In the absence of state pensions, sons are often expected to provide for their parents in old age. The practice of dowry moves capital between families. Where dowry is practised; the birth of a female child suggests the eventual loss of resources to a family (Harriss-White, 2001: 146–7). The Jha *et al.* study 'suggests that prenatal sex determination and selective abortion probably account for nearly all of the deficit in the number of girls born as second or third children' (2006: 217). But they also noted that they could not 'exclude selective abortion' as the reason for the differential in numbers of male and female births for first births (2006: 217). Again it is important to stress that these are not uniform practices or outcomes, but the sex ratio is sobering statistical reflection of a variety of patriarchal assumptions. Given the prevalence of ultrasound machines that can show the sex of an unborn child, it has been estimated that over 10 million female foetuses have been terminated since the mid 1980s, despite it being a criminal offence since 1994 to use these technologies for the purposes of sex-selection (BBC, 2006a; Jha *et al.*, 2006).

The gendered differences in adult literacy are just as striking. The 2001 census recorded the male literacy rate at 75.3 per cent in contrast to 53.7 per cent for females. Again there are important variations. The gap between men (86.3 per cent) and women (72.9 per cent) in urban areas is narrower. Regional variations are striking, with Kerala having a small gap between men (94.2 per cent) and women (87.7 per cent) whereas in Bihar the divide between male literacy (59.7 per cent) and female literacy (33.1 per cent) is vast (Government of India, 2001b). Many poorer families struggle with the cost of their children's education – either in terms of a direct financial cost or because of the loss of earnings from the child (either directly or in terms of using this child for childcare/domestic help). Families with limited resources are often reluctant to make such investments because a female child will be married into another family and her education will therefore not benefit the family. More prosperous families do not face these constraints, and education is seen as an asset, which may be a consideration when it comes to securing an advantageous marriage alliance. The work participation rate between men and women varies significantly, with fewer women than men in paid employment. Women are more likely to fall into the more disadvantaged categories of casual or self-employed workers. It has been estimated that women constituted 32.5 per cent of the paid workforce in 2004–05 (Sundaram, 2007: 3124).

The Indian economy is heavily shaped by gendered assumptions. The Shramshakti Report, published in 1988, revealed a wide range of gendered disadvantages. Land titles are usually in the name of male family members, and banks give priority to male borrowers. Not all of the work that women do is recognized. Household work can extend to gathering firewood and drawing water. Other unpaid work includes tasks such as farm labouring or tending cattle. Where this work is part of a family enterprise, women might not be paid, which results in serious undercounting of the contribution women make to the economy. It is also reflected in the limited income that women

Illustration 4.3   Women working on the tea plantations in the Nilgiri Hills, Tamil Nadu

Women's work is often defined by gendered assumption. On tea plantations women are routinely assigned the arduous work of tea plucking. It is assumed they are better qualified for the precision of this work. Higher wages are paid to the factory workers.

control. Where work is paid, men usually get paid at higher rates. Working conditions in the informal economy are poor. So the majority of Indian women who have paid employment have little social insurance, struggle to find adequate childcare facilities and face many health and safety hazards (Spodek, 1990: 897–8). Unequal wage rates are often reinforced by the allocation of tasks on a gendered basis. In the textile industry men usually occupy the higher-paid role of master tailor, with women and children taking on lower-paid work deemed to be less skilful.

The Indian legal system gives some insight into the diversity of approaches to gender issues. A critically important area is the personal law that regulates marriage, divorce, inheritance and the guardianship of children. There is no single legal framework governing personal law in India. Instead there are laws based on different religious traditions. The legal system recognizes personal laws for Christians, Muslims and Parsis. All other religious groups are governed by Hindu personal law that was codified in the 1950s.

Women are treated unequally by all forms of personal law in India. Men are privileged as inheritors of property by the Hindu Succession Act and are assumed to be the default guardian of children. Not all marriages have to be registered, which makes bigamous marriages easier and creates problems, mostly for women, in situations of divorce and separation. Unsurprisingly many argue that personal law in India is badly in need of reform. Some argue for bringing together all personal law into a Uniform Civil Code (UCC) that would disregard the religious backgrounds of individuals in the operation of the law. The politics of this issue are intricate and difficult to resolve. The 1985 *Shah Bano* case demonstrates the intricacies extremely well. Shah Bano, a Muslim woman, was divorced by her husband, who refused to pay alimony. The Supreme Court ruled that by civil law her husband was required to pay alimony. However, under pressure from some Muslim leaders who claimed that the judgment undermined the right to be governed by their own personal law, Rajiv Gandhi's Government passed the Muslim Women (Protection of Rights on Divorce) Act, 1986. Although Shah Bano received her alimony, Muslim women divorced after this Act was passed would not. The case demonstrates the tensions between gender equality and community rights. Many proponents of a UCC merely want to stigmatize minority groups. Minorities fear a UCC would give state institutions legal ways of interfering in their community life. For this reason most feminists are uncomfortable with the enthusiastic support given to the idea of a UCC by Hindu nationalists. Most women's organizations are more concerned about substantive reform that would give women more legal protection on family issues (Menon, 1998: 245, 248, 259).

The Indian state is aware of these differences in outcomes between men and women, and between female and male children. A landmark government report, *Towards Equality*, was published in 1974. The Shramshakti Report, discussed above, encouraged the Indian state to pay attention to the conditions under which women were employed. The National Commission for Women was formed in 1992. In 1995 the Government of India sent a delegation to the UN Fourth World Conference on Women in Beijing. In 2001 the National Policy for the Empowerment of Women was produced to recognize commitments made in Beijing (Spary, 2009). The Indian state has gone beyond merely recognizing inequality. A number of policies have been introduced to promote equality. Five-Year plans look more at issues of concern to women. The central government has taken up a number of initiatives, including the scrutiny of its budgets to reveal potential gender bias in spending allocations. The state governments in India's federal system have their own policies and their own commissions for women. Some states have introduced affirmative action quotas for women in government employment. Parastatal organizations have been formed in many states. These autonomous government bodies work to advance the development of women and they usually encourage small Self-Help Groups (SHGs) to form. These SHG groups enable women to act collectively to promote their welfare, for example, they might manage small development projects or form businesses funded by micro-credit. What is notable, however, is that the Indian state has struggled to come to terms with the notion of gender and the dynamics of relations between men and women. Instead, the prevailing state discourse encourages the idea of female vulnerability and inspires paternalist policy responses (Spary, 2008).

The governing bodies at every level of the Indian political system seem to favour men. The majority of elected representatives are men. Though the number of women getting elected has increased marginally in recent years, the imbalance is still striking. The highest number of women MPs elected was 58 in 2009 (plus one nominated woman), 11 per cent of the total Lok Sabha. This begs the question of what it is about political parties in India that results in so few women being nominated for parliamentary election. Political authority is understood in gendered terms and mostly in ways that work to the advantage of men (Spary, 2007). In Chapter 3 we discussed the Seventy-Fourth Amendment to the constitution, which reserved 33 per cent of seats for women in the panchayat village councils. This resulted in a sharp increase in the number of women being elected. The proposal has been criticized by parties representing the lower castes, who have demanded 'a quota within a quota' so that lower-caste women get a share of the reserved seats. These parties have protested in parliament when the legislation has been debated but are not able to outvote the large parties who have said they are committed to a 33 per cent quota for women (Randall, 2006).

Conclusion

Indian society has experienced important changes since 1947. Changes to the economy have had some impact on social relations with regard to caste, class and gender. Wider access to education has encouraged some social mobility and created more opportunities.

Attitudes have changed, with previously subordinate groups seeking more autonomy. Part of the process of social change has been driven by political efforts at reform. In some areas the state has been able to lead opinion and shape social attitudes. The 1950 constitution granted formal equality in terms of caste and gender. The constitution also assumes that all citizens, regardless of their wealth (or poverty), have equal standing before the law. Giving citizens a shared, equal status was an important part of the process of nation building. A nation that is less divided should be more cohesive. However, significant inequalities persist. Subordinate groups with lower social and economic status are not treated equally by society or, very often, by state institutions like the judiciary and the police. These inequalities inhibit a sense of shared purpose. Some groups, such as the Dalits, still feel alienated from Indian society. The nation-building project has therefore had mixed outcomes and India still is a divided society. That said, the promise of formal equality is significant. For example, the presumption is that caste discrimination and untouchability are illegal. Where the political will is present, laws that give protection to subordinate groups have been used as they were intended. Some upward mobility has occurred and important elements of social hierarchy have been weakened.

While the promise of the 1950 constitution has not been fully achieved, the document has been used as a benchmark for those seeking greater equality. The institutions of democratic politics have provided opportunities for subaltern groups, including Dalits, women and the lower castes, to claim more equal treatment. Political changes have had unintended consequences as well. For example, caste has taken on a new meaning in India's democratic system. A ritual hierarchy that gives privilege to a few cannot survive by itself in a political system that rewards numerical dominance. This development is explored in the next chapter.

5

Politics and Society

It would be surprising if contemporary India's politics and society were not very different than they were in the middle of the twentieth century. These differences are a result of not only endogenous changes within India, such as the introduction of universal suffrage and competition between different political parties, but also structural changes in the polity, for example the linguistic reorganization of states in the 1950s, as well as changes in the economic model that India managed itself by – most notably after the economic liberalization of the early 1990s. Still other changes have occurred because of exogenous changes such as increasing globalization and technological innovation. This is seen most markedly in the fields of technology and the media, which have had a dramatic impact on politics, society and the structure of the media itself. The image of India's position in the world has also changed (as we discuss further in Chapter 8). Contemporary India as a nation is arguably as divided as it was at independence, despite (or maybe because of) the nation-building project pursued by different elites. The democratic articulation and representation of the different sections of Indian society are indicative of a vibrant society but many sections of that society feel excluded from the 'mainstream', as we discuss below.

Party Politics

India's constitution-making process was less fraught than in neighbouring Pakistan and India was able to hold competitive elections under universal suffrage within four years of gaining independence. As with many former colonies, in the first elections the organization most associated with the movement for independence, the Indian

National Congress, reaped the benefits, winning 73 per cent of the seats with 45 per cent of the vote. But its success was not only due to enhanced legitimacy from its involvement in the struggle for independence, nor from the countrywide profile of many of its leaders such as Jawaharlal Nehru or Sardar Patel (although these undoubtedly helped). What was just as important was its strong organization – penetrating into all India's states and active at a local level. As noted in Chapter 1, Congress was formed in 1885 and evolved from an elite movement into a political party with a mass base. It was facilitated in this by its reorganization along linguistic lines in the 1920s. This enshrined its status as a movement that could truly represent all areas of India, but it was less successful at representing all religious groups. Its status as a mass party was consolidated by Mahatma Gandhi's mass mobilization campaigning strategy. It also benefited from the simple plurality electoral system – discussed later in this chapter.

The Congress's heyday was between 1947 and 1977 when it governed in Delhi. India's first Prime Minister, Jawaharlal Nehru ruled from 1947 until his death in office in 1964. But even in this period of dominance, the Congress was not unopposed. A total of 53 parties, not including independents, contested the 1952 elections. After the 1957 elections, as can be seen in Table 5.1, the number of parties contesting elections rose gradually, and proliferated exponentially after 1989; a phenomenon that is discussed in more detail below. The electoral success of Congress was also due to the fact that it was a middle–of-the-road party able to accommodate a wide range of political views. In 1964 Rajni Kothari famously coined the phrase the 'Congress system' to describe the nature of one-party dominance in India (which must not be confused with a one-party system). He described Congress as 'the party of consensus, [that] functions through an elaborate network of factions which provides the chief competitive mechanism of the Indian system' and that opposition parties, who had no chance of coming to power, would 'influence it by influencing opinion' and threaten to displace it should Congress stray too far 'from the balance of effective public opinion' (1964: 1162–3). Many of these opposition parties and movements not only had their ideas accommodated, but also in some cases they were absorbed within the Congress itself (for example, agitators for linguistic states), further strengthening the party. Within its ranks it was therefore extremely factionalized – not only at the centre, but also at different levels of its party – from the centre to the states. This

Table 5.1   Number of officially recognized parties in Indian national elections 1952–2009

Election year	National parties	State parties	Total no. of parties (not including independents)
1952	14	39	53
1957	4	11	15
1962	6	11	27
1967	7	14	25
1971	8	17	53
1977	5	15	34
1980	6	19	36
1984	7	19	35
1989	8	20	113
1991	9	28	145
1996	8	30	209
1998	7	30	176
1999	7	40	169
2004	6	51	230
2009	7	30	n/a

Note: An earlier version of this table appeared in Adeney (2007: 127).

Sources: Data on the numbers of national parties from 1952–2004 adapted from Election Commission of India (ECI) (Election Commission of India, 1952–2004). Data from 2009 have been taken from Press Information Bureau (2009). The ECI report has not yet been published for 2009, but over 360 parties participated. These data for 2009 are the number of state parties that won seats – data for earlier years provided by the ECI include state parties that did not win seats, so these data are not directly comparable.

enabled it to accommodate tensions in the short term but, as we shall see below, state-level challengers emerged.

As noted in Box 5.1, in early 1966 the leadership of the Congress Party passed to Indira Gandhi. Following (relatively) bad election results in 1967, especially at the state level, the party establishment, or 'Syndicate' as they were known, blamed Indira. These elections saw Congress lose power in a large number of important states. After a conflict over the choice of Congress president – Indira Gandhi was determined that her power as prime minister would not be limited by a powerful Congress president nominated by her political enemies – over 60 Congress members left the party to sit in opposition in the Lok Sabha, leaving Indira Gandhi with the support

Box 5.1 The Nehru–Gandhi Dynasty

Democratic institutions do not prevent families from becoming influential (as the Kennedy and Bush families have shown in the US). Some politicians gain name recognition from famous political parents. In some cases parents actively promote the political careers of their children and other close family members. This pattern is not uncommon in India. In Chapter 1 we showed how Jawaharlal Nehru followed his father into Congress politics. Jawaharlal had no intention of building a political dynasty, but during his time as India's first prime minister opportunities were provided for his daughter Indira to gain experience. Indira Gandhi (she acquired her surname through marriage to Feroze Gandhi – she is not a relation of Mahatma Gandhi) was elected President of Congress in 1959. After Nehru's death, the prime ministership did not directly pass to Indira, but after the death of Prime Minister Lal Bahadur Shastri in 1966 Indira was elected as leader of Congress (and effectively prime minister) by the Congress parliamentary party. Gandhi was not a political novice – she had held office during Shastri's premiership as Minister for Information and Broadcasting. Indira Gandhi was prime minister of India from 1966 to 1977 and again from 1980 to 1984 until she was assassinated. On her death, a coterie of senior Congress leaders decided that her son, Rajiv Gandhi, should assume the leadership of Congress. This was a definite case of dynastic succession – until the early 1980s Rajiv had no interest in a political career. It was only after the death of his younger brother, Sanjay, in 1980 that his mother sought to groom him for public office. Rajiv became prime minister in 1984 and governed until 1989. He was assassinated while campaigning during the 1991 elections. Upon his death, the Congress Party tried to persuade his widow, Sonia, to assume the mantle. She refused. In 1998 when the party was in serious danger of atrophying, she agreed to become President of Congress. Her motivations for assuming the leadership of Congress in 1998 have been hotly disputed; many have assumed that she wished to keep Congress a viable organization for her two children, Rahul (born 1970) and Priyanka (born 1972). Initially Priyanka looked the favourite to assume the mantle, but in a surprise move in 2004 Rahul stood for (and was elected to) the Lok Sabha. He has gradually moved to take positions of responsibility in the party and is widely tipped to be its future leader; and possibly India's next prime minster when Manmohan Singh retires. Priyanka, in contrast, continues to work behind the scenes. Congress is not alone in this regard. Other parties have seen the leadership pass from one generation to the next. We do not wish to overemphasize the prevalence of dynastic succession in Indian politics. Some parties are not dominated by one family. Where dynasties have been established, their ongoing success is not guaranteed – other leaders wait in the wings prepared to contend for leadership. Attempts to build a dynasty have failed in other parties and voters do not automatically vote for a political heir.

Illustration 5.1   Teen Murti, New Delhi

Prime Minister Nehru reluctantly moved into Teen Murti, the former
residence of the British Commander-in-Chief in India, in 1948. It became
his official residence until his death in 1964. It is now a museum and
housed in an adjacent building is the Nehru Memorial Library.

of over 200 (Hardgrave, 1970: 260). This loss of the organizational
wing of the party had far-reaching ramifications. Indira Gandhi
chose to appeal directly to the people – circumventing the organization. Together with her more populist strategy, she adopted a radical
programme of nationalization and portrayed herself as the champion
of the poor.

The Congress slogan of *Garibi Hatao* (Abolish Poverty) emerged
dominant in the 1971 election and Indira Gandhi's wing of the party
was re-elected to power with 352 seats and 43.7 per cent of the votes.
However, Congress ran into political difficulties. Indira had an over-
bearing style of leadership within the country and within Congress.
Indira worked to destabilize opposition parties and gained notoriety
for dismissing many state governments using the device of
President's Rule. Inside the party it became clear that power was
concentrated in Delhi, and Congress state chief ministers who
appeared to be too independent or too popular found themselves
replaced. This further undermined the Congress organization. The

political system was stretched by a series of events in the early 1970s, including war with Pakistan, rising food prices, and increases in the price of oil. The tendency to rule from Delhi had its limits and the regional character of Indian politics asserted itself. The imposition of a State of Emergency in June 1975, discussed in Chapter 3, kept Indira Gandhi in power but, in 1977 when she was persuaded to fight elections, Congress was soundly defeated by a combination of opposition parties fighting under the Janata Party banner. This party represented the aspirations of the upwardly mobile backward castes and brought together a number of political leaders alienated from the Congress Party. However, it was heavily factionalized and hostility towards Congress did not provide a sufficient policy programme to keep it together.

The return of Indira Gandhi to power in 1980 marked the temporary resumption of Congress dominance at the centre. The centralization continued, as did attempts to intervene in the politics of states (such as the Punjab) in support of the Congress. Indira's support of the Sikh radical, Bhindranwale, against the more moderate Akali Dal party as a means to increase the likelihood of Congress winning power in the state dramatically backfired. Bhindranwale's secessionist movement used violent methods and spiralled out of control. He based himself in the Sikh holy shrine, the Golden Temple in Amritsar. Indira Gandhi decided to use the army to resolve the crisis and the attack on the Golden Temple in June 1984 led to the death of Bhindranwale but alienated many Sikhs not connected to the secessionist movement. Not long after, in October 1984, Indira Gandhi was assassinated by two of her Sikh bodyguards. Sikhs were even more alienated by rioting and revenge attacks, which saw thousands of Sikhs killed and in which Congress workers were implicated. The subsequent election, fought under the leadership of Indira's son, Rajiv Gandhi, saw Congress returned to power for a five-year term, partially on a sympathy vote. However, it lost power at the national level again in 1989. Congress returned to power in 1991 but, lacking a majority, it was obliged to form a minority government. This government lasted until 1996 but it became abundantly clear that Congress was no longer a dominant party and since 1996 its share of the national vote has not risen above 30 per cent. Congress was slow to adapt to the new context of national coalitions as its leaders assumed that it was still the natural party of government. In contrast, the much more ideological BJP realized that coalition politics had arrived and was quick to form alliances of convenience.

Box 5.2   Anti-defection legislation

Political instability has been caused by splits in ruling parties. This was an occasional feature of state and national politics. A party can lose its ruling majority if some of its legislators defect to the opposition. It was often alleged that defections were driven by personal ambition or bribery. Various attempts have been made to deal with the problem. In 2003 the Ninety-First Amendment to the Constitution was passed. This provided for several things, including a curb on the size of the Council of Ministers, but also to clarify the legal status of those parliamentarians who choose to leave a political party and join another. The Tenth Schedule to the constitution, enacted by Rajiv Gandhi in 1985, had penalized individual defectors with disqualification from the legislature (and from holding any other remunerative political position). The changes introduced in 2003 extended this provision to include situations when a group of legislators broke away to form a new party or to merge with another (unless two-thirds of the original party were in favour of the breakaway or merger). Controversially, the disqualification applied also to those who were deemed to have voted against their party in the legislature (or abstained) without permission, even if, on other matters they supported their original party. The matter of what constituted a defection was left to the speaker of the particular legislature to decide. This provision has been criticized for being undemocratic in that it restricts the free vote of individual legislators.

By 2004 the Congress had adapted to the dynamics of the new situation and, surprising many observers of Indian politics, the Congress-led United Progressive Alliance (UPA) defeated the BJP-led NDA coalition. Manmohan Singh became the first Sikh Prime Minister of India in 2004. It was thought by many that Sonia Gandhi, the Italian-born widow of Rajiv Gandhi, would take the office. She was, after all, the leader of Congress. However, the vitriolic resentment expressed by some opposition politicians encouraged Sonia to take a (highly influential) back seat. The Government was supported from outside by the Samajwadi Party (SP) and the Bahujan Samaj Party (BSP) (the latter withdrawing their support in June 2008). It was also extended support by the Left Front, which includes the Communist parties, which withdrew support in July 2008 over the nuclear deal with the US, discussed in Chapter 8. Despite this, the Government was able to last its full five-year term in office, and elections were held in April and May 2009. In another surprise result, Congress was returned to power with a more definitive mandate. It won 206 seats, and the UPA alliance won 262 seats, requiring the support of only ten more parliamentarians to govern. The UPA includes mainly regional parties, Congress offshoots, as well as small Muslim parties. The 2009 coalition was different to the UPA that fought the 2004 election. It lost some allies, notably the RJD and the Lok Janshakti Party (LJP), but added the Congress breakaway party, Trinamul Congress. Another change in 2009 was a more flexible, or even atomized, approach to the forming of electoral alliances. Congress gave up on the idea of a national alliance and instead it cooperated with parties in individual states. The BJP adopted a similar approach. As such, no common political programme was projected, and an alliance in one state did not preclude competing against the same partner in another state. This allowed the leading parties to fine-tune their alliances so that they could achieve a minimum winning coalition. If necessary, they could add extra partners after the elections to get a ruling majority (Kailash, 2009: 55).

Congress has been opposed by a number of parties claiming to be national parties, including the Communist parties: the Communist Party of India (CPI) and CPI(M). Some parties with a national outlook, including the Communist parties, are in practice regionally confined. A few parties have made serious attempts to rival Congress as a national party. Most have failed. The Swatantra Party was briefly influential in the 1960s and the Janata Party, as we noted above, actually formed a government in the 1970s. The principal national rival to Congress is the Bharatiya Janata Party (BJP), which is an offshoot from the Jana Sangh. The BJP was formed in 1980. Unlike Congress it espouses a Hindu nationalist ideology that is 'not so much a clearly defined movement and ideology, as a broad field of thought' (Zavos, 2005: 37). This is primarily based around the notion that India's political institutions and society should reflect Hindu culture. We elaborate on this ideology in Chapter 6. The BJP was helped by both Indira and Rajiv Gandhi's cultivation of the north Indian 'Hindu vote' as a space opened up for the religious mobilization of voters. Political parties have to take some care when doing this because the first clause of the Election Commission's Model Code of Conduct states that parties and candidates should not 'aggravate existing differences or create mutual hatred or cause tension between different castes and communities, religious or linguistic' (2007). In 2009, a BJP candidate, Varun Gandhi (grandson of Indira Gandhi and cousin to Rahul and Priyanka Gandhi), was censured by the Election Commission of India for violating these provisions and inciting communal feelings, leading the BJP to distance themselves from his remarks (although he was elected as a BJP MP shortly afterwards) (BBC, 2009a).

Box 5.3   The ongoing controversy over the Babri Masjid

In 1986 the Babri Masjid in the north Indian town of Ayodhya (in the state of Uttar Pradesh) was reopened for worship. This mosque was the object of controversy and its reopening had important consequences. Hindu nationalists claimed that the site was the birthplace of Lord Ram. A temple commemorating this event is said to have been destroyed by the Mughul Emperor Babur in the sixteenth century and later replaced by a mosque. The reopening of the Babri Masjid reinvigorated a Hindu nationalist campaign to have the temple rebuilt. The issue was a boon to the BJP in the late 1980s as the campaign to build a Ram Temple helped the BJP increase its tally of 2 seats in 1984 to 85 seats in the 1989 national elections. The BJP returned to the campaign in 1990 and the conflict over the issue, discussed in Chapter 2, intensified. The BJP caught public attention and were elected to office in the states of Rajasthan, Madhya Pradesh and Himachal Pradesh in 1990, and Uttar Pradesh in 1991. The mosque was attacked and torn down by a mob in December 1992, leading to the dismissal of all four state governments, ostensibly for failing to protect the mosque (although the Congress minority government at the centre, headed by Narasimha Rao, did not intervene to stop the demolition). The status of the site has not been resolved and the site itself is sealed. One Hindu nationalist organization, the Vishwa Hindu Parishad (VHP) is prepared to build a temple, but has been prevented from doing so. Several BJP politicians still face prosecution for their role in the demolition, including L. K. Advani who in September 2009 renewed his commitment to build a temple on the site. In 2002 a coach on a train carrying Hindu pilgrims returning from a visit to the site was set alight – 58 people were killed. Muslims were blamed for setting the fire and reprisal attacks killed up to 2000 people in the state of Gujarat, as well as displacing 150,000 others.

Support for the BJP increased in the 1990s, even as interest in the Ram Temple issue declined slowly after December 1992 (see Box 5.3). In 1996 the BJP won the most seats in the general election but was only able to govern for 13 days. When it failed to put together a viable coalition it was replaced by the United Front coalition government of Deve Gowda. By the time of the 1998 elections the BJP was fully alert to the necessity of adapting to coalition politics and, despite the paradox of a Hindu nationalist party in alliance with lower-caste and regional parties, successfully made several pre-election alliances. These produced a workable coalition for a few months but the formidable leader of the AIADMK, Jayalalithaa Jayaram, ultimately withdrew her support over a dispute concerning cabinet places. The 1999 elections saw a more stable governing coalition elected, with a common manifesto. The National Democratic Alliance governed from 1999 to 2004, ultimately defeated by a resurgent Congress, now woken up to the coalition politics game.

Regional Parties

Although the Congress dominated at the centre until the late 1970s, at the state level the picture was very different. Regionally based political parties began successfully to challenge its dominance in elections for the state legislative assemblies, succeeding in defeating Congress in a large number of important states in 1967 (triggering the split in Congress discussed above). Therefore party systems diverged among states, and diverged further as many of these regional parties developed national aspirations. As Manor notes, 'India has not one party system, but many' (1995: 107). Defining regional parties is not straightforward. Some parties are regional parties in the sense that they appeal to regional culture or sentiment. Examples include the Akali Dal in the Punjab, several political parties in Tamil Nadu, and the Telugu Desam Party in Andhra Pradesh. Some parties do not appeal to regional identity but are still regionally bounded because they choose to work in one or two states or appeal to a caste identity which is confined to one or two neighbouring states. Examples include the Samajwadi Party in Uttar Pradesh or the Pattali Makkal Katchi (PMK) in Tamil Nadu. In addition, the Communist parties are in no sense ideologically regional, but their support is primarily concentrated within the states of Kerala and West Bengal. As seen in Table 5.1, the number of state parties has massively increased since independence. The importance of the regional parties began to be felt at the national level in 1989 when a national coalition government was formed. The DMK, a regional party from Tamil Nadu, held a post in the cabinet. In 1991, a rival party from Tamil Nadu, the AIADMK, supported the minority Congress government without a coalition being formed. Since 1996 no coalition has been formed without the participation of regional parties; they have become fundamentally important in national politics.

Regional Parties: Creative Campaigners

The dominance of Congress meant that the early regional parties had to compete against a well-established party that had good access to patronage and campaign funds. The regional parties used creative

Illustration 5.2   Campaign posters, Tamil Nadu

This poster, photographed during the 2006 state assembly election, shows how Congress seeks support. The pictures of Indira and Rajiv Gandhi in the top left-hand corner recall the history of the party. The election symbol of the Congress, the open palm which can be seen in the bottom centre of the poster, is a visual prompt that ties up with the electronic voting machine. The election symbol helps identify the party and is a useful tool for guiding illiterate voters in the voting booth. Also prominent on the poster are images of the regional party leaders allied with Congress. The fragmentation of the party system means that elections are fought between coalitions of parties in alliance.

ways to communicate their message and define issues. In the southern state of Tamil Nadu the DMK argued in favour of a distinctive southern or 'Dravidian' identity. They argued that south India was exploited by north Indian interests that were hegemonic in politics (via the Congress Party) and business. Short of money they used ingenious methods to sell their message. Several DMK leaders also worked in the film business and they inserted their messages into film scripts. The stars of those films campaigned for the party and political images abounded. Between elections the parties in the state fly flags, cover the walls of buildings with cheaply printed posters and commission colourful murals. Many parties have since moved on to using television for promoting their image but the old methods remain in use. In the western state of Maharashtra a regional movement, the Shiv Sena (Shivaji's army), was formed in 1966. The founder, Bal Thackeray, was a newspaper cartoonist and is adept at getting publicity for his movement. The Shiv Sena focused on the flow of migrants into the rapidly growing economy of what was then the city of Bombay. Using the slogan of Maharashtra for the Maharashtrians, the movement argued in favour of localism. It also questioned the loyalty of Muslims to India and formed a long-term alliance with the BJP. The Sena moved into electoral politics but has remained active in street politics. Activists have ransacked the offices of newspapers and have used violence against opponents. In the southern state of Andhra Pradesh the Congress Party enjoyed a very long period of dominance. This came to an end in 1983 when it was successfully challenged by a new regional party, the TDP. The party was led by the filmstar N.T. Rama Rao (NTR) who was well known for playing religious figures in his films. NTR played up to this image and took care to make public appearances clad in the saffron robes worn by many Hindu holy figures. We need to stress that the cinema does not provide an automatic route into Indian politics. Many filmstars have failed to convert their popularity into votes, such as the Tamil star, Sivaji Ganeshan, in 1989. An ambitious actor has to become a professional politician who speaks to the concerns of voters and is able to run a well-organized campaign. Many have tried. A few have succeeded.

Caste-Based Political Parties

The strength of social ties based on caste means that politicians in India have frequently used caste as a way of mobilizing support. Often this has been done by matching candidates of a particular caste background to constituencies where that caste is known to be numerous. In some cases parties have formed with the objective of getting the support of a single caste group. A number of these parties formed in the 1950s but most of them faded away in the face of Congress dominance. As Congress controlled the government it could undermine caste-based parties by making concessions to that caste, promoting members of that caste within its own party or encouraging the party to merge with Congress. Part of the story of Congress decline is the way in which it neglected important caste groups. In the state of Uttar Pradesh the Congress Party did little to reach out to the numerically important backward castes. In other states this group was cultivated by using the full range of concessions that could be given under the OBC affirmative action schemes and by making sure that politicians from these backgrounds held important positions in Congress. Few concessions were offered to this group in Uttar Pradesh and upper-caste politicians held most of the senior positions in Congress. Another point of contention was the treatment of Dalits by Congress. This section of society were given some benefits and held some posts in Congress. However, Congress did not do all that it could have done to promote the interests of this group. As we noted in Chapter 4, many schemes intended to ameliorate the consequences of untouchability were not properly implemented. Also, it was usual for senior Dalit politicians in Congress to hold only token responsibilities. Dalits rarely held senior cabinet posts in state governments or acted as Chief Minister. This neglect cost Congress dearly as Dalits turned to other parties.

Many of the new caste parties are confined to one or perhaps two states. They have gained electoral success as the demands of the lower castes within Indian society have become more prominent and assertive. The decline in Congress's organization was important because the demands of the lower castes became more prominent at the time when Congress was least equipped to deal with them. The reservation schemes led to 'the emergence of an educated generation of Scheduled Castes' who were to become leaders of parties such as the BSP (Chandra and Laitin, 2002: 28). Examples of caste-based political parties include the BSP in Uttar Pradesh, led by Mayawati, and the RJD in Bihar led by Laloo Prasad Yadav. They have been vitally important to national coalitions, for example the RJD was a member of the UPA Government from 2004 to 2009, and the SP and BSP both extended support to the UPA from outside. These caste-based parties have often controlled state governments, either on their own or in coalition, and the RJD in Bihar and BSP in Uttar Pradesh are two recent examples of this.

The Bahujan Samaj Party (BSP) was formed in 1984 claiming quite credibly that Congress had neglected its loyal Dalit supporters. The BSP gained core support from the Chamars, a Dalit caste that is fairly populous across north India. The BSP also added support from Muslim voters, other Scheduled Caste groups and some minor backward caste groups. The BSP picked up support in Uttar Pradesh and

Box 5.4   Mayawati: India's first Dalit woman Chief Minister

Mayawati Kumari is the Chief Minister of India's most populous state, Uttar Pradesh. She is a remarkable female politician who is hailed as an example of the success of Indian democracy and of its affirmative action policies. Rising from humble origins, she is a Dalit from the Chamar community; she benefited from the Scheduled Caste quotas and was originally employed as a teacher. She is the current leader of the BSP and became Chief Minister of Uttar Pradesh in 1995 at the age of 39, the youngest person to hold this position in such a politically vital state. Mayawati's original campaigning issues and support base focused on the Dalits. Mayawati has a lively campaigning style and became known for her fiery speeches. She came to national prominence in the mid 1990s in the midst of controversy over outspoken remarks made about Mahatma Gandhi. Mayawati's elevation to the post of Chief Minister was psychologically important for Dalit voters because they had been accustomed to being kept at the margins of politics. Mayawati forced the state bureaucracy to implement neglected policies designed to protect and compensate Dalits who have been the victims of caste discrimination. She secured a loyal following, and became known by supporters as *behenji* (older sister). In recent years she has widened the caste support base of the BSP – to higher-caste voters – and also extended campaigning to states other than Uttar Pradesh. Mayawati's career has continued to be controversial, with some seeing her as having an extravagant ruling style that focuses on generating spectacle and creates a cult of personality. Statues of Mayawati have already been erected in the state of Uttar Pradesh. Much attention focused on her decision to allow a gigantic shopping mall to be built next door to India's Taj Mahal – India's most famous landmark. Investigations have also been carried out into the vast personal wealth that she has amassed (*The Independent*, 2008). In this, however, she is hardly alone among Indian politicians.

was able to win enough seats to become the junior partner in a number of coalition governments at the state level (Wyatt, 1999). The BSP was very careful to allocate seats according to caste background and then publicize this widely. Most recently the BSP reached out to upper-caste Brahman voters. The combination of good organization and a broad caste alliance meant that the BSP was able to win enough votes to form a majority government in Uttar Pradesh in 2007. However, Mayawati's aspirations of becoming the first Dalit prime minister of India have yet to be fulfilled. The party contested the vast majority of seats in the 2009 election and increased the vote share of the party, gaining 6.2 per cent of the national vote, an increase of almost 1 per cent from 2004 (Yadav and Palshikar, 2009: 36). However, this increase in vote share failed to lead to a massive increase in seats, with the BSP gaining only one more seat in the Lok Sabha. The BSP failed to extend its broad caste alliance.

Regional and caste-based political parties have continued to increase their support, and raised their ambition to a share of power in New Delhi. These parties hold the balance of power and now, in contrast to the 1970s and 1980s, the regional pattern of politics has reasserted itself. It remains unlikely that a single party government will ever be able to be formed again in India. However, two coalition governments have completed full terms in office, albeit with internal tensions, demonstrating that the sometimes tricky process of coalition formation need not lead to federal instability.

The Electoral System

As mentioned in Chapter 3 the vast majority of elections in the Indian political system are carried out using a single member simple plurality (SMSP) system. The electoral rules are straightforward and it is not difficult for independents or new parties to get themselves on the ballot. Actually getting elected is more difficult of course! In practice it takes a good deal of organization, ingenuity and money for a candidate to get elected. The task of organizing a national party in a country the size of India is truly daunting. As noted above, most parties have tended to organize locally and often opt to work in only one or two states. The states of the federal system are attractive units to organize in. They are manageable in terms of size and the dominance of a single language adds to the convenience of forming a regional party or working in a single state.

In a country that in many areas still has low levels of literacy, the parties campaign on the basis of a symbol. These symbols are allocated by the Election Commission. They are used by candidates on their campaign material (posters, leaflets) and at rallies. The party symbol appears next to the candidate's name on the ballot paper or voting machine; therefore, even if the voter is illiterate, he or she can identify the party that he or she wants to vote for. The current symbol of the Congress is the palm of the hand (as seen in Illustration 5.2) and that of the BJP is the lotus flower.

Despite its dominance of the Lok Sabha, Congress never won a majority of the votes at the all-India level, although the simple plural-

Table 5.2   The leading party's share of the seats and votes in national
elections 1952–2009

Year	Leading party	Percentage of seats	Percentage of the vote
1952	Congress	73.0	45.0
1957	Congress	72.7	47.8
1962	Congress	72.5	44.7
1967	Congress	53.7	40.7
1971	Congress (R)	67.8	43.7
1977	Janata	54.4	41.4
1980	Congress (I)	67.0	42.7
1984	Congress	76.6	48.1
1989	Congress	37.2	39.5
1991	Congress	44.5	36.4
1996	BJP	29.7	20.3
1998	BJP	33.5	25.6
1999	BJP	33.5	23.8
2004	Congress	26.7	26.5
2009	Congress	37.9	28.6

Note: Data adapted from Election Commission of India.

ity electoral system translated its vote share into a comfortable seat majority. For example, as can be seen in Table 5.2, Congress won very handsome seat majorities in 1952 (73 per cent of the seats with 45 per cent of the votes) and 1984 (76.6 per cent of the seats with 48.1 per cent of the votes).

Political scientists take a close interest in electoral systems as a factor determining the shape of party systems. Duverger (1964) famously claimed that the SMSP system would lead to the formation of a two-party system. The need to win the largest number of votes cast in each constituency sets a high threshold for parties to cross. Even where there are four fairly strong parties in a constituency, which is not unknown in India, a party has to achieve between 25 per cent and 50 per cent of the vote to have a chance of being elected. This is a colossal task for a new party and most fail to persuade voters to support them. This in part explained the early success of the Congress Party, and indeed its dominance, in the 1950s. However, the Indian case has proved somewhat problematic for Duverger's theory as a two-party system has not emerged. India, as noted, has a frag-mented party system, with 38 parties being represented in the Lok Sabha in 2004. Duverger's advocates argue that the two-party system operates at the level of the constituency, with the number of parties being reduced by electoral alliances that restrict competition between parties (Sridharan, 2002). Indeed many states have something approximating a two-party system. However, there are a number of states where three or four parties are strong contenders and defy the logic of Duverger's prediction. The most prominent of these is Uttar Pradesh in northern India.

Civil Society

Civil society can be broadly defined as a collection of voluntary associations that stand between the family and the state. However, it is a matter of debate whether all associations should be included within this definition. Some would rule out associations that do not conform to a definition of civility. They would discount associations that seek to usurp the political authority of the state and/or act illegally (Whitehead, 1997). Others such as Jenkins (2005) would rule out associations that are not formally organized. We take a pragmatic view. We include trade unions in our discussion of civil society because individuals choose to join them. As businesses consist predominantly of paid employees, we do not consider them as part of civil society. Therefore we treat business and the media in India in separate parts of the book. We relax the civility qualification when discussing civil society in order to give a comprehensive picture of India's rich associational life.

Civil society in India developed in unusual circumstances in the nineteenth and twentieth centuries. Many Indian activists were enamoured by the formality of civil society organizations in western countries and adopted them as tools for pressing their own concerns. A number of notable religious and social reform movements emerged in the nineteenth century. However, the British colonial regime distorted the context in which civil society and politics developed in India. Many normal political activities were deemed illegal and activities that involved formal organizing were often repressed by the colonial authorities. Furthermore, politics in India was understood, and influenced, by very broad social and cultural forces. Nationalist movements in British India were not easy to separate from social movements. So, for example, during the first half of the twentieth century the Congress movement engaged in a very broad range of activities, including running schools and cooperatives. Similarly, the

Hindu nationalist movement has its origins in nineteenth-century movements for religious reform such as the Arya Samaj. Formal organizations, like the Rashtriya Swayamsevak Sangh (RSS), which was formed in 1925, articulated political objectives and nationalist views. However, it was only in 1951, and with some reluctance, that the RSS agreed to support a new Hindu nationalist political party, the Bharatiya Jan Sangh (BJS). The RSS is also associated with trade unions, schools and development projects. These organizations seek to transform India into a more Hindu society. Politics, especially when understood as a project of social transformation, cannot easily be 'kept out' of civil society in India. Not all civil society organizations are linked to political parties and movements by any means, but the boundary between civil society and political organizations is heavily transgressed. Trade unions, discussed in more detail below, are another very obvious example of this. The trade union sector is fragmented as trade unions have proliferated, usually encouraged by political parties that want to promote *their* union.

India's civil society is distinctive in other ways. It reflects India's regional diversity as most associations are local in orientation. As we shall see below, they organize around issues of local concern and concentrate their membership within one or two states and there are relatively few national organizations (Jenkins, 2005). As mentioned, some elements of civil society have a considerable history but recently there has been a proliferation of development oriented non-governmental organizations (NGOs). A full census of NGOs has not been carried out but those registered to receive foreign donations increased from 16,740 in 1995–6 to 30,321 in 2004–5 (Jayal, 2007: 152). It is often observed that civil society is fractured by social distinctions, with class being the usual suspect. Civil society in India is also often internally divided but with a wider range of stratification. Many organizations, including religious organizations and caste associations, reflect India's religious, cultural and social diversity.

Civil Society and Caste

The links between caste and civil society are multiple. At the lowest level of Indian society informal caste-based entities are potentially important. These include kinship networks and bodies that regulate or discipline behaviour within a caste group. The effectiveness of these associations varies over time and between different caste groups. Another caste-related aspect of civil society is the formal caste association, many of which were formed from the late nineteenth century onwards to promote the interests of particular caste groups (Rudolph and Rudolph, 1967). The associations have an internal and an external function. An association would often encourage the reform of internal caste traditions, such as the adoption of vegetarianism, to enhance their status. This is a good example of the impact of associational activity and political aspirations on social practices. Externally, caste associations lobby the government and political parties for recognition and material benefits, such as jobs. In recent years these functions of the caste association have often been usurped by political parties that incorporate caste considerations into their organizational structures. Caste associations have their critics who consider that they divide society but there is no denying that even in contemporary India these associations continue to have a profound impact on Indian society and politics.

Civil Society and Religion

Religious belief inspires a good deal of associational life in India. Various organizations exist to reform, protect and promote religious practice in India. Charitable activities have also been inspired by religious belief and organized by religious bodies. Temples are an important part of religious observance for many Hindus. The larger temples and noted pilgrimage sites are run by formally constituted trusts. These trusts are regulated by state governments and often control substantial resources, including land and money, used to pay for activities which often go beyond ritual activity and include education and poor relief. Apart from temple trusts, there are numerous Hindu religious societies which promote religious ideas and education.

Other religious groups have contributed to the diversity, and complexity, of associational life in India. Christian churches have gained respect by providing high-quality education and healthcare under charitable auspices. As discussed in Chapter 2, some Christian groups have recently attracted criticism for propagating their religious beliefs (even though it is a constitutional right to do so). A lot of Muslim charitable work is associated with the principle of *waqf*, making pious bequests. Bequests are made to trusts that hold endowments for the purpose of poor relief (Awn, 1994: 74). The status of these funds has sometimes been controversial and each state government convenes a Waqf Board to regulate the trusts and resolve disputes.

The Shiromani Gurdwara Parbandhak Committee (SGPC) was given legal responsibility for managing Sikh shrines in 1925. Not all Sikh Gurdwaras are under SGPC control but it controls a large number, including the 10 most historic ones. The Gurdwaras, with SGPC support, also run schools and employ workers to propagate the Sikh religion (Nayar, 1966: 177–80). The SGPC and its associated Gurdwaras make a major contribution to civic life in the state of Punjab, also funding hospitals and charitable trusts (SGPC, 2009). It is also worth noting how it is integrated into politics. Most of the committee are elected and elections to the SGPC are contested by candidates affiliated to parties, including Congress and the Akali Dal. However, the Akali Dal makes a special claim to represent the Sikh community, and the SGPC elections have allowed the party to dominate the organization (Byala, 2009; Mahaprashasta, 2009). In 2009 a controversy emerged over the Haryana Government's plans to create a separate SGPC to look after the Sikh Gurdwaras located in Haryana (formerly part of the Punjab). As the state government is Congress controlled, some have alleged that this division is a ploy to divide the Sikhs. The Akali Dal is strenuously resisting the proposal (Financial Express, 2009).

Renewed Interest in Movement Politics

The early 1970s marked an important juncture in Indian politics. An economic crisis helped crystallize a number of trends. The optimism generated by the nationalist movement in the 1940s and 1950s was beginning to dissipate. Congress was increasingly regarded with cynicism and mistrust because the Indian state had not been able to eradicate poverty or bring about rapid development. In the early 1970s a slowdown in the industrial sector was matched by drought and poor harvests in the countryside. Public disaffection was manifested in protests on the streets, strikes and growing interest in alternative approaches to politics. Movements were certainly not new to India but interest in movement politics was boosted by the events of the early 1970s.

These developments were prefigured by developments in leftist politics. In 1967 another split occurred in the Indian Communist movement. A number of activists spurned the formal political process and turned to armed resistance. A focal point of this activity was the district of Naxalbari in West Bengal. The original movement was heavily repressed but the term 'Naxalite' lives on as a way of referring to various leftist insurgents who use force in pursuit of their revolutionary objectives. Some of those involved in the Naxalbari revolt were drawn into the Communist Party of India (Marxist-Leninist) (CPI(ML)), which was formed in 1969 (Omvedt, 1993: 40–2). The conventional Communist parties tended to draw their support from peasant farmers who owned some property. In contrast, the CPI(ML) argued that a genuine leftist movement needed to organize among the very poorest, including the Dalits and landless labourers. These ideas were expressed by loosely connected disparate movements in the 1970s and 1980s.

In recent years leftist insurgents have become much more active and groups have merged, culminating in 2004 with the formation of the Communist Party of India (Maoist) (CPI (Maoist)). This group poses a serious challenge to the authority of the Indian state in central and north India, including parts of the states of Andhra Pradesh, Karnataka, Maharashtra, Madhya Pradesh, Orissa, Bihar and Jharkhand (Menon and Nigam, 2007: 118–24). The CPI (Maoist) was banned in several states such as Bihar, Andhra Pradesh, Chhattisgarh, Orissa, Jharkhand, Madhya Pradesh and Tamil Nadu, and in June 2009 the central government extended this ban, classifying it as a 'terror organization' (Rediff.com, 2009). Naxalites are estimated to control almost a third of the districts of India. They have a strong presence in many states, including Jharkhand, Bihar, Andhra Pradesh, Chhattisgarh, Madhya Pradesh, Maharashtra and West Bengal (BBC, 2009b). They seek to foment revolution against 'the semi-colonial, semi-feudal system under the neo-colonial form of indirect rule, exploitation and control' (Press release 2004, cited in South Asia Terrorism Portal, SATPO, nd). They are extremely active in contemporary India and seek to join up the territory under their control, from Nepal to Karnataka.

In September 2009, Prime Minister Manmohan Singh re-described the Naxalite violence as the 'gravest internal security threat' and conceded that levels of violence continue to rise (BBC, 2009b). The draconian legislation enacted to deal with the threat, including the right to interrogate without formally arresting a person, has outraged human rights activists (The Telegraph, 2009). More than 6,000 people have been killed in the conflict, which has worsened in recent years (BBC, 2009b). In the first ten months of 2009, it has been estimated that 765 people were killed (including civilians, security forces and Naxalites) (SATPO, 2009). A senior retired policeman with experience of fighting the Punjab insurgency, K. P. S. Gill, opines that the

Naxalites' 'ideology is that the manner of killing should frighten more than the killing itself' (*The Economist*, 2006). In September 2009, Manmohan Singh conceded that the problem was not solely a law-and-order one (BBC, 2009b).

There are a plethora of Dalit movements and organizations active in different parts of India. Few of these organizations have a national presence, as is common with civil society formations in India. However, taken together, Dalit human rights groups, advocacy organizations, journals and magazines have done much to make caste a political issue.

Issues of particular interest to women were taken up with renewed enthusiasm in the 1970s. This built on a tradition of women's activism. The All-India Women's Conference was formed in 1927 and came to be seen as the key organization representing women. However, some viewed it as too closely linked to the Congress political establishment and in 1954 the National Federation of Indian Women was formed by more left-inclined activists (Kumari and Kidwai, 1998: 26–9). The 1974 report from the Committee on the Status of Women in India, *Towards Equality*, expressed disappointment that the status of women had not substantially improved in spite of the official drive for national development. This encouraged Indian feminists to be more critical of the Indian state. They have argued for greater recognition of the work that women do, both in the household and in wider society (John 2001: 107–10). Various women's organizations have campaigned against domestic violence and lobbied for legislative changes that would promote equality. Movements with more grassroots orientation have campaigned against the sale of liquor, arguing that it diverts money out of the household and increases the risk of domestic violence. A notable campaign was conducted in the state of Andhra Pradesh between 1991 and 1995. Local protests by women against liquor sales grew into a state-wide campaign, which resulted in a brief period of prohibition (Larsson, 2006). State governments are reluctant to yield on this issue because, as we noted in Chapter 3, they gain a large amount of revenue from taxes on alcohol. It is also an area in which parties generate illegal income. Current areas of concern are multiple – as discussed in Chapter 4 the reported rate of dowry deaths has increased substantially in the last twenty years. Other major concerns include the spread of HIV/AIDS (to women who are unable to insist that their husband use a condom), the trafficking of girls and women (as the ratio of women to men falls) and increasing female education: the

Delhi-based Centre for Social Research estimates that 20 per cent of school-age girls are not in school (Centre for Social Research, nd). As with other NGOs, women's organizations are often based locally or regionally rather than nationally and are often divided along caste lines.

India faces a number of pressing environmental problems. These include deforestation and habitat destruction, particularly in areas with adivasi populations. The state of Orissa provides several examples of this trend (Menon and Nigam, 2007: 65–6). The 'green' revolution of the 1960s has brought with it depletion of groundwater and pollution from the overuse of pesticides and fertilizers. Urban areas are blighted by airborne pollution and polluted rivers. A number of movements and organizations have formed to address these problems and oppose what they see as the crude developmentalist mentality of the state. Gandhian ideas inspire some campaigners. Some movements have a grassroots character as they seek to protect local livelihoods, such as fish stocks, from immediate threats. Activists of the Chipko movement, in the Himalayan foothills of the Tehri Garwhal, embraced trees to stop them from being felled (Omvedt, 1993: 132–4). There is also an urban middle-class strand to the environmental movement, which emphasizes the dangers of excessive consumption.

The vast dam project in the Narmada Valley has become a prominent issue for a number of movements and organizations. A series of dams was planned that involved cooperation between the states of Maharashtra, Madhya Pradesh and Gujarat, which were interested in the irrigation schemes and hydroelectricity that would come from the project. In spite of international concerns about the environmental assessment, the project was aggressively pushed forward by the Indian state in the 1990s and work continues on the project. The project has been strongly opposed on environmental and humanitarian grounds. As well as habitat loss, an estimated 400,000 people will lose their homes to the waters of the newly created dams. The Narmada Bachao Andolan (NBA) has been the key movement opposing the project. Other NGOs have joined the campaign, raising concerns about environmental issues and the inadequacy of rehabilitation for the displaced (Menon and Nigam, 2007: 69–72). The misgivings about these mega-projects were eloquently expressed in Arundhati Roy's (1999) controversial essay, 'The Greater Common Good', on the topic. The Narmada issue is a poignant one and shows how environmental issues are intertwined with other concerns in the movement politics of contemporary India. The NBA failed to prevent the construction of the dam but made the authorities 'pay more attention to compensation and rehabilitation'. It has partially done so by campaigning internationally, expressing 'its concerns not merely in terms of immediate social and environmental impacts, but link[ing] these to questions of biodiversity, corruption within government, and democratisation' (Williams and Mawdsley, 2006: 667).

Non-Governmental Organizations

India has an extremely diverse range of non-governmental organizations (NGOs) that are active. Many are small and active within a well-defined locality (as is much of civil society within India). Others are nationally organized and work with very large budgets. The orientation of NGOs varies greatly, with some being little more than businesses that provide social goods or act as contractors for other agencies. The voluntary sector not only mobilizes but also seeks to network and engage in 'advocacy in an effort to shape social and policy agendas' (SDSA, 2008: 104). However, the 'movement' orientation is often apparent among NGOs, many of which provide social services *and* press for social change. The Association of Rural Education and Development Service (AREDS) in the southern state of Tamil Nadu illustrates how organizations have a range of objectives. Formed in 1980, the organization works in one district in the state and focuses on the welfare of Dalits, women and children. It provides non-formal education and some health services, and supports micro-enterprises that create jobs. At the same time, AREDS works as an advocacy group encouraging its members to claim entitlements from the government and lobbying the government for policies that favour the poor (AREDS, 2007).

The mix of social and service activities carried out by many organizations has not prevented NGOs from being heavily criticized by figures on both the left and the right. It is frequently assumed that NGOs in receipt of foreign funding are suspect; this assumption has been written into government policy regulating foreign contributions. Critics on the left see NGOs as having given up on progressive politics, and they accuse NGOs of having 'sold out' (Jenkins, 2007: 64). Some observers have seen in the growth of NGOs a new approach to social action and politics. Citizens from an urban middle-class background are often prominent in NGOs (Harriss, 2007: 2717–19). Some critics argue that a 'shift away from mobilisation to advocacy and

---

Box 5.5   SEWA: Success story

The Self-Employed Women's Association (SEWA) is another civil society organization that provides services, and works for social change. It was formed as a trade union in 1972 representing women textile workers but has broadened out its activity considerably since then (Spodek, 1994). SEWA was formed in the Ahmedabad in the state of Gujarat and is influenced by Gandhian ideas including religious tolerance, non-violence and local self-sufficiency. Its members are self-employed and, given their place in the informal economy, comprise a group that is not well represented by conventional, workplace-oriented trade unions. Some SEWA members work at home doing outsourced piecework for garment manufacturers or making *bidis* (homemade cigarettes). Other members work as street vendors or manual labourers. A lot of SEWA's work is concerned with gaining full employment for women and protecting their employment rights. However, SEWA also runs a bank, and this reduces the dependence of poor families on usurious moneylenders. It has also organized cooperatives to create livelihoods and it provides easily accessible medical services. SEWA shows something of the geography of Indian civil society as its activities are regionally concentrated. In 2006 it had 959,698 members with just over half living in the state of Gujarat. Most of the rest lived in the adjacent state of Madhya Pradesh (SEWA, 2006).

---

agenda setting has . . . succeeded in drawing in a new middle class of professionals, usually less comfortable with, if not dismissive of, political parties and electoral politics' (SDSA, 2008: 104). While there are tensions between some movement activists and some NGOs, different organizations often complement each other. This has been the case among Dalit organizations where the educational and social work of formally organized NGOs complements the activism of more loosely organized movements. NGOs provide detailed reports and information that can be used to give substance to claims made by movement activists. NGOs build political capacity by providing education and organizing workers into unions (Gorringe, 2005: 76).

Trade Unions

Associations representing the interests of workers have a long history in contemporary India. Trade unions grew as Indian industry developed in the early twentieth century. An apex body, the All-India Trade

Union Congress (AITUC) was formed in 1920. The Congress nation-alist movement was anxious to curtail strikes and limit labour mili-tancy during the 1940s. Congress leaders also resented Communist influence over the labour movement. Accordingly an alternative body, sponsored by Congress, the Indian National Trade Union Congress (INTUC) was formed in 1947. The Congress government also introduced legislation that controlled and limited the ability of the trade unions to take strike action. These moves weakened the trade union movement and gave political parties greater influence, for instance the Congress formation of INTUC gave the Communist Party of India control of AITUC. The trade union legislation of the 1940s gave state governments, and thus the parties that control them, great power over the activities of trade unions (Chhibber, 2004: 116–22). Other political forces insinuated themselves into trade union movements over time. In 1955 activists from the RSS formed a trade union, the Bharatiya Mazdoor Sangh (BMS), committed to the prin-ciples of Hindu nationalism. The BMS avoided the leftist orientation of most other unions, favouring a less confrontational approach to employers (Andersen and Damle, 1987: 129–33). The Centre of Indian Trade Unions (CITU) was formed in 1970. It is affiliated with the CPI(M) and has overtaken the AITUC as the largest trade union federation with a leftist orientation. Regional political parties have also formed connections with trade unions. It is not uncommon for several rival unions to be active in the same workplace and workers can be members of several unions simultaneously. Unions affiliated with political parties have lost credibility with many workers, given that the leaders have divided loyalties and appear to have been co-opted by the party. Independent unions not affiliated to political parties have been formed to provide better representation for workers. These are usually confined to one workplace. They tend to have a better record of recruiting members but they lose influence because they are not connected to a large apex organization (Ramaswamy, 1995: 103–7).

Agricultural workers have also organized to demand better working conditions but have faced even more obstacles. The reasons for this are partly structural. Agricultural workers are not as geographically concentrated as urban workers and members are dispersed and easier to intimidate. The All-India Kisan Sabha was formed in 1936 to represent peasants. Agricultural unions have worked to promote the interests of farm labour, for example campaigns have been launched for minimum wages and the enforcement of these wages. However, these organizations have had varying degrees of success. Also, they have not always been purely labour unions. Peasant farmers have been encouraged to join some unions, which has required unions to take up a broader range of issues, often at the expense of those whose only income is from labouring. Agricultural unions have been actively discouraged by landlords, with coercion used and in some cases union members murdered (Gough, 1989). Where minimum wages have been determined by state governments, they have not always been implemented as the authorities have been scarcely more enthusiastic about rural equity than the landlords themselves.

The trade union movement faces great difficulty in contemporary India. The movement is politically divided and much activity is duplicated. Trade unions have been criticized for overly centralized and unimaginative leadership, and a poor record of representing women workers (Sinha, 2002: 4). Union membership is concentrated in the sector that is easiest to organize, that is, in large-scale workplaces where workers are relatively well protected and have formal employment contracts. The industrial sector remains relatively small. Many workers are employed on informal contracts but it is easier for trade unions to represent the minority of workers with formal contracts and those who have well-defined benefits to protect. The vast majority of workers in India, an estimated 457.9 million in 2004–5, are not unionized. Initial figures for the last count of membership (for 2002) show only 24.6 million members affiliated to the main apex organizations and only a minority of those members, 7.5 million, were employed in agriculture and related work (John, 2007). In contrast, over half of the workforce, 258.7 million in 2004–5, is still employed in this sector (Sundaram, 2007). The economic reforms since 1991 have resulted in large-scale redundancies. The Government of India has been under pressure to reduce the legal protections offered to workers.

Media

The reach of the broadcast media (radio, television and satellite) has been extended since 1947. The press has kept pace with advances in literacy, and newspapers and magazines in regional languages are very popular. Numerous broadsheet newspapers and magazines published in English are widely available. The print media have a good record of promoting accountability and stimulating debate, though there have been some notable failures. At the time of independence there were a number of quality publications. Many had played a role in the independence struggle, found it difficult to adjust to the role of a critical press and were supportive of the Nehruvian government. This had changed by the 1970s as a new generation of journalists and politicians emerged. Indira Gandhi's relationship with the press was more difficult than her father's, and she had less tolerance for dissent. This was manifest during the Emergency of 1975–77 when hundreds of journalists were detained (Sonwalkar, 2002: 824–5).

The regionalization of politics has also contributed to a regionalization of the print media, encouraged by the advances in literacy (Sonwalkar, 2002: 822). In 1998, the predominant language of publication was Hindi, with 2202 dailies. Urdu dailies numbered 509, and English dailies numbered 353. However, the regional language press is vitally important; for example, in 1998 there were 344 Tamil, 302 Marathi, 208 Malayalam, 106 Punjabi and 106 Gujarati dailies. In addition to the dailies, there are numerous fortnightly and monthly publications, a substantial number of which are in English (Sonwalkar, 2002: 826–7). Many of these publications are news magazines, such as *Frontline* and *Outlook*, which include high-quality reporting and in-depth analysis of political and social issues.

There have been several prominent exposés in recent years. In the late 1980s, *The Hindu* exposed Rajiv Gandhi's alleged involvement in the Bofors corruption scandal, contributing to his defeat in the election of 1989. In 2001 the *Tehelka.com* tapes caught members of the ruling NDA allegedly taking bribes in return for awarding defence contracts. This scandal cost Samata Party Chairman, George Fernandes (then defence minister), his job. More recently (2007), *Tehelka* published allegations concerning the active role of Hindu nationalist organizations, including the Bharatiya Janata Party, in the 2002 Gujarat riots.

Unlike the independent print media, All India Radio (AIR), established in 1936 had 'clear objectives to inform, educate and entertain the masses' even though at the time of independence its broadcasts could reach only 11 per cent of the population (All India Radio, nd). It 'was to be used as a powerful educational tool in a hugely illiterate country' (Thussu, 1999: 126). As the Government of India states, '[t]he commitment of All India Radio to the rural audience dates back to more than 50 years . . . These programmes not only provide information about agriculture but also create awareness about the ways and means to *improve the quality of their lives*' (our emphasis) (Government of India, nd-a). Together with the other national broadcaster – the state-run TV station, Doordarshan, discussed below – AIR's mandate was to promote national integration. The first three Ministers of Information and Broadcasting 'were upper-caste Gandhians' seeking to implement a nation-building project and 'a policy of high culture' (Jeffrey, 2006: 212–13). As part of this project AIR adopted a Sanskritized version of Hindi in Hindi-speaking areas, prompting Nehru to complain that he 'could not understand the language in which his Hindi speeches were reported' (Jeffrey, 2006: 205). As will be discussed further in Chapter 6, the choice of language used in India is not only cultural, but it also has political as well as communal associations – such a decision promoted the interests not only of the Hindi-speaking north but also of Hindus over Muslims. Today AIR claims to serve over 99 per cent of the population, broadcasting home services in '24 languages and 146 dialects' (as well as several foreign languages) (All India Radio, nd). Close links with the government meant that AIR was used as a propaganda tool by successive governments (Thussu, 1999: 126), especially during the Emergency when, during a two-week period, AIR broadcast 192 news items about Sanjay Gandhi (Frank, 2001: 409). In recent years it has maintained its national integrative function and remains an important outlet for the government of the day, although many other sources of information are now available.

Between 1959 and 1991, India possessed one television channel, Doordarshan, 'a notoriously monotonous and unimaginative state monopoly which was uncharitably labelled as being a mouthpiece of the government of the day' (Thussu, 2007: 594). As was the case with AIR, Doordarshan not only tended to be supportive of government, but also endowed itself with a nation- and state-building mission 'through images of a unified and progressive nation' but one that was 'always having to catch up with the industrialized countries' (McMillin, 2001: 48 and 51). As Farmer points out, Doordarshan used 'heavily Sanskritised Hindi, particularly for news broadcasts' (1996: 100) as part of this nation-building project. One of the successes of Doordarshan had unintended consequences. The extended serialization of the Hindu epic, the *Ramayana*, between 1987 and 1990 proved to be enormously popular. The Hindu nationalist movement was able to exploit the imagery of the programme in support of its own ideology and campaigns (Farmer, 1996: 102).

India was slow to allow the use of personal satellite dishes, giving cable television operators an advantage. In 2000 government policy was changed and in 2003 Zee TV began offering a direct-to-home (DTH) service. Several other broadcasters have taken this route; consumers get better picture quality and DTH improves access to television in remote areas.

Illustration 5.3   The proliferation of satellite dishes

Doordarshan came under challenge with the decision in 1991 to liberalize the economy. A swift expansion of cable and satellite operators occurred – in 2000 the number of cable connections had reached 30 million compared to 20 million telephone connections (McMillin, 2001: 46). Challengers such as Star TV moved in. In 1992 only 1.2 million homes had access to satellite television; in 2005 this had increased to 61 million (Thussu, 2007: 594). These viewers were predominantly middle-class and urban – targeted by a different set of advertisers to those that advertised on Doordarshan.

In 1993 Doordarshan launched regional channels in Indian states, many of them focusing on entertainment in an attempt to compete with the cable networks (McMillin, 2001: 53). But its nation-building project remained. Multiple regional channels launched themselves at the same time. Thussu notes that there were over 200 digital channels by 2005, many aimed at the South Asian disapora (2007: 594). The liberalization of the economy has also regionalized television production – notable examples are Sun TV and Udaya TV. Many of these regional channels had powerful political backers, for example Sun TV was owned by close family members of the leader of the DMK regional party, M.K. Karunanidhi (McMillin, 2001: 48). However, although the satellite stations do well, Doordarshan still retains the highest audience share – 400 million people watch the channel DD-1 (Thussu, 2007: 606). Despite the competition, it is still committed to a public service ethos. As the Government of India website states:

> Doordarshan has contributed significantly towards the acceleration of socioeconomic change, promotion of national integration and stimulation of scientific temper in the country . . . its mandate is to carry . . . messages on population control and family welfare, preservation of environment and ecological balance, highlighting the need for social welfare measures for women, children and the less privileged. (Government of India, nd-c)

Interestingly, the liberalization of the Indian television sector has not resulted in an 'Americanization' of television. Both Thussu and Juluri note that channels have branded themselves as Indian – the case of MTV India is an example of this (Juluri, 2002: 368; Thussu, 2007: 596). Channels such as Zee TV have also promoted 'Hinglish' as a medium of communication (a mixture of Hindi and English) popular among the 'urban youth', particularly in the north of India (Thussu, 1999: 127). However, the 'Murdochisation' of news has resulted in less attention on international affairs and more on indigenous stories, and on those that support the free market rather than the concerns of the rural population (Sonwalkar, 2002; Sainath, 2004; Thussu, 2007: 600 and 605). As Thussu notes, 'the increasing marketisation of television seems to have left out of the picture the majority of India's citizens – the poor – especially those living in the countryside' (2007: 607).

Conclusion

India's politics and society have changed dramatically since independence. At the time of independence the Congress dominated the political landscape, and its vision of how to bring India into the modern age was promoted through several all-India organizations. Although India at the time of independence was extremely diverse and many of these differences were politicized (without such politicization the partition of India could never have occurred), the presumption of many in the Congress was that these differences would become less salient. Instead, the reverse has happened. Societal cleavages have introduced themselves into the political arena. Universal suffrage changed the dynamic of society – those with numerical power who are organized (such as the lower castes) now have electoral power. This has translated into positive policy outcomes for these groups such as the extension of reservations for OBCs. The proliferation of political parties has generally increased the voice of the more marginalized sections of society, and sources of information are much more widespread than they were. But it is important to note that many groups within all sections of Indian society remain vulnerable. Lower-caste women and those in rural areas are more vulnerable than educated urban women, but, as the increase in reported dowry killings indicates, even they are not safe from harm.

India's constitution has been adapted to take into account many of the changes in the political sphere (such as the anti-defection legislation and the extension of reservations). But the political system, as discussed in Chapter 3, has generally accommodated the changes informally. Party politics remain in flux – there has been too much change in recent years for us to predict its future direction with certainty. However, it is likely that the different nationalist traditions represented by Congress and the BJP will continued to influence Indian society for the foreseeable future. In addition, a plethora of political parties and movements are likely to remain and contest for influence. The old Nehruvian adage that India achieves unity in diversity also remains true – although the diversity has achieved more political and social expression than it did at independence. This has been despite certain nation-building measures intended to promote standardization and convergence on a shared national character. We develop this theme in the next chapter.

6

Nationalism and Culture

A key theme of this book has been the diversity of India, in many different spheres. The commonly used term 'the Indian subcontinent' recognizes this size and diversity. How then does this diversity fit with nationalism? There is something approximating a pan-Indian culture that is consumed, to a greater or lesser extent, across all Indian regions. In this category we can talk of sport, literature, film, as well as the national media discussed in the previous chapter. Much, but not all, of this material is communicated in English and is accessed by middle-class consumers in India and elsewhere. Some cultural forms, including sport and some films, depend less on language. There are flourishing popular cultures across India and in each of the major regional languages there is serious cultural production in the forms of literature, film, popular music, broadcast and print media. Improvements in communications technology mean that these products are also consumed by members of the diaspora. As we will discuss in this chapter, Indian nationalism is strong, especially when directed externally, against Pakistan. It is also very evident at the time of major sporting fixtures, especially those involving cricket. A sense of Indian identity, however imperfectly communicated, can be seen in the juggernaut that is the Bollywood film industry. Just as important are the attempts of the Indian state to foster and standardize a strong sense of identity. The components of that identity have political implications, as we shall see. They are also contested – and have changed over time.

Nationalism and National Identity in India

The Indian state in its present form was born out of a contested national identity. After independence (and indeed, today), the idea around which the Indian state was legitimized, and membership of the state community defined, was highly controversial. While the states of India and Pakistan were ostensibly created around the idea of two nations, Congress never accepted the two-nation idea, and refused to create a 'Hindustan'. Instead, Congress created a secular constitutional framework, rejecting the institutionalization of the different religious elements within the composite culture, albeit with elements of minority protection. This secularism was conceptualized differently from the secularism of the United States as well as other western countries – that of the separation of state and religion. The Indian version of secularism meant the *neutrality* of the state between different religions. Thus, it retained provisions that permitted it to fund religious schools (of all major denominations) that French legislation prohibits because of its rigid separation of the two spheres. But Muslim demands for reserved seats in the parliament were rejected (though Congress had accepted these before independence). Reserved seats for Muslims would have guaranteed Muslims a certain number of representatives in the parliament (as well as state legislatures), although groups other than Muslims would be able to vote in these constituencies. Reserved seats were rejected on the grounds that 'the granting of political safeguards to minorities would . . . undermine national unity and cohesion' (Bajpai, 2000: 1839). Sikh demands for the redrawing of the borders of the Punjab to create a Sikh majority state were also rejected, also on the grounds that such a state would undermine the 'unity' of the Indian nation. Although ostensibly neutral, the practice of secularism in the daily administration of the Indian state was uneven after 1947 (G. Singh, 2000). Some Congress politicians had Hindu nationalist sympathies and at the state level it was not unknown for Hindu interests to be championed at the expense of other religious minorities (Hasan, 1998). As Judith Brown notes, many of Nehru's colleagues felt that 'community [was] . . . an essential part of national identity' (2003: 185 and 189).

However, the government under Nehru's leadership still favoured an 'inclusive' approach to nation building, which was not just equated with the equal treatment of religious groups. Overall, the Indian state articulated a version of nationalism and national identity premised on a territorial and civic identity. Membership of the civic 'nation' was defined by residence within the state borders regardless of religious, linguistic or regional affiliation. But this does not mean that different groups had nothing in common – culture was vitally important to this conception of national identity – this culture developed as a result of

Box 6.1 Controversies of the Indian census

The Indian census is one of the largest censuses in the world. It is a complex operation that requires two million enumerators (Harding, 2001). Census results have been controversial ever since the census was introduced to India in 1871. The enumeration of the demographics of different religious communities both at the all-India and the local level contributed to tensions between all religious communities. These tensions continue today – along both ethno-linguistic and religious lines. An example of this was seen at the time of the 2001 census. The data from the 1991 census had counted the Hindu community as 82 per cent of the population and Muslims as 12.1 per cent of the population. In 2001 a radical change was seen – Hindus had dropped to 80.5 per cent of the population and Muslims had increased to 13.4 per cent. This resulted in sensationalist headlines in the Indian press including 'Muslim growth rate up by 1.5 pc' (Times of India, 2004). However, what the 'headline figure' had failed to reveal was that in 1991 no census was held in Kashmir because of the security situation existing in the state at that time. As Jammu and Kashmir is a Muslim majority state, this reduced the Muslim population in the 1991 census. 'Adjusted figures' revealed that the Hindu population had reduced somewhat – down to 81.4 per cent – but that Muslims had increased only 0.3 per cent to 12.4 per cent. Of course, in a country with a population as large as India, the absolute numbers indicate an increase of the Muslim population of 36.5 million, but as the Hindu population increased by approximately 140 million there was no significant change in the overall demographic balance.

living within a shared territory (Sridharan and Varshney, 2001: 225–6).

This secular version of national identity cannot be divorced from Nehru's vision of creating a strong and modern Indian state – strongly influenced by the Soviet Union and his own socialist beliefs. Nehru's views closely resembled the ideas of British Fabian socialists who favoured a strong central state to direct economic development. Identities that detracted from this centralization were viewed as anathema to Nehru's project. In addition, it was assumed that these identities, whether based on language, religion or caste, would lose their salience and maybe even fade away with the onset of modernization and economic development. This did not happen.

Hindu nationalists have contested this version of the Indian nation, from the Jana Sangh during the 1950s to the BJP of today's India. The BJP argues that India as a Hindu state does not preclude minority protection but those minorities must accept that the national culture is a Hindu one. Hindu nationalists also argue India is not merely a territory but the cradle of Hindu civilization (Savarkar, 1999). Therefore, in the Hindu 'motherland', a secular state espousing neutrality between religions is inappropriate. The BJP, and various attached organizations, such as the VHP, make a distinction between 'indigenous' religions such as Buddhism, Sikhism and Jainism and those that have 'affiliation' elsewhere – by this they mean the Christian and Muslim faiths. Although the vast majority of Christians and Muslims are indigenous to India, their loyalties are the subject of Hindu nationalist innuendoes. Other attempts at minority stigmatization include alarmist suggestions that inattention to birth control will enable Muslims to overwhelm the Hindu majority.

Other versions of the nation have been articulated by various ethno-nationalists who did not subscribe to the civic nationalist vision, Hindu nationalism or the two-nation theory (Chadda, 1997). They rejected the Nehruvian argument that identity politics were irrelevant to membership of the Indian nation. They also rejected the Hindu nationalist assertion that non-Hindu identities were either inferior or Hindu 'in essence'. The campaign for a Sikh state in the 1940s and again in the 1980s are examples of a movement against Hindu domination, just as the Tamil agitation in the 1950s and 1960s against the dominance of the northern-Hindi speakers (although this agitation also had a caste dimension, discussed below) were both ethno-nationalist movements. Another basis of ethno-nationalist sentiment has been the defence of local identities against 'encroachers'. The 'sons of the soil' campaign in Assam is an excellent example of this (Weiner, 1978). This campaign defined itself against the Bengali community, a minority in the state of Assam, who were perceived to be taking jobs through their higher educational qualifications (Price, 1997).

Not all ethno-nationalists in India have sought independence. As we shall see, many nationalist movements have been content with autonomy within India – when demands have escalated, this has normally been due to clumsy handling by the centre (Adeney, 2007). When the Indian state has perceived its territorial integrity to be threatened (which is often when such demands are couched in religious terminology), it has cracked down with force. The surprise of the 1990s was that the BJP and some regional forces associated with minority religious communities, such as the Akali Dal and the Jammu and Kashmir National Conference (though both would reject the

Table 6.1   How proud are different groups to be Indian?

	Very proud	Proud	Not proud	Not at all proud	No opinion
Upper-Caste Hindu	73	22	1	0	4
Peasant Hindu	69	24	0	1	6
Hindu OBC	60	29	2	1	8
Hindu Dalit	56	29	3	2	10
Muslim	57	31	1	2	9
Adivasi	44	37	2	1	15
Christian	75	23	0	0	4
Sikh	66	27	3	2	2
India	**60**	**29**	**2**	**1**	**8**

Note: N = 5227.
Source: Adapted from SDSA (2008: 257–9).

claims that they only represent Sikhs and Muslims respectively), joined forces in opposition to the 'national', secular Congress Party (G. Singh, 2000). In a survey taken in 2005, the vast majority of those interviewed were 'proud' or 'very proud' to be Indian. As can be seen in Table 6.1, this pattern was replicated across different groups. However, there is a marked difference among different religious groups – only 57 per cent of Muslims were very proud to be Indian, compared to 73 per cent of upper-caste Hindus.

All three versions of the nation discussed above have been contested by Dalit activists. As discussed in more detail in Chapter 4, Dalit is the preferred term for former 'untouchables'. They claim that 'Indian' national identity reflects the interests of the upper castes and that while caste oppression continues, the formal declaration of independence from Britain is meaningless (Joshi, 1986). Dalit activists claim that India is profoundly fractured by caste divisions and the socio-economic inequality that follows from it. As long as the legacy of caste persists, they argue that India cannot be united as a national community. Dalit activists also take issue with the larger narratives favoured by Hindu nationalists. Some argue that Hinduism, connected as it is with ritual caste practice, is a minority concern of the minority of the twice-born, upper castes (Illaiah, 1998). It has long been debated whether Dalits are formally Hindus. Nationalists, like Gandhi, have been anxious to claim Dalits as Hindus and prevent the proliferation of identities that might become the basis of alternatives to nationalist politics (Galanter, 1997). Dalit activists tend to

Dr Ambedkar was a notable political leader who campaigned against untouchability and caste discrimination in the mid-twentieth century. He has literally become an icon who symbolizes Dalit aspirations. Ambedkar statues are a common sight in contemporary India. Activists erect his statue as a way of asserting their identity and claiming recognition in their locality.

Illustration 6.1   Ambedkar statue

reject Hindu nationalism because they see it as a hegemonic project favoured by the upper castes, designed to secure the acquiescence of the backward castes and Dalits. In recent decades hundreds, if not thousands, of Dalit organizations have been formed across India. Increasingly powerful Dalit political parties have been formed and see themselves as rivals of other nationalist parties. The most notable Dalit party is the BSP, which is currently governing India's largest state of Uttar Pradesh. Dr Ambedkar, famous for his role in drafting the 1950 constitution, has become a national Dalit icon. The strength of Dalit identity in contemporary India suggests further fragmentation of support for civic and Hindu nationalism. As Table 6.1 demonstrates, 56 per cent of Hindu Dalits feel very proud to be Indian compared to 73 per cent of upper-caste Hindus.

Government Institutions and the Indian Nation

After independence the government was well aware of the challenges of unifying the diverse state, and worked hard to promote standardization in several areas. One of these was the national language. As noted in Chapter 2, India is a multilingual polity and the issue of what language should be the national language achieved prominence during the Constituent Assembly Debates. Several options presented themselves. Hindi was the language spoken by the largest number of speakers and had the advantage of being an 'indigenous' language. However, although spoken by the largest number of speakers it was a diverse language – 'Hindi' spoken in Bihar and 'Hindi' spoken in Rajasthan are very different creatures. In addition it cannot claim to be a majority language. Finally, although it can claim indigeneity, in this it is rivalled by all other Indian languages, which, while they may not have a similar number of speakers, are important languages in their own right. Many of these languages claim a prouder and more ancient status than Hindi. There was therefore great resistance to the adoption of Hindi as the national language. The only other option was that of retaining the link language of English. However, as well as being the language of the colonizers, English was not spoken by a large enough proportion of the population to be a viable choice as a national language.

A compromise was eventually reached. Hindi and English were accepted as official languages (but the term 'national' was rejected on the grounds that all languages of India were 'national languages'). English was accepted as a joint official language for a 15-year period. A decision also had to be made on the script in which Hindi was written. Hindi was commonly written in the Devanagari script – which has its origins in Sanskrit, the ancient language of India in which the Veda are written – rather than the Persian script in which Urdu is written. The Devanagari script was chosen. In terms of nation building and national identity this was controversial. Devanagari is a script of northern India, which served to highlight the distinction between the north and the south. These decisions had implications for the inclusivity (or otherwise) of the Indian nation.

The final debate concerned the status of the other languages of India such as Tamil, Telugu, Marathi and Gujarati. What rights would be conferred on speakers of these languages? This was an important point. What language should government business be conducted in? What language should government examinations be taken in? If the government recognized only Hindi and English as the languages of official discourse, then this had major implications for the rest of the population who did not speak these languages. Were these speakers of different languages to be disadvantaged compared to their Hindi- and English-speaking compatriots? Following serious riots in the south of the country in 1965, especially in Tamil Nadu, the 'three-language formula' was agreed. Speakers of any of the languages

Table 6.2   How do Indians identify themselves; by their national identity or by their regional identity?

	Only national	*More national*	*Equally national and regional*	*More regional and less national*	*Only regional*	*No opinion*
North India	41	7	20	5	10	17
East India	26	19	15	13	17	10
NE India	20	7	32	9	15	17
West India	42	7	27	5	10	10
South India	23	22	15	20	13	7
India	**32**	**12**	**21**	**10**	**12**	**13**

Note: N = 5227.
Source: Adapted from SDSA (2008: 256–7).

recognized in the Eighth Schedule of the Indian constitution could sit government examinations in their own language (although few avail themselves of the opportunity), English or Hindi. Business in parliament could be conducted in any of these languages. Obviously, given the benefits that derive from inclusion in this group, linguistic communities have continued to press for recognition on this list. The number of languages recognized in the Eighth Schedule increased, from 14 plus English at the time of constitution formation in 1950, to 22 plus English in 2003. The last four, Bodo, Dogri, Maithili and Santhali, were added by the BJP-led NDA coalition – partially for electoral reasons and partially as an addition to the peace agreement between the Bodos and Assamese (Adeney, 2005: 110).

In addition, linguistic reorganization in 1956 redrew the boundaries of the states of India to make them conform more closely to linguistic lines. Although this reorganization was undertaken with great reluctance as many of the central elite, Nehru included, were worried that this would lead to the Balkanization of India, the opposite effect has occurred. India has been a successful multilinguistic state; survey data demonstrate that regional linguistic identity is easily compatible with membership of the wider 'Indian nation' (Mitra and Singh, 1999; SDSA, 2008).

As can be seen in Table 6.2, in India as a whole, 22 per cent of respondents reported that they felt more regional than they did national, or felt only regional. There were substantial variations. In the north of India (not including the north east) this reduced to 15 per cent whereas in the south of the country it increased to 33 per cent. However, even in the south of the country 45 per cent of respondents felt only national or more national than provincial, compared to 48 per cent in the north. The north east reported only 27 per cent felt only national or more national but the largest number (32 per cent) reported that both identities were equal. The fact that regional political parties, which have become more prominent since the 1960s at the regional, and then the national level (as discussed in Chapter 5), seek power at the centre rather than seeking to break away from it, is another sign of the strength of the Indian Union.

State Emblems

The Indian nation is visualized for domestic and international consumption around some very powerful images. Emblems were carefully chosen for their symbolism of all-Indian unity, as was the interpretation given to the design. Prime Minister Jawaharlal Nehru was profoundly aware that for the nation to come alive it had to be visualized in the imagination of its citizens. He wrote at length in *The Discovery of India* about how images of the Indian landscape should be used to conjure up a picture of the nation. The website of the Government of India states that 'symbols are intrinsic to the Indian identity and heritage. Indians *of all demographics* [sic] *backgrounds* across the world are proud of these National Symbols as they instill [sic] a sense of pride and patriotism in every Indian's heart' (Government of India, nd-b) (authors' emphasis). Three symbols that make this point well are that of the national flag, the national anthem and the national emblem.

A state's flag projects an image of the state externally as well as internally. The tricolour flag (saffron, white and green) was developed in the 1920s to be symbolically inclusive of Hindu and Muslims; the white stripe symbolizing the existence of minorities. This was a conception favoured by Gandhi – although this subsumed all religious communities other than Muslim or Hindu into the 'white' band, to the chagrin of many (Roy, 2006: 503). In the 1930s, Nehru moved away from the religious interpretation 'as we wanted it to be considered the common national flag of all' (Nehru, 1938: 34–5). This version was upheld by the Constituent Assembly (Government of India, 1947: 764) where it was adopted unanimously 'in a matter of moments' (Roy, 2006: 509). Representatives from different religious and regional backgrounds pledged their allegiance to the design.

In a significant change, the new insignia on the national flag would no longer be the Gandhian *charkha*, or spinning wheel, a sign of how Indians could liberate themselves from economic exploitation, but the Ashoka chakra, a reminder of an 'international period in Indian history' (Roy, 2006: 511) as well as a reference to a period epitomized by Buddhist tolerance and enlightenment. The flag continues to be an important symbol of India. It has increasingly been appropriated by commercial cinema and politicians 'as the primary sign of Indian identity' (Roy, 2006: 517 and 519). It is also used as a symbol of protest – burning the flag is a regular feature of anti-Indian protests in Kashmir – seen recently on Independence Day in 2008. To do so is to face a charge of dishonouring the Indian flag, for which imprisonment is a real possibility (The Hindu, 2003).

Similarly, the Indian national anthem, *Jana Gana Mana*, has an important pan-Indian dimension. Written by the Bengali freedomfighter (and Nobel laureate), Rabindranath Tagore, it was adopted by the Constituent Assembly in 1950. The shortened English version (Government of India, nd-b) reads as follows:

> Thou art the ruler of the minds of all people, dispenser of India's destiny.
> Thy name rouses the hearts of Punjab, Sind, Gujarat and Maratha, Of the Dravida and Orissa and Bengal;
> It echoes in the hills of the Vindhyas and Himalayas, mingles in the music of Jamuna and Ganges and is chanted by the waves of the Indian Sea.
> They pray for thy blessings and sing thy praise.
> The saving of all people waits in thy hand, thou dispenser of India's destiny.
> Victory, victory, victory to thee.

As can be seen it directly evokes many of the regions, such as Gujarat, and the peoples of India, for example the Dravidian people of south India, and refers to some areas that did not remain within India after 1947, for example parts of Bengal, Punjab and Sind. The choice of national anthem was contested. Many felt that *Bande Mataram* should be the national anthem (Sen, 2003: 160). Written by another Bengali, Bankimchandra Chattophyay, in a book as a protest song against the British Raj, it translates as 'Hail to the Motherland'.

However, the song was (and remains) controversial partly because Muslims objected to the equation of the motherland with a Hindu goddess, but also because of the anti-Muslim sentiments of the book (Noorani, 1999). As we saw in Chapter 1, the objections raised by Muslims against singing this song in schools under Congress provincial governments in the late 1930s had been one of the catalysts for unifying under the Muslim League. It remains the national song of India, but not its national anthem, although the Government of India website notes that the song 'was a source of inspiration to the people in their struggle for freedom. It has an equal status with *Jana-gana-mana*' (Government of India, nd-b). Controversies relating to the song continue in contemporary India. In September 2006 Sonia Gandhi's absence from a ceremony marking the centenary of the song was used by the BJP to make political capital during the state elections. The recommendation of the central government that the singing of the song be compulsory in schools on the song's centenary day was rejected by most non-BJP-led state governments, and leaders of the Sikh and Muslim communities vociferously objected (Rediff.com, 2006).

The state emblem was also chosen for its symbolic resonance, making use of the art from Ashoka's Lion Capital. To quote from the Government of India website again:

> The state emblem is an adaptation from the Sarnath Lion Capital of Ashoka. In the original, there are four lions, standing back to back . . . In the state emblem, adopted by the Government of India on 26 January 1950, only three lions are visible, the fourth being hidden from view. The wheel appears in relief in the centre of the abacus with a bull on right and a horse on left and the outlines of other wheels on extreme right and left. The bell-shaped lotus has been omitted. The words *Satyameva Jayate* from *Mundaka Upanishad*, meaning 'Truth Alone Triumphs', are inscribed below the abacus in *Devanagari* script. (Government of India, nd-b)

The state emblem implies that India is a tolerant state with an international outlook. This links back to the conception of Indian secularism and also to India's worldview, discussed in Chapter 8.

The state emblem is important; it appears on all government publications and the currency. The images on postage stamps and bank notes were (and are) just as important for transmitting political nation-building messages – a longer version of this argument was

Images of the Sarnath Lion Capital of Ashoka are reproduced on official publications, some stamps and signboards of government ministries. Sculptural images of the capital are sometime displayed on public works like bridges or on a pillar at a road intersection (as shown here). Like the national flag the state emblem was intended to evoke a secular image for the Indian republic.

Illustration 6.2   India's state emblem

originally published in Wyatt (2005a). Stamps are especially important bearers of nationalist ideology as they project the image of the nation both internally and externally. They are a form of what Michael Billig calls 'banal nationalism' (1995). For example, the territorial basis of nationalism (as understood by Nehru) was proclaimed in the Map of India series, issued in 1957. The maps featured on this set of stamps highlight the main river systems and mountain ranges. Territory is a fundamental component of the claim to nationhood and these and other stamp series were a deliberate attempt to build a national community around the three themes of a shared culture, a self-reliant economy and a common territory. In 2009 a holographic first-day cover was released of the face of Mahatma Gandhi to mark his 140th birth anniversary. This demonstrates the relevance of the person of Gandhi and of the independence struggle to the idea of the 'Indian nation'. The independence struggle remains relevant for understandings of the Indian nation, as demonstrated by the recent stamps in the 'Builders of Modern India' series.

Politics and the Indian Nation

It is important to note that visions and visual representations of the Indian nation, which as we have seen are heavily contested, have political implications. Differences in understandings of which group 'belongs' to a state, and has rights (and duties) within it, affect the policies of the state – in all countries. Some are historical legacies – the prohibition of a Catholic acceding to the throne of Britain; others are more recent – the decision of many of the Baltic states to prohibit ethnic Russians from voting in elections. Policies may not only exclude or include but may also seek to regulate particular communities, and not only minority ones. This is pertinent in India when discussing the so-called Hindu Code Bill.

Box 6.2   The Hindu Code 'Bill'

The Hindu Code Bill is actually a set of laws introduced in the 1950s which meant that members of the Hindu religion were subject to certain civil laws, particularly in relation to marriage and property. It was controversial for a number of reasons. First, conservative Hindus resented state interference in matters of religious custom and the legislation was opposed by senior members of the Congress Party. Secondly, the legislation implied greater homogeneity among Hindu traditions in the area of family law than actually applied in practice. Furthermore, minority religious groups including Buddhists, Sikhs and Jains were considered to be 'Hindu' for the purposes of the legislation. Thirdly, the codification of Hindu personal law built elements of legislation into it that favoured men in certain family disputes. Fourthly, the provisions did not apply to Muslims or Christians: minority religious communities which were seen by Nehru as deserving of 'protection'. In reaction to this, Hindu nationalist political parties and movements have called for the introduction of a uniform civil code that would apply to all religions. As discussed in Chapter 4, feminists face a dilemma as they want the legislation revised but they are reluctant to join cause with Hindu nationalists, whose motives they question (Menon, 1998).

The secular, territorial, civic version of the Indian nation articulated under Nehru sought to include all religions. However, when in power the Congress Party has not been entirely consistent in the application of civic principles. The 'concession' of minority rights was reflected in policies relating to secularism: the neutrality of the Indian state to different religions, citizenship, and in relation to its diaspora (Adeney and Lall, 2005). In contrast, the Hindu Nationalists reject the 'appeasement' of minorities and charge that civic nationalists have been only 'pseudo-secularists' seeking to win the votes of minorities. However, when in government Hindu nationalist politicians have for the most part continued the policies designed to conciliate and protect minorities (although not religious minorities), and in the case of federalism even extended them (Adeney, 2005). Controversies over the uniform civil code are as pertinent in contemporary India as they were at the time of independence. In 2003, a Supreme Court judgment noted that it was 'a matter of regret that Article 44 of the Constitution has not been given effect to' (Rahman, 2003). Article 44 provides that '[t]he State shall endeavour to secure for the citizens a uniform civil code throughout the territory of India'. However, this article is within the section concerning the 'Directive Principles for State Policy', which is not enforceable by 'any court' (Article 37). In June 2008, the BJP sought to bring the issue of the uniform civil code to the forefront as a campaign issue again, after relegating the issue to satisfy potential coalition allies in recent years (Express India, 2008). Such debates contribute to the insecurities of religious minorities in the country.

Sport

Cricket occupies a special place in the sporting affections of the Indian nation. It is a truly national sport. As in many other countries, sport is a powerful integrative force, drawing together people from all sections of society. But cricket has a privileged place in the Indian national psyche. Cricketers are feted as national heroes. However, there is a feeling within India that the team rarely reaches its potential as a side. Perhaps more than anything that builds interest in cricket is this (often elusive) pursuit of success. Immense potential in the team, narrow margins of defeat and occasional victories keep fans in a permanent state of suspense (Bhattacharya, 2006: 17–20). That said, India battled its way to the top of the test cricket ratings in December 2009. It was rated as the number one side in the ICC ratings after series victories over Pakistan (2007), Australia (2008), England (2008), New Zealand (2009) and Sri Lanka (2009).

As well as being an important sport in India, cricket is avidly followed in the wider South Asia region. Pakistan and Sri Lanka have highly competitive sides and Bangladesh achieved test status in 2000. Unsurprisingly, the matches between India and Pakistan attract special interest. The scheduling of matches has been caught up in the politics of the region and a few xenophobic activists in India have

Illustration 6.3   Cricket in a park

The popularity of cricket is revealed in the enthusiasm of young players who colonize any open space they can find for an impromptu game.

used fixtures in India as the backdrop for attention-grabbing protests against Pakistan. In recent years the BJP and its allies have made divisive accusations that Muslims within India fail what the British Conservative MP, Norman Tebbit, called the 'cricket test' – supporting Pakistan rather than India. These allegations tend to be more prominent during times of high tension with Pakistan. Cricket has an important international dimension and rivalry between India and Pakistan is replicated on the field. When tensions are high between the two countries, cricket matches have been cancelled, as in the 1960s. It is common to hear games described as 'playing out war' (Mitra, 2009). In recent years the warming of relations between the two countries resulted in a successful test cricket tour of Pakistan by the Indian team in 2004. In 2007 India beat Pakistan in the final of the World Twenty20 cricket tournament. An occasion of national jubilation, the reporting in the Indian press was positive rather than anti-Pakistani. Therefore, in spite of the baleful consequences of partition, at times cricket has become an important cultural bridge between India and Pakistan. However, the terrorist attacks on elite hotels in Mumbai in November 2008, killing over a hundred people, forced the relocation of the Indian Premier League's second series to South Africa in April–May 2009. Security concerns were particularly high because the timing of the series clashed with the Indian general election, when security forces were acutely stretched.

The success of cricket in India requires some explanation. Soccer was more widely played in India before 1947 and the iconic sporting victory of an Indian team over an English one was not, as in the film *Lagaan: Once upon a time in India* (Gowariker, 2001), a cricket match but the triumph of the barefooted Mohun Bagan team in the 1911 Indian Football Association Shield final (Bose, 2002: 16–18). India has enjoyed great international success with hockey, collecting no less than eight Olympic gold medals (although the team failed to qualify for Beijing 2008). India dominated international hockey between the 1920s and 1950s, at the very time that a competitive Indian cricket side was struggling to emerge. Hockey is officially India's national sport, yet cricket is now seen as *the* Indian game.

The growth of cricket in India mirrors the development of the Indian nation. Indian cricket emerged in the first half of the twentieth century just as the nationalist struggle against the British peaked. In an interesting echo of the political struggle there were 'loyalists' (loyal to the British that is) who ignored the fledgling Indian game and fulfilled their ambitions playing for English county sides and the England team. Cricket was played in India with early teams divided along regional and religious lines. An Indian national team was assembled in the 1930s and was keen to challenge England but the English were reluctant to recognize the newcomer. Under-strength teams were sent from England to India, and India struggled to compete when they toured England. Behind the scenes the team and the Indian cricket establishment were troubled by personality clashes and ambitious patrons of the game. The popularity of the film *Lagaan* may have reflected a desire to wipe those troubled moments from the national memory. Partition brought with it the loss of talented players to Pakistan and a new, and somewhat narrower, meaning to the term 'Indian cricket'.

At independence, appropriately enough, India came into its own as a cricketing team and cricket continues to play an important role in shaping the sense of Indian national identity. Majumdar exaggerates when he writes: '[c]ricket is the only realm where Indians can flex their muscle; it is India's only crack at world domination' (2004: 2) but it speaks to a national need to be recognized as internationally important. The politics of the game in contemporary India are fascinating. There is an expectation that the team should represent India in the sense of reflecting India's social diversity. To an extent the team has done this with players from different religious backgrounds working effectively together. As in *Lagaan*, the Indian team has regularly had notable Hindu, Muslim and Sikh players. The side also reflects regional diversity, with particular players backed by fans, politicians and pundits from their home regions. However, the critics still note that the game is dominated by players from relatively wealthy, urban backgrounds, a point made in the film *Iqbal* (Kukunoor, 2005). The socio-economic imbalance correlates with a caste profile such that players from Dalit backgrounds are extremely rare at the highest levels of the professional game (Anand, 2003). Despite this, cricket has been consciously used by politicians of all hues as a symbol of Indian unity.

Cricket in contemporary India is in a strong position. The current Indian team includes a number of truly world-class players. The batting averages of Rahul Dravid (53.6), Virender Sehwag (52.5) and Sachin Tendulkar (54.7) reflect exceptional talent; Tendulkar, at the time of writing, has scored 44 centuries. Anil Kumble, having taken over 600 wickets, was one of the world's leading bowlers until his retirement in 2008. The financial strength of Indian cricket, based on extremely lucrative television rights, has meant that the centre of gravity of world cricket has shifted towards South Asia. Advertisers are avaricious for celebrity endorsements from leading cricketers. India is reshaping the format of the game as it favours shorter versions over the five-day test match format. One day and Twenty20 cricket appeal to a large television audience. The gap between each over that is bowled provides space for two or three highly prized ad slots. The Indian Premier League's Twenty20 cricket tournament attracts players from around the world, commanding salaries of almost £700,000 for six weeks. Nationally it is also popular, despite concerns being raised about whether city teams, especially with so many foreign players, would be as popular as the 'national' team. The financial backing and high levels of involvement of Bollywood superstars such as Shahrukh Khan has also enhanced its prestige, and it has been extremely financially lucrative for all involved.

Popular Culture

India has a rich and changing culture. The term 'Indian culture' has to be treated with care because of the diverse forms of cultural

expression. It is important to stress that although it is possible to identify all-Indian cultural references, as our discussions of religion and
language in Chapter 2 revealed, regional factors shape cultural forms.
The breadth and depth of India's cultures mean that we simply cannot
provide a comprehensive catalogue of cultural life in India. We have
had to be selective and concentrate our attention on a few salient
aspects of Indian culture, including cinema, literature, storytelling,
music, dance and food. We show how each of these forms reflects
some aspects of India's diversity. We say something about the intersection of religion and caste with some of these cultural practices. We
also show how regional differences contribute to the variety of
cultural life in India.

Cinema

Indian cinema has remarkable depth and diversity. Popular Hindi
films have the highest profile outside of India but to focus only on
these 'Bollywood' films would give a misleading picture of Indian
cinema. Regional cinema is very important and alternative cinema
makes a small but notable contribution to the diversity of film
production. India's vibrant and prolific film industry produces around
800 films a year, the majority of these being produced by regional
studios. Even in an era where satellite dishes have proliferated,
cinema attendance has remained high and, in fact, India has the
highest rate of cinema attendance in the world: 2860 million cinema
attendances per year (an average of 3 per person). When you consider
that the vast majority of India's population lives in rural areas and the
high levels of poverty within many urban areas, these figures show
how popular cinema is. Western films have a following among the
upper middle class which, until recently, tended to disdain popular
Indian films (Bose, 2006: 33). Although some have raised concerns
about the proliferation of American culture in India (a concern that
has also been voiced in relation to the MTV generation), Indian
cinema continues to adapt and thrive.

The part of the Indian film industry that is based in Mumbai picked
up the popular tag 'Bollywood'. Before the city of Bombay was
renamed, the 'B' from Bombay replaced the 'H' in Hollywood. Hindi
cinema, somewhat controversially, is considered by many to be
India's national cinema (Dwyer and Patel, 2002: 16–19). The term
'Bollywood' has to be treated with care, however. It suggests paral-
lels with Hollywood that are not there, and can be seen as a derisory

Illustration 6.4   *Avatar*

Hollywood blockbusters are popular in India – *Titanic* was a major
success in the subcontinent, many people viewing it multiple times. A
dubbed version of *Jurassic Park* also attracted a large audience. A recent
film, *Avatar*, was also very popular.

term. Hindi films have a style of their own. They commonly include
lavish sets, leading stars, and song and dance routines. The combination of romantic drama, action and comedy can result in a seemingly
disjointed product which is not always attractive to a middle-class or
overseas audience (Dwyer and Patel, 2002: 30–1). Music is very
important for aesthetic and financial reasons. The songs, which
usually go on sale several months before a film is released, mean that
the producers are not solely reliant on ticket sales. Songs, displayed
in elaborate song and dance routines, feature prominently in most
Bollywood films. We say more about this below.

Hindi films have a very wide audience, appealing to many groups
within Indian society, including different religious communities,
different castes, the poor and the rich, as well as elements of the
Indian diaspora. Hindi films also appeal to the people of Pakistan,
and it is significant that one of the signs of the rapprochement in
recent years between the two countries has been talk of lifting the ban
on the screening of Bollywood movies within Pakistan (which, in any

case, can be seen on satellite TV). Bollywood has reached out far beyond the shores of India, in particular to south-east and western Asia, Europe and East Africa (Booth, 1995: 170). Many Hindi filmstars are famous overseas. Since the mid 1990s a great deal of attention has been paid to the audience among the diaspora. This is a minority audience for Hindi cinema but higher ticket prices bring lucrative returns. *Lagaan* was an important 'cross-over' film that achieved critical acclaim and commercial success in the West.

Hindi cinema illustrates our argument that questions of national identity have been very important in modern India. Key films of the 1950s picked up important nation-building themes. Contemporary films show that national concerns are still important in India. The theme of patriotism features in many films, as do the implications of migration for Indian identity and culture. In the decades after independence the inclusion of different religious and linguistic communities was considered a priority. Bollywood exemplified this, with Hindus and Muslims working closely together (Bose, 2006: 191). In *Mughal-E-Azam* (Asif, 1960), the film speaks of an India ruled by a Muslim known for his religious tolerance (the Emperor Akbar). The film communicates 'messages of Hindu-Muslim brotherhood'. The opening credits show a map which suggests India 'has always been the same . . . [p]olitical lines are drawn to separate people but nature/land knows no such difference' (Chakravarty, 1993: 170). In other words, the film rejects the argument of the Muslim League that India is irredeemably divided between a Hindu and a Muslim nation (Bose, 2006: 219–20). Another foundational film of Indian cinema is *Mother India* (Khan, 1957). It tells the story of Radha, who, deserted by her husband and in debt, has to raise her young sons alone. She saves the livelihood of her village after a disastrous flood and Radha thus becomes both a virtuous and selfless mother to her family and the village. The story closes with an optimistic picture of independent India (Chatterjee, 2002: 72). The Congress government, by building dams, can tame the forces of nature and bring development to India's villages. The icons were deliberately constructed in such a way as 'to serve Nehru's political vision of the nation state' (Schulze, 2002: 74). The film made a positive impression on overseas audiences.

Hindi films of the 1970s were much less idealistic. The problems of corruption, drought and economic crisis were reflected in Hindi cinema. The time was ripe for the rise of the anti-hero. This rootless, angry figure intervened (in film) to wreak revenge and intervene where the state was indifferent or corrupt. Amitabh Bachchan emerged to make this role his own, including in the remarkable *Sholay* (Sippy, 1975) and *Deewaar* (Chopra, 1975; Kabir, 2001: 39–41). Bachchan went on to become a giant of Hindi cinema and was the popular host of the Hindi version of the television quiz show *Who Wants to be a Millionaire* between 2000 and 2006.

Hindi cinema seemed to lose its way in the 1980s. It proved difficult to attract a broad audience to films that were frequently gritty and violent. However, Bollywood reinvented itself. Hindi films returned to many of the homely conventions of earlier periods. Romantic comedies, such as *Hum Apke Hain Koun* (*HAHK*) (Barjatya, 1994) and *Kuch Kuch Hota Hai* (Johar, 1998) peopled by suave cosmopolitan characters, proved popular with middle-class audiences. The post-1991 economic reforms gave producers new opportunities, such as shooting in locations outside of India, and a new mood to explore. Indian heroes and heroines, with a nod to so-called Indian traditions, were depicted as enjoying the benefits of prosperity and global mobility. Sudhanva Deshpande (2001) terms this the rise of the 'consumable hero'. Since the turn of the millennium Bollywood has continued to adapt and production values have continued to improve. *Lagaan* was just one example of a film made to very high standards. Further attempts have been made to produce films that would appeal to western audiences.

Yash Raj films, the most professionally organized of India's studios, has been adept at producing films that satisfy the shifting tastes of middle-class audiences in India and in the diaspora (Dwyer, 2002). Subtle but important innovations have helped them achieve many commercial successes. The film *Kal Ho Naa Ho* (Advani, 2003) is a smooth rendering of the classic Bollywood love triangle. The film is unusual for being set entirely in New York and it refers to the complications of suicide and adultery. Much of the plot of *Kabhi Alvida Naa Kehna* (Johar, 2006) concerns an extra-marital affair and the subsequent divorce and the film breaks with the staid, socially conservative genre of the Bollywood romantic drama.

Aside from these recent exceptions, Bollywood films tend towards safe subjects and not raising difficult questions. Controversial and taboo topics are more likely to feature in the films of the parallel, or alternative, cinema. An example is a recent film by Benegal, *Welcome to Sajjanpur* (2008): a rural comedy that satirizes attempts by local landowners to exert control over their village. The film has a sharp edge as it touches on caste violence and political corruption. The film,

Mr and Mrs Iyer (2002), directed by Aparna Sen, probes the politics of communal violence between Hindus and Muslims. A number of highly talented actors are associated with this alternative film-making, including Shabana Azmi, Naseeruddin Shah and Om Puri (Thoraval, 2000: 167–9).

As we have noted, Bollywood helps create a sense of national identity but it is not a particularly nuanced identity. Many social identities are simplified or simply ignored. The topic of caste is rarely given explicit treatment, partly because of rules intended to stop films from encouraging caste tension but also because film-makers censor themselves (Bose, 2006: 35). The regional and ethnic diversity of India is another topic that is rarely broached in Hindi films. As Velayutham comments, 'Hindi cinema more often than not represents an "Indian" without an ethno-specific identity. The characters of Bollywood cinema are supposedly pan-Indian' (2008: 7). The action in Hindi films usually takes place in geographically vague locations. Exceptions to this dominant trend are films set in Mumbai and those concerned with the conflict in Kashmir. *Chak de India* (Amin, 2007) is a rare film which acknowledges the fact that India is composed of many different states. The film depicts the travails of a fictional Indian women's hockey team in which members from different Indian states struggle to cooperate. The treatment of religion in Hindi films is an object of controversy and can be connected to larger debates about national identity. Some argue that recent films tend to have Muslim characters as villains (Deshpande, 2003). It has also been argued that film-makers depict Indian culture as Hindu culture. Many family dramas, like *HAHK*, are entirely concerned with the fortunes of devout Hindu families. On the other hand, some films depict India as religiously diverse and promote secular values. Several recent films celebrate the patriotism of Indian Muslims, for example the popular historical drama *Jodhaa-Akbar* (Gowariker, 2008) depicted the Mughal Emperor Akbar as a devout and tolerant Muslim ruler.

Among regional cinemas, Tamil cinema has particular strength. There is a long tradition of film-making in the Tamil language that stretches back to 1917. The Tamil film industry attracted a great deal of attention in the 1950s as it was drawn into the struggle between the nationally dominant Congress Party and the regional Dravidian movement. These films were popular and politically oriented. Tamil films tend to identify closely with their own region both through the use of language and the distinctive locations. The portrayal of rela-

Box 6.3   Talent in contemporary Tamil cinema

Tamil cinema has produced a number of highly talented individuals with national and international reputations. The filmstar Rajnikanth is popular for his action films and his distinctive mannerisms or 'style'. He has a massive following. The majority of his fans are in south India but they can also be found among the Tamil diaspora and he has a following in Japan. Nearing the end of his career Rajnikanth now concentrates on a smaller number of high-impact projects. The release in 2007 of *Sivaji: The Boss* (Shankar, 2007) was a major event. The film was said to have had the largest budget of any Indian film to date. In addition to the star's fee, the budget secured: the services of a leading director (Shankar), the talent of India's leading music director (A.R. Rahman), world-class special effects, and elaborate song and dance routines (Vijayabaskar and Wyatt, 2007). Among many other things, Rahman provided music for the film *Slumdog Millionaire* (Boyle and Tandan, 2008), for which he won two Academy Awards at the 2008 Oscars. The director, Mani Ratnam, established his reputation in Tamil cinema and he has a talent for making films that find a national audience. His films, including *Roja* (1992) and *Bombay* (1995), are often controversial. Recently he has made films in Hindi as well as Tamil. Ratnam's films are aesthetically interesting, engage with political issues and are popular.

tions between men and women tends to be highly hierarchical and films reflect a conservative social order (Velayutham, 2008: 5–9). Notable stars who began their careers in the 1950s include M.G. Ramachandran (MGR), also a very successful politician, and Shivaji Ganesan (a much less successful politician).

Andhra Pradesh is another southern state with a strong regional cinema. A large number of films are made for a Telugu audience. In some years the largest number of films made in any Indian language have been of those produced in Telugu (Thoraval, 2000: 344–5). The connections with Tamil cinema are strong and even today some Telugu films are made in Chennai. The immense popularity of cinema in Andhra Pradesh helped the star N.T. Rama Rao to build a political career which saw him elected Chief Minister in 1983. Another notable star of Telugu cinema is Chiranjeevi. He has a distinctive style as a dancer and has won admiration for his heroic roles (Srinivas, 2000: 299–300). Chiranjeevi has an extensive network of fan clubs, which were used as the basis on which to contest elections in 2009.

Rajnikanth celebrated his 60th birthday in December 2009. His fans marked the moment by producing and pasting up posters paying homage to their star. Rajnikanth projects a younger persona in films like *Sivaji*, but he is relaxed about his public image as can be seen in photographs like this one that reveal the physical effects of his age.

Illustration 6.5   Rajnikanth

Music and Dance

Music in India is as diverse as other forms of culture in the country, and some forms of music 'have origins that stretch back thousands of years' (Farrell, 1990: 7). There are many regional variations, the most basic divide being that between the north and south of the country. We concentrate on three forms of music here: the first is Indian classical music; the second, qawwali, is 'a dynamic and popular Muslim devotional genre . . . often employing Urdu gazal as texts' (Manuel, 1988: 95); and the third, linking to the discussion of cinema above, is the role music that has played in the movie industry.

Classical music in India has a long history and is one of 'the major expressions of Indian culture abroad' (Farrell, 1990: 8). It was made famous outside India by performers such as Ravi Shankar who use the sitar, an instrument that has become associated with the northern Indian music tradition. Instrumental traditions are the most popular form in the north of the country, the music of which has been influenced by Islam and music from Persia. Ragas, an important element of Indian classical music, are best described as melodies. They 'set an emotional mood as well as become a complete and identifiable musical world'. There are thousands of ragas; about a hundred are 'ubiquitous' (Morris, 2001: 75). Each raga can be performed at only a certain time of the day or year. Those who attend classical music concerts tend to be well versed in ragas 'and will show their approval by exclamations and affirming gestures of the hand when some particularly subtle or exciting phrase is played' (Farrell, 1990: 8 and 10). Improvisation around a particular raga is very important, demonstrating the skill of the performer.

In the south of the country Carnatic music dominates. Although the musical traditions of the north and the south share the same 'melodic and rhythmic principles, their specific ragas, talas and performance practices are different' (Morris, 2001: 74). One major difference is that north Indian music is based around improvisation much more than in the south (Morris, 2001: 74). There are many styles of Carnatic music. Kriti is one of these – 'a three-section, vocal composition that sets a text in Sanskrit or a South Indian language [often alluding to] . . . Hindu myths and religious lore' (Morris, 2001: 75). Carnatic music is often devotional. Ragas are an important part of the musical tradition in the south, just as they are in the north of the country.

Qawwali, as noted above, is a 'devotional genre' of Sufism, generally sung 'by a group of singers and accompanists' (Manuel, 1988: 95). Qureshi notes that until recently qawwali was probably 'the most popular genre of recorded religious music in South Asia' (1992: 111) and that after independence in India it 'embraced a general humanism extolling all religions' (1992: 115). The most famous qawwali singer, Nusrat Fateh Ali Khan (died 1997), established an international reputation. Despite being born in Pakistan, he is extremely popular in India. His music is well known among the diasporas of South Asia and he made a major contribution to the soundtrack of the Hollywood films *Dead Man Walking* and *Natural Born Killers*, among others.

Music is an essential part of Indian cinema. Many songs have borrowed heavily from the Indian classical tradition (Farrell, 1990: 2), although westernized influences are now as strongly felt. Most Indian films include 6–9 songs that typically last between 5 and 6 minutes (Sarrazin, 2006: 27). The songs are usually not important for plot development but they are integral to the film. They are normally accompanied by an elaborate dance routine. Villains do not sing in the films – to do so would be to humanize them (Sarrazin, 2006: 29). Long-standing favourites include *Meera Joota Hai Japani* ('My shoes are from Japan') from the film *Shree 420* (Kapoor, 1955). As Sarrazin notes, this song must also be seen as part of the nation-building project because the song concludes that despite his clothing his heart belongs in India (2006: 28). Movie songs are usually sung by professional playback singers, and not by the actors and actresses (who mime to them). Many playback singers are famous in their own right, having recorded songs for films over several decades, for example Lata Mangeshkar and Asha Bhosle. These songs are often integral to the success of a movie (Morcom, 2001: 63) – songs from movies prominently feature on MTV India and soundtracks sell well. Sarrazin notes that 70 per cent of all music sales are of film music (2006: 27). MTV India is an important cultural phenomenon. Indian pop music is as varied as the rest of the country, and certain musical styles, such as the Punjabi Bhangra, have been successfully exported to the West. MTV India programming prominently features 'the best of Hindi Film Music, Hindi pop and International videos' as well as 'Style Checks' aiming at 'giving viewers tips on how to dress right for any occasion' (MTV India, 2009).

Indian dance traditions are also the product of centuries of development. For example, Kathak, the northern Indian dance tradition, existed before the rise of Buddhism in the fifth century. '[P]rofessional storytellers, known as *Kathakas*, sang, danced, and recited the tales of the ancient epics and myths' (Coorlawala, 1992: 88). 'Present-day Kathak has been adapted both for the concert stage and for more informal and traditional intimate gatherings of dance-lovers. Its outstanding characteristic is its emphasis on fast, complex, rhythmic footwork while the hands trace circular and spiral forms around the moving body' (Coorlawala, 1992: 88). Facial expressions are vitally important in Kathak dancing, and training to become a dancer is onerous. There is also a strong tradition of Indian folk dances, many linked to seasonal festivals, myths and epics, as well as devotional dances (Renouf, 1978: 327). Folk dance traditions are also regionally varied, as one would expect. Many of these dance traditions have informed the song and dance numbers in Indian film, discussed above.

The South Indian dance traditions of Bharatha Natyam and Kathakali are both narrative traditions (Wade, 1987: 9). Bharatha Natyam emerged in South Indian temples. 'The *devadasi*, literally "servant of God" danced and sang the stories of God before temple deities to propitiate and entertain them' (Meduri, 1988: 4). Hand gestures and facial expressions are prominent features of this tradition. '[A] *bharata natyam* dancer expounds upon and interprets poetic text, melodic contours, and rhythmic patterns; but also, if she

The colourful Kathakali dance is a southern Indian dance tradition.

Illustration 6.6   Kathakali dancer

is adept, creates a commentary on these elements' (O'Shea, 1998: 51). The *devadasi* system, where pre-pubescent girls were 'married' to the deity of the temple, fell into public disrepute in the late nineteenth/early twentieth century. The system was accused by Indian social reformers, as well as British missionaries, of being a form of prostitution. The dance tradition of Bharatha Natyam continued, but was reinterpreted by Brahmanical dancers such as Rukmini Devi, seeking to make the dance 'respectable' (Meduri, 1988: 9). This reinterpretation was resisted by Balasaraswati, among others, who sought to retain the *Sringara* sensuality of the dance (O'Shea, 1998: 48).

Literature and Storytelling

India has an abundant literary culture which is enriched by India's many languages and various religious traditions. An important influence on this culture comes from the Hindu epics, the *Mahabharata* and the *Ramayana* first mentioned in Chapter 2. The stories have been told and re-told in many formats and both were serialized on Doordarshan in the late 1980s. The novelist R.K. Narayan translated both epics into English. The Congress leader, C.R. Rajagopalachari, produced a version of each, achieving more fame as a storyteller than as a politician! The initial versions were written in Tamil and translations have been reissued many times. Rajagopalachari was paid a curious compliment when a political rival, E.V. Ramaswami Naicker, produced another version of the *Ramayana* with the villain, Ravana, converted into the hero (Waghorne, 1981: 592-4). Versions of the *Mahabharata* and the *Ramayana* are widely on sale as cheap paperbacks in many different languages. The epics have been made accessible to children by the popular Amar Chitra Katha series that tells short episodes in colourful comic book form. Films often make allusions to key characters from the epics such as Krishna and Radha.

A residue of Persian culture can be seen in the Urdu ghazal, popular since the eighteenth century. These poems are short enough to be easily memorized, usually no more than a dozen couplets. Most ghazals celebrate the joys or regret the disappointments of love, though some are given over to philosophical conjecture and others are satirical (Kanda, 1992: 4–10). Some have been set to music and widely popularized. Versions of ghazals feature in many Bollywood films, indeed Manuel argues that the formal structure of ghazal 'lends itself well to commercialization' (1988: 106). The ghazal was celebrated in one of India's notable contributions to world literature, Vikram Seth's *A Suitable Boy* (1994). This massive novel is a family epic and found a receptive audience. The family epic, involving several generations of one or more families, is a staple of Indian literature in English. Seth's novel is a variation on this format compressed, chronologically at least, into 12 months that span 1951 and 1952. *A Suitable Boy* includes highly readable digressions on caste, religion, cricket and shoemaking that evoke the optimism of newly independent India.

India is *implicated* in the production of many notable novels, and we choose our words carefully here because there is some controversy as to what constitutes an Indian novel. It has not gone unnoticed that several very successful authors, including Salman Rushdie and Rohinton Mistry, no longer live in India. Rushdie defends himself, claiming that migration breaks the 'shackles of nationalism' and argues that '[t]o see things plainly, you have to cross a frontier' (Rai, 2002: 217). Rushdie's *Midnight's Children* (Rushdie, 1981) tells the story of Saleem Sinai and his family against the background of India's modern history. Or, it might be said, Rushdie tells a story of the Indian nation against the background of Sinai's family history. The novel eschews realism in favour of a fantasy packed full of clever wordplay and conceits. Sinai is born at midnight on 14 August 1947, so his life span is identical to that of the new Indian state. He establishes telepathic contact with the others born at the same time and has an overview of their plight. The novel despairs at the declining vitality of the Indian nation. Key parts of *Midnight's Children* deal with the 1975 Emergency and the turn towards authoritarianism, which is symbolized by Rushdie 'when the midnight's children are castrated to prevent the hope and optimism they epitomised from reproducing' (S. Singh, 2000: 164). The narrative moves across much of the subcontinent but the city of what was known as Bombay is an important location, with references to the linguistic reorganization of the state of Bombay and the city's film industry. In another family saga, *The Moor's Last Sigh* (1995), Rushdie engages in a satirical attack on the regional politicians of the city. Bombay/Mumbai is also an important feature of Rohinton Mistry's work. *Tales from Firozsha Baagh* (1987) is an impressive collection of short stories. A later novel, *A Fine Balance* (1995), depicts the city during the Emergency. The novel shows the human cost of attempts to beautify cities and solve India's population 'problem'.

A vast amount of literature is written and published in India's regional languages. The Sahitya Akademi, the national academy of letters, provides official recognition of these literatures and sponsors translations among a variety of languages to build connections among literary traditions in India's many languages. The question of caste has been taken up in Marathi literature by a number of Dalit writers. A collection of stories, translated into English, are included in the volume *Poisoned Bread* edited by Arjun Dangle (1992). The stories, often stark and simply written, explore the deep psychological pain that follows from caste discrimination. The experience of Indian diasporas has been explored in a number of novels. Amitav Ghosh's sweeping family saga, *The Glass Palace* (2000), reminds us that the British Empire encouraged the migration of Indian labourers to Burma and Malaya. A significant part of the book tells of the horrific experience of civilian refugees fleeing to India following the Japanese invasion in 1942. The experience of a new migrant adjusting to the awkwardness of American culture is a central part of Anita Desai's *Fasting, Feasting* (1999). A similar theme was developed further in Kiran Desai's novel *The Inheritance of Loss* (2006), which includes narratives set in the Gorkha hills of West Bengal and an important strand following the experience of a migrant in the US. The celebrated short stories of Jhumpa Lahiri consider the position of newly migrated and settled migrants to the US as well as their reencounter with India as they travel again in the subcontinent. Her first volume of stories, *Interpreter of Maladies* (1999), was followed up by *The Namesake* (2004) and *Unaccustomed Earth* (2009).

India's recent experience of rapid economic growth surfaces in a number of books. Chetan Bhagat's novels have proved very popular. *One Night at a Call Centre* (2005) is a lively story in which almost the entire narrative is contained in just one 12-hour shift! The novel concentrates on the ambitions of six members of one team and includes some amusing commentary on the dependence of the US on Indian talent. Aravind Adiga won the 2008 Man-Booker prize with *The White Tiger* (2008). Adiga takes the extreme case of Bihar as the starting point for a story focused on the newly rich in the liberalized economy. *The White Tiger* is written in an unusual style; it is an epistolary novel. It makes the point that in spite of liberalization, old-fashioned methods of making money are still prevalent. Readers are introduced to a combination of brutal landlordism and businessmen using connections to corrupt politicians. *The White Tiger* uncovers the seamier side of Indian life but, unlike *A Fine Balance* (Mistry, 1995), it is a story without nuance, and so presents a simplified picture of India.

Food

There is no Indian cuisine as such; food in India is as diverse as the rest of the country. On one level this is not surprising given the regional diversity already commented on, India's size, or the invasions and conquests different parts of the country have experienced. On the other hand, given the importance of Hindu traditions that are 'so concerned with food as a medium of communication on the one hand and with matters of hierarchy and rank on the other', it is curious that there is not 'a significant textual corpus on cuisine' (Appadurai, 1988: 11). Many Hindus are vegetarian, although not all, and orthodoxy prohibits eating beef because the cow is sacred. Muslims will not eat the pig because it is said to be unclean. Culinary tensions can and often have been politicized between the two groups. Jains and Buddhists are also often vegetarian.

Staples of Indian cuisine include rice and different types of bread. These breads are made by different methods and with different types of flour. In north India, the chapatti, a small round of flat bread, is made with *atta* (wholemeal wheat flour) and cooked on a *tawa* (a flat

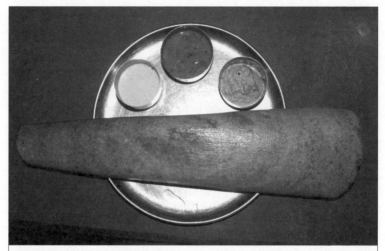

Illustration 6.7   A dosa

Dosas are made from ground rice and lentils. They are usually served with a selection of chutneys and are offered with a mixture of fillings. The dosa has become a popular form of fast food across India.

frying pan). The more elaborate *naan*, which can also be made with *atta* or plainer *maida*, is leavened so that it rises when baked in a *tandoor* (clay oven). In south India rice is *the* staple ingredient. It is used very creatively, including as flour. A combination of ground rice and urad lentils are used to make batter. The mixture is left to ferment overnight and can be fried to make a pancake-like *dosa*. Variations include steaming, to produce an *idli*, usually eaten for breakfast. A slightly different batter is cooked in a special dish to produce the cup-shaped *appam*. In Bengal, rice is a staple of another distinctive regional cuisine. Indian cuisine is known for being spicy, but spiciness does not always equate to being 'hot'. Many Indian foods are flavour-some without the heat of the chilli (which Nandy notes was imported from South America (2004)). Other foods are extremely hot. Outside of India, the word 'curry' is indelibly associated with Indian food. The link is unhelpful, first as the regional diversity of India means there is no single national cuisine that could be labelled 'Indian food', but instead a range of different regional cuisines within India. Secondly, the term 'curry' is a generic term referring to many different gravy sauces with spices. The mix of spices varies from dish to dish and from region to region; in the north extensive use of cumin can be found, while the south uses more mustard and coconut (Chandra, 1991: 1). The regional cuisines often reflect the ecology of the area, thus Bengali cuisine is heavily dependent on fish, and the cuisine of Kerala makes use of coconut milk. Within India stereotypes abound about different regions' cuisine that are less than complimentary (Appadurai, 1988: 18).

The closest India has to a national cuisine is the one introduced to India by the Mughals, which is closely associated with formal food when eating out in India, especially in the north of the country (Appadurai, 1988: 5; Nandy, 2004: 13). This is why this 'national cuisine' is primarily an urban middle-class phenomenon (Appadurai, 1988: 5). Economic liberalization and urbanization have provided new opportunities for wealthier middle-class consumers. Food fashions have spread, with restaurants and shops selling regional delicacies in cities far from the region of origin. Multinational eateries have proliferated in the urban areas of India. Brands such as Pizza Hut, McDonalds and Ben and Jerry's ice cream parlours are seen by some as fashionable places to visit (Nandy, 2004: 12). Different kinds of 'ethnic' cuisine, including Japanese, Chinese, Italian, Lebanese and Thai food, are available to wealthy customers in fashionable restaurants. Expensive clubs and bars are proliferating within urban areas. India, as Nandy reminds us, has its own fast food. These include North Indian snacks such as *samosas* and the increasingly popular southern Indian fast food such as *idli*, *dosa*, *vada* and *uthappam* (2004: 12–13).

Discussions of India's fast evolving and very diverse culinary culture need to be kept in context. Many people live a hand-to-mouth existence and struggle to access very basic staples like flour, rice and lentils. Recent bouts of inflation have put the poor under great pressure. At the end of November 2009 the Food Inflation Index was showing an annual rise of nearly 20 per cent. As we will discuss in Chapter 7, the Indian state is losing its enthusiasm for keeping the prices of these staples at levels that the poor can afford. There have been no famines in India since independence but rural distress has been severe in times of drought. Even in 'ordinary' circumstances there have been reports of starvation deaths. Chronic malnutrition is a recognized problem and poverty is still prevalent, a theme we return to in Chapter 7.

Conclusion

'Indian' culture is therefore as diverse as its society. Concerns to promote a sense of nationhood have been at the forefront of government efforts since independence, even if these governments have differed on what they understand the Indian nation to be. Conflicts have arisen between different groups and the centre over the terms in which the dominant narrative of the nation is expressed. Religious, linguistic and caste groups have at various points objected to the way in which the national community is defined. Many of these dissenting groups have been accommodated and drawn into the national mainstream. Cultural activities, including national sporting events, do bring Indians from many different backgrounds together. Hindi cinema gives cultural expression of national identity even if it is not particularly nuanced. Survey data show there is a strong sense of being 'Indian' as well as strong attachment to regional identities. But, importantly, the sense of being Indian is strongest when there is recognition of the diversity of its peoples.

7

Political Economy

India's policy-makers have tended to view the international economy cautiously. This was especially true before 1991 when multinationals, foreign investors and even expatriate Indians were commonly treated with disdain (Kumar, 1996; Lall, 2001). These policies can be traced back to the nationalist critique of colonialism. Attitudes among policy-makers relaxed after 1991 when market friendly reforms were introduced. However, the transformation has been gradual and policy-makers are keen to shield India from instabilities in the global economy. As we shall see, India remains quite inwardly focused. Attempts by the Indian state to direct economic development have had mixed outcomes. On the positive side, India has modest external debts and a stable currency. The economy has developed substantially since the British colonial period. Indian industry has depth and breadth that is unusual for a developing country. Inflation has been kept within tolerable limits and economic growth has been achieved. Until the late 1970s economic growth was modest, with GDP growth averaging 3.7 per cent in the period 1950–64 and 2.9 per cent in the period 1965–79. Critics dubbed this the 'Hindu' rate of growth. The GDP growth rate was an impressive 5.7 per cent between 1980 and 2004 (Kohli, 2006: 1254). These are average figures and Kunal Sen shows that growth actually began to accelerate in the late 1970s (Sen, 2009b: 2–3). On the negative side it can be said that after 1947 India did not do as well as other developing countries, particularly the export-oriented economies of East Asia (Bhagwati, 1993). Heavy investments were made in state-owned enterprises that achieved very low rates of return or were loss making. Levels of poverty, though reduced since 1947, remain high. Economic liberalization from 1991 has accentuated differences between states in India, and economic expectations between different sections of Indian society differ markedly.

191

India's economy is distinctive, partially because the role of the state in the economy has been, and remains, very important. The legacy of several decades of economic planning means that the state is both an owner of important economic assets and a regulator of the economy (even if this task is carried out unevenly). India has been slow to follow the neo-liberal trend towards down-sizing the state. Levels of imports and exports are relatively low. Even after nearly two decades of impressive export growth, India's exports were valued at only 13.3 per cent of Gross Domestic Product (GDP) in 2006. Imports were somewhat higher at 19.2 per cent of GDP. India's economy is not export-oriented and this has often meant that India has struggled to pay for its imports.

This inward orientation is shown when we note that African states like Ghana and Cote D'Ivoire exported a much larger proportion of their economic output in the same year – 27.5 per cent and 49.9 per cent respectively (World Bank, 2007). As we will demonstrate, Indian agriculture remains very important as an employer although the sector is in decline. The outlook is much more positive for Indian industry and the service sector. Economic growth has been strong in these sectors over the last decade. However, in per capita terms India is still among the poorer economies of the world. The World Bank measured India's Gross National Income (GNI) per capita at US $950 in 2007 (World Bank, 2009b). This measure includes the wealth produced domestically, but also includes income earned overseas. This basic measure does not give a good sense of what India's wealth will actually purchase but, even when the GNI is adjusted for purchasing power parity (PPP), a modest figure of $2,740 was estimated in 2007. Of course, income distribution is not uniform and many in India subsist on much less than these averages suggest. We discuss the issue of poverty in more detail at the end of the chapter.

Indian nationalism has long had an economic dimension. Nationalist critics argued that the British drained resources from India and were barely competent administrators who failed to deal properly with several severe famines before 1947. Nationalists complained about a tariff regime that allowed cheap British imports to flood the Indian market and drive local producers out of business. In addition, it was argued that the British did not sponsor economic development. Nationalists responded by running *swadeshi* campaigns to promote local consumption. So when independence came it was an opportunity to build a *national* economy. For Nehru, economic development and India's position in the world were intimately linked (Chaudhuri,

Box 7.1   India's formal and informal economies

One way of categorizing economic activity in India is to use the distinction between formal and informal economic activity. The informal sector can be defined as consisting of economic activity that is not taxed or regulated by the state. The formal sector is easier to study because it is more obviously organized and regulated by the state. It includes India's largest companies that are listed on stock exchanges, file accounts and are widely commented on in the press. In contrast, an estimated 93 per cent of the population work in the informal sector (Adams, 2007: 251), and produce 60 per cent of GDP. The informal economy can also have an illicit dimension. Labour laws are often flouted and in the worst cases workers are tied, or 'bonded', because they owe debts to their employer. This practice occurs in the brick-making industry where entire families work to pay off the debt (Ghosh, 2009). Many businesses increase their profits by avoiding tax and failing to comply with state regulation (Harriss-White, 2003: 5–7). The informal economy vaults over the divisions of agriculture, industry, and services we use below. There are formal and informal elements in each of these sectors and even inside individual businesses. For example, a large corporation might have some staff with formal contracts but also use workers who do not have contracts and therefore few legal rights.

1988: 272). Nationalists firmly believed that India was a world power robbed of pre-eminence by colonial rule. Nehru subscribed to this view and argued that Indian technological inadequacy allowed the British to dominate India. As such, independent India could only be secure if it had a robust economy and modern industry.

A very deliberate strategy was pursued after 1947 to promote economic development and encourage self-sufficiency through the production of key industrial goods. The objectives were to promote a strong economy to solve the massive problem of poverty, and to increase India's independence in international politics. To achieve this, the Government of India invested heavily using a series of five-year plans. Heavy industry was especially favoured by this system. This strategy and the complex system of planning had significant shortcomings. Export growth was sluggish and India's share of world exports declined from about 1.5 per cent to 0.6 per cent by 1978 (Srinivasan, 1990: 113). Persistent droughts in the mid 1960s prompted a new focus on agriculture. The application of new technology and subsidies helped India to achieve a 'green revolution' that boosted output and enabled India to achieve food self-sufficiency by

Illustration 7.1   Brick factory

Brick making is an activity that exemplifies many aspects of the informal economy. The work is seasonal, labour-intensive and workers are driven hard. The workers, who are often migrants engaged by labour contractors, are vulnerable to exploitation.

the 1980s. However, increased production has not been matched by increasing equity in food consumption and rural poverty continues to be a severe problem. Many of the large public sector enterprises set up under the planning system were inefficient. A perception of economic underperformance, encouraged by comparing India with China and East Asia, has been used to justify policies used to reform the economy (Alamgir, 2009). The balance of payment crisis of 1990–91 helped reform-minded policy-makers gain the initiative and since 1991 India has been pursuing a series of reforms that make it easier for the private sector to operate. The economy is now much more open to global forces.

The Government of India uses the three broad categories of agriculture, industry, and services as an aid to describing India's massive economy. This three-fold division is used by many when preparing statistics and this helps when describing the structure of the Indian economy. We begin with agriculture.

Agriculture

India's physical environment (discussed in Chapter 2) influences economic possibilities. Large parts of India receive only seasonal rainfall and good arable land is in short supply. Farmers gain some advantage over these obstacles by making use of irrigation and fertilizers. These techniques have long been in use in parts of India. The Indian countryside has changed substantially since independence. In 1950, agriculture contributed 53 per cent of India's GDP. In 2007–08 this had fallen to 17.8 per cent (Government of India, 2009a). However, the declining proportion of wealth produced in agriculture is not matched by a corresponding sharp decline in agricultural employment. The majority of the population still depend on the land for a living, approximately 52 per cent of the workforce (Government of India, 2009a). In 1947 India's villages were fairly self-contained even if they were not exactly the unchanging mini-republics that Gandhi eulogized (Gupta, 2004). Unemployment, under-employment, and low productivity on farms were (and are) causes of large-scale rural poverty.

Congress argued that British deindustrialization and neglect had exacerbated poverty in the countryside. To rectify this, Congress promised to modernize the Indian village. Those with socialist inclinations, including Nehru, hoped for substantial land reform that would have redistributed land from the large landed estates, and large and medium-sized farms. The departure of the British deprived the large landowners of political support. Congress was closely allied to the owners of medium-sized farms and the tenant farmers working larger plots on the landed estates. So there was a good deal of political support for abolishing the landed estates and passing ownership of the land to the tenants, but great hostility to land ceilings on large and medium-sized farms. The Indian federal system also reduced the chances of land reform. Responsibility for agriculture was assigned to state governments. These state governments were controlled by state Congress parties supported by the numerically important tenant cultivators and wealthy farmers who owned medium-sized farms. The abolition of the large landed estates was generally straightforward, but land reform legislation intended to introduce land ceilings on other farms often failed to get passed into law by state legislatures. In the cases where legislation was passed, various means were used to prevent implementation. Therefore, effective steps to help the majority of the landless out of poverty were rarely taken.

The end of the landed estates was a boon for those tenants who became owners of the land they had formerly rented. These farmers were set on the road to become prosperous owner-cultivators and became the backbone of the rural middle class discussed in Chapter 4. Their fortunes were further improved by the green revolution. In the mid 1960s new high-yielding varieties (HYVs) of various crops became available. In 1965 the Congress Government decided to exploit this technology to modernize Indian agriculture and increase food production. Subsidies were given to farmers for the irrigation, pesticides and the fertilizers essential for the successful use of new HYV seeds. The headline results of the strategy were impressive. Many farmers enthusiastically adopted the technology. India achieved food self-sufficiency in production by 1980. The increasingly prosperous owner-cultivators became a powerful political force in many states in India (S. Sharma, 1999, 120 and 136–7).

However, the green revolution was not without its problems and critics. Large farmers were best placed to use the new technology and absorb the costs. Farmers with small plots usually lacked the financial resources and the political connections needed to get access to the subsidized technology. Critics of this agricultural policy have argued that state governments are too attentive to wealthy farmers. They object to the wasteful use of subsidized inputs and the overregulation of agricultural markets (Srinivasan, 2000: 20–3). A particular point of contention is the supply of free or very heavily subsidized electricity that farmers use for drawing water out of (increasingly) deep tube wells that tap water from underground aquifers. The intensification of agriculture has created environmental problems. Pesticides and fertilizer have been overused and tube well irrigation has contributed to severe depletion of the water table in states such as Tamil Nadu.

The social effects of the green revolution were very uneven and varied by district and state. In some areas landless labourers secured better wages or more days' work as larger farms moved to several harvests a year. Often the wage increases were secured through bitterly fought struggles between farmers and unions. In other cases labourers gained because of labour shortages (Oommen, 1984). In some districts of India there are a lot of employment opportunities and employers have to pay well to attract workers. A 'tight' labour market has been created in the Punjab and some areas close to Delhi by the combination of good irrigation systems and new seeds that allow for several crops to be harvested a year. This means that work is available for most of the year (Jhabvala, 2005: 145). There are also jobs in nearby industrial centres that give workers more freedom to choose whether or not they want to work in agriculture. The picture is complex but what is clear is that the green revolution did not *by itself* substantially reduce rural poverty across India. It is still the case that many landless labourers remain below the poverty line and are unable to consume the food surplus created by the green revolution.

The Indian countryside has witnessed mixed fortunes since 1991 as the consequences of long-term changes in the economy have become clear. Growth rates in agriculture 'have remained at an average of 2 to 3 per cent per annum over the five decades since independence' (K. Sen, 2009b: 18). At the same time, the fast-growing sectors have not created enough employment to draw labour away from the land. This means that agriculture, the least productive sector, carries the burden of providing employment. The number of landholdings has increased at the same time as the amount of land available has declined. Between 1960 and 2003 the amount of land under cultivation was reduced from 133.5 to 107.6 hectares, while the number of farms increased from 50.8 to 101.3 million (Government of India, 2007: 23). This has increased the number of farms that are 'marginal', or unable to provide a living income for those who farm them. The government has withdrawn support from the countryside in several key respects since the early 1990s. Government investment in rural development has been scaled back and governments have been much more reluctant to guarantee remunerative prices for farmers. Banks have been allowed to concentrate lending on urban customers, making it difficult for farmers to get credit. Farmers that wish to innovate and find more productive activities face great risks (Government of India, 2007: 20–3). New World Trade Organization (WTO) rules have been disruptive for some farmers. Cheap imports of certain foodstuffs, such as edible oils, hurt Indian producers. In addition, the introduction of Monsanto's genetically modified seeds to the Indian market has caused problems. These seeds are expensive, non-reseeding and have not produced the promised yields, meaning that farmers have not been able to pay the seed producers after the harvest. In recent years there have been tens of thousands of cases of suicide by farmers who have been bankrupted by these changes. The UPA Government responded with a central aid package in 2004 (BBC, 2004), and the 2008 budget included a large fund to pay the cost of waiving debts owed by small farmers (Buncombe and Hardikar,

Illustration 7.2   Rural India

Irrigation is an essential part of agriculture in India. Electric pumpsets, such as the one pictured here, give farmers greater flexibility and they can grow a wider range of crops. However, these pumpsets, powered by heavily subsidized electricity, threaten the water table as water shortages spur farmers to sink even deeper tube wells.

2008). Uncertainty in the countryside has increased pressure on labourers to migrate, often great distances, in search of work. The optimism generated by the green revolution has now faded and has been replaced by a crisis in agriculture.

Industry

India has a long industrial history but its fortunes were eclipsed during the colonial period when British administrators introduced manufactured imports from Britain. Before 1947, family-owned industrial houses dominated India's industrial development (see Box 7.2). These houses often emerged from smaller trading or banking concerns. For example, the Tata family made a seminal contribution to the development of Indian industry. Jamsetji Tata founded a trading company in 1868 that extended into hotels (in 1902), steel (1907), electricity (1910) and chemicals (1939). Another family

---

Box 7.2   Family firms

Family-owned businesses are an important feature of India's corporate sector. The firms often started small, using family contacts to raise capital, and family members were key managers of the business. Some remain under private control while others have issued shares in order to raise money to grow the business. Family-owned businesses often struggle with the issue of succession as the business is handed from one generation to the next. Siblings and relatives often prefer to divide up the company and have closer control over a smaller part of the business. It is relatively rare for a business conglomerate, like the Tata group, to remain jointly owned by a family over several generations. The Birla group was divided into several different businesses in 1986. Although the Birla group was divided in an orderly fashion, other businesses have been damaged by rancorous arguments over the share of assets. The division of the Reliance companies in 2005 between Anil and Mukesh Ambani took six months to conclude and damaged the image of the main protagonists. Family businesses continue to be an important feature of India's corporate sector. The response to globalization has been interesting. One defensive move commonly adopted by stock market listed firms has been to buy back shares to make it easier to resist hostile takeover bids from overseas competitors (Srinivas, 2005: 229). In anticipation of competition some families have withdrawn from day-to-day management and given more responsibility to profes-sional managers. Other businesses have entered joint ventures with overseas companies in order to help modernize their operations (Harriss-White, 2003).

---

member, J.R.D. Tata, who founded India's first commercial airline in 1932, drove the company forward for much of the twentieth century. The entrepreneur G.D. Birla was another of India's industrial pioneers. He established successful jute mills in Calcutta in the 1920s and built up a range of businesses including the very successful Gwalior Rayon in 1947.

J.R.D. Tata and G.D. Birla were members of the group of seven businessmen who proposed the 'Bombay plan' in 1944. This docu-ment accepted the need for economic planning and some state controls that would help promote industrialization. The Congress leader Nehru, working from a socialist outlook, supported even stronger state intervention. Business leaders saw things rather differ-ently but realized that the public mood was hostile to unfettered capi-talism. The nationalist leadership avoided radical changes but agreed to redirect the economy to meet the needs of the population.

Illustration 7.3   Tata trucks

The Tata group is active in many different areas of the Indian economy. Its trucks (colourfully decorated by their owners), pictured here, and cars are a ubiquitous sight on India's roads. The service industries of the Tata group include the luxury Taj hotels and software.

Congress leaders saw industrial development as a remedy for the harmful legacy of colonial rule. The system of planned development created a mixed economy. The state invested very heavily in new industries through the system of five-year plans. The private sector was recognized and given a lot of freedom but it had to work alongside a large public sector and accept state controls (for example, new factories could not be opened without a government licence). Private enterprise was not penalized by random nationalization of companies; the taking of private business into public control was quite rare in India. The nationalization of Tata's airline business and the state takeover of private banks announced in 1969 were exceptions to the general rule. There were compensations for the private sector but there was little competition from overseas businesses. Foreign imports were controlled and subject to high tariffs and the policy of import substitution encouraged companies to produce domestic substitutes for overseas manufactures. These substitutes, sheltered by the steep tariffs, were very profitable for private businesses manufacturing in India. The private sector was also helped by lending from government-run banks (Tripathi, 2004). Indian business was generally able to expand. Existing business houses added new companies, developed new products and increased sales. Industrial pioneers found a way through the maze of regulations. Over thirty new industrial groups emerged between 1947 and 1984 (Tripathi, 2004: 298). Both the Tata and Birla groups continued to diversify after 1947 and were the two largest business groups in India in the 1980s. They have both become successful multinational companies.

Political connections were immensely useful under the so-called 'licence-permit-quota raj'. The licensing system was often (ab)used to gain an advantage. Privileged access to rare imported raw materials or being the sole holder of a licence to develop a particular product were just such routes to profit. The Reliance group was extremely adept at manipulating the system of bureaucratic controls to its advantage (Srinivas, 2005; Tripathi, 2004: 302). Reliance was able to access the latest technology and develop very profitable textile and petrochemical interests. The founder of the group, Dhirubhai Ambani, began business in 1958, and in his lifetime the family business became a massive conglomerate.

National economic planners intended that the emphasis on the heavy goods sector, such as machine tools and railway stock, would help other industries develop. Planners hoped that new industries would create jobs and relieve pressure on the poverty-stricken countryside. Planners preferred an inward focus in their development planning. It was feared overseas trade would leave India dependent on the former imperial powers and limit the gains from political independence from Britain. The inward strategy required Indian industry to be built up to make the country self-reliant in the production of key goods, including heavy goods, such as steel and chemicals. These items would also be useful for an indigenous defence industry.

The industrial policy pursued by the Indian state had very definite effects. Critics have pointed to the inefficiency of public sector enterprises. They have also complained that private businesses were stifled by the close regulation of business. It is certainly true that some state-owned businesses produced poor-quality goods (as did many private businesses). The profits of many public sector companies were not especially impressive. Private businesses were protected from overseas competitors and were able to produce expensive goods of indifferent quality to sell to customers who had very little choice. The neglect of exports created problems, including a persistent shortage of foreign exchange needed to pay for essential imports. Participating in competitive export markets would have encouraged higher-quality standards for the companies involved. However, in the period 1947 to 1991, India achieved remarkable depth in the industrial sector. India could produce many of the basic goods, such as cement and machine tools, which had to be imported by other developing countries. Some of these goods were produced by public sector undertakings and others were produced by the state-directed private sector. Public investment over a long period also changed the ownership structure of Indian industry. By the mid-1980s it was remarkable that a large proportion of India's largest companies were state-owned. Of India's leading 100 companies in 1983, 47 were in the public sector. Strikingly the state dominated the larger firms with only 6 private sector firms in the top 30 leading companies (Rudolph and Rudolph, 1987: 403–6).

A number of apex organizations represent the collective interests of Indian industry and business. The two oldest organizations are the Associated Chambers of Commerce and Industry (Assocham) and the Federation of Indian Chambers of Industry and Commerce (FICCI). Assocham was associated with the interests of overseas (especially British) owned businesses whereas FICCI spoke for larger Indian enterprises. After 1947 FICCI emerged as the stronger organization. It was known to be dominated by the large established, family-owned businesses and to be hostile to liberalization. The bias towards older industrial houses based in Bombay created a gap for a new organization. The Confederation of Indian Industry (CII) was formed in 1992. The forerunner to this body was formed in 1974 as a representative of smaller engineering companies uncomfortable with the Bombay orientation of FICCI. The CII considered itself to be a representative of modern, technology-based industries. The CII argued for economic reform and deregulation that would attract foreign investment to India (Pedersen, 2000).

The Post-1991 Economic Reforms

A small but influential group of economists were critical of planned development. They received a sympathetic hearing from Indira Gandhi, who introduced some cautious reforms and took a loan from the International Monetary Fund (IMF) in 1981. Rajiv Gandhi was also attentive to reformist economists and adopted some liberal reforms but these were slowed down as they proved unpopular

(Kohli, 2006: 1257). In early 1991 India was desperately short of foreign exchange reserves and was in danger of defaulting on its overseas loans. The background to the crisis was an increase in government spending unmatched by tax increases. This fiscal deficit was partly paid for by overseas borrowings. Servicing this debt cut into the already scarce supply of hard currency and left India vulnerable when the 1991 Gulf crisis reduced the inward flow of remittances from migrant workers *and* increased the cost of India's oil imports (Harriss-White, 2003: 60). The possibility of a balance of payments crisis created a sense of urgency which senior policy-makers used to justify a series of reforms. In 1991 a newly elected Congress Government pushed through a series of measures to reduce state controls and help integrate India with the global economy. India's currency, the rupee, was devalued. This made exports more competitive. Rules on investments were relaxed to encourage foreign investors to do business in India. The policy of using state planning to shape the Indian economy was heavily revised; there is now little direct state investment in industry. India ratified the agreement that founded the World Trade Organization in 1994 and has reformed its trade policy so that it is easier to import goods into India.

The political aspect of the post-1991 reforms must not be overlooked. Advocates of reforms tend to see their favoured policies as technical corrections to an economic system in which price mechanisms are distorted. However, so-called 'technical' adjustments can have a dramatically adverse impact in a country in which a large proportion of the population live below or just above the poverty line. Reforms, such as cutting food and fuel subsidies, cause inflation which will meet with resistance. As such, governments have an incentive to conceal the extent to which they have implemented unpopular reforms. A variety of methods have been used, including incremental changes that slowly move the economy in a more liberal direction. Jenkins (1999) argues that the 'reform by stealth' approach goes a long way to explaining how unpopular reforms have been sustained in a democratic political system that has the potential to unseat a government which follows policies that are too unpopular. Examples of reform by stealth include changes to labour markets and regulations on land transactions. India has strong labour laws but state governments often choose not to implement them and so create a more 'flexible' labour market in which firms can shed staff if they so choose. In other cases, legal limits on the corporate purchase of agricultural land were waived on an ad hoc basis. In both cases the

Table 7.1   Foreign direct investment and foreign
institutional investment in India since 1991

Year	FDI US$ millions	FII US$ millions
1991–2000	15,483	-
2000–01	4029	1847
2001–02	6130	1505
2002–03	5035	377
2003–04	4322	10,918
2004–05	6051	8686
2005–06	8961	9926
2006–07	22,826	3225
2007–08	34,362	20,328
2008–09	35,168	-15,017

Source: Compiled from Government of India (2009b);
the figures for 2007–08 and 2008–09 are provisional.

official policy stands but the actions of the state governments show a
different policy at the implementation stage (Jenkins, 1999: 194–6).
Further evidence of the political management of reforms is provided
by the policy on the privatization of state-run industries. Relatively
few state-owned companies have been converted to private companies or sold off to private sector bidders. Instead, state-owned companies have tended to sell a minority of their shares to private investors
producing a compromise outcome of state control but partial private
ownership.

The consequences of reform for Indian industry have been mixed.
The reforms were slow to dispel the doubts of overseas investors.
Overseas investments are separated into two kinds, short-term 'portfolio investments' or foreign institutional investment (FII) in stocks
and bonds, and longer-term foreign direct investment (FDI) used to
buy Indian companies or investment in plants and machinery. FDI
should generate employment and in some cases might enable technology transfers that spill over into the wider economy. The long-term
nature of FDI makes it a more desirable form of investment in contrast
to potentially speculative and destabilizing portfolio investments.
Among the post-1991 reforms were measures that gave greater

freedom to FII. The general upward trend in Indian stock markets has been a pull factor among overseas investors seeking a place in India's 'emerging market'. Investors are not completely free to speculate, with shares being limited to only 70 per cent of investments. The rest has to be invested in government and corporate bonds (Chakrabarti, 2007). One of the consequences of the global credit crunch was that overseas investors sold stock market investments in India and repatriated their funds, though this sell-off did not result in a financial crisis of the type seen in East Asia in 1997. Overseas investors still have confidence in Indian financial markets. Growth in FDI has been uneven. Amounts were low in absolute terms, for example China attracts far larger amounts than India, but in proportional terms, which make for a clearer comparison, the gap is not so marked. In terms of overall investment in the Indian economy FDI is a small proportion. Between 2004 and 2006, FDI was only 5.2 per cent of overall investment. The equivalent figure for China was 8.3 per cent (Nunnenkamp and Stracke, 2008: 57). Only very recently has the level of FDI picked up (see Table 7.1). Investors are deterred by remaining government regulation and poor-quality infrastructure, perceptions of corruption and unreliable electricity supplies.

However, as we discuss below, some of the states in India's federal system are seen as more desirable investment locations than others. Foreign investments are regionally skewed with Delhi and the states of Goa, Haryana, Karnataka, Maharashtra and Tamil Nadu attracting more than five times the average per capita investment than the rest of India's states. Even within these states investment was highly concentrated in the period between 1993 and 2005. The leading cities of India attract high proportions of the total invested in their state as a whole: Mumbai (60.1 per cent), Bangalore (89.3 per cent), Chennai (63.8 per cent), Kolkata (70.2 per cent) (Nunnenkamp and Stracke, 2008: 63–6). The process of economic reform since 1991 exposed many Indian firms to overseas competition. This competition obliged Indian firms to improve their products and provide more responsive service. Indian companies have undergone technological and organizational change leading to increased output and many redundancies (Harriss, 2003: 341 and 345). These changes help to explain the paradox of what critics of the reforms call 'jobless growth'. The Indian economy has grown very rapidly but employment growth in the formal sector in the 1990s lagged behind. As well as the number of redundancies, growing productivity meant firms were able to increase output while not hiring many new workers. It is only since

2000 that employment has shown noticeable signs of expansion and even then wages for ordinary workers have not been that buoyant (Sundaram, 2007). The reform process has been challenging for industry but it is widely recognized that there is a much more business-friendly environment in contemporary India.

An indication of the growing confidence of Indian industry lies in their overseas activity. The Tata group bought the British-based Tetley tea group in 2000. Another part of the group, Tata Motors, was listed on the New York Stock Exchange in 2004. In January 2007, Tata Steel bought the European steelmaker Corus, in the largest overseas acquisition made by an Indian company. Tata followed this up with the purchase of the British-based carmaker, Jaguar, in March 2008. The United Breweries Group, manufacturer of Kingfisher beer in India, has built a large conglomerate within India. Recently it has sought to expand overseas. In 2006 it made an unsuccessful bid for the champagne producer Taittinger and settled instead for buying Bouvet Ladubay, a wine-making subsidiary of the parent group. In 2007, United Breweries Group (UBG) acquired the UK whisky distiller, Whyte and Mackay.

Services

India's service economy has grown rapidly and it has made an important contribution to India's high growth rate in recent years, with finance, communication and IT being critically important given that other services like retail, hotels and restaurants follow growth patterns in other areas (K. Sen, 2009b: 20). The service economy is extremely diverse. If we sort workers according to earnings we can identify an elite who work in cities, are often employed by large companies, possess formal contracts and earn regular salaries. Among this group are the software engineers who have become national heroes in the last decade. In contrast, the majority of those who work in services are employed by small family-run businesses. These workers do not have formal contracts and are usually badly paid. Services based on informal employment are provided in many ways, ranging from the very small concerns run by single self-employed individuals to small enterprises like wholesale trading, shop-keeping and transport companies. Even though this sector escapes media attention, it is also dynamic and can be the source of considerable prosperity for the owners of small businesses (Harriss-White, 2003).

Illustration 7.4   Roadside restaurant

Many service enterprises, such as this roadside restaurant, are small
concerns that employ a few workers in an informal way.

Banks are a critically important service. Much of India's banking is
in the public sector. In 1969 the Congress Government led by Indira
Gandhi decided to nationalize 14 large private banks. An important
outcome of this change was that the nationalized banks were required
to work to certain social criteria which included opening more
branches and making loans in specific categories (including agriculture). Nationalization was followed by a substantial increase in the
savings rate, better access to credit and a larger pool of funds to make
loans with. Kunal Sen argues that this contributed substantially to
investment in industry and increases in economic growth in the 1970s
(2009b: 13–14). Making sure that the poor have access to the banks is
considered a priority, given that one alternative is a loan from a private
moneylender at a usurious rate. Credit unions have been one mechanism whereby small groups of savers, usually women participating in
an SHG, can get bank loans. However, banks have not always been
helpful. Poorer customers often need intervention by a politician to get
a loan agreed and SHGs are put under pressure by aggressive bank
managers. In some cases debts owed by relatives of SHG members
have been transferred to the SHG. SHGs have at times been obliged to
take unnecessary loans so that bank managers can reach targets.

Since 1991 the banking sector has been reformed gradually. Fewer restrictions limit the operations of private banks, and overseas firms have an expanded presence in India as rules on FDI in the sector have been relaxed. Banking practices have been modernized. Branches are more efficient and middle-class consumers have easier access to personal loans and credit cards. Private banks, in particular, have moved aggressively into the market for home loans and unsecured personal loans, causing some to fear that India may experience a banking crisis of its own (Ghosh and Chandrasekhar, 2009: 733–5). Further changes lie ahead. The sector is quite fragmented and it is very likely that mergers and takeovers will reduce the number of domestic banks.

India's software industry has been especially vibrant since the late 1990s. The sector has grown rapidly and enjoyed a great deal of export success. The success is reflected in the volume of exports and in the fact that the leading exporters are Indian companies. Multinational companies and joint venture operations do export software but in smaller quantities. The Indian companies Tata Consultancy Services, Infosys and Wipro headed the list of exporters in 2008–09 (NASSCOM, 2009b). As Indian companies gained a reputation for employing highly skilled staff and completing high-quality work, they have moved up the value chain. Initially the focus was on supplying staff to work as onsite consultants, so-called 'body shopping', for projects managed by customers. As time passed more projects have been handed over to Indian companies that work on projects in India and deliver a completed product to overseas customers. Some multinationals have established their own software development centres to take advantage of the same conditions that give Indian companies an export advantage (Balakrishnan, 2006). These advantages include skilled workers fluent in English, good communication links, and dedicated software parks with excellent infrastructure. Most of India's software exports (60 per cent) are bought by US customers. The time difference between the two countries means that a team split between them can work on a project around the clock (Narayana Murthy, 2007: 490–1). India has become a world leader in producing animation for international films as well as computer games, with Indian companies such as Toonz Animation and Maya Entertainment being commissioned to complete projects for companies such as Walt Disney and Sony. Maya Entertainment worked on *The Mummy* as well as *Stuart Little*.

A logical extension of software development was offering to run the process the software was designed for, and so some Indian companies have moved into the related areas of consultancy and business process outsourcing (BPO) (Balakrishnan, 2006: 3868). BPO has grown strongly. In 2008–09, exports from the IT sector totalled $46.3 billion of which BPO contributed $12.7 billion (NASSCOM, 2009b). The rapid growth of software exports has seen the share of IT-BPO exports rise from 'less than 4 per cent in 1998 to almost 16 per cent in 2008' (NASSCOM, 2009a). The improvements in telecommunications and information technology vital for the software industry have allowed other IT-enabled services (ITES) to be exported. Among other things, Indian call centres are used for providing customer service, telephone sales, insurance and banking services. India's software companies are globally recognized as effective providers of services and have well-recognized brands. Infosys has its shares listed on the NASDAQ stock market and Wipro is listed on the New York Stock Exchange. Despite the scandal relating to Satyam's creative accounting to hide losses (which broke in 2009, so-called 'India's Enron') (Vaswani, 2009), the success of larger companies has given the software industry confidence and has become a source of national pride.

In global terms the salaries for workers in the IT and ITES sectors are low, which gives the industries a cost advantage. Within India there is high demand for skilled workers and salaries for skilled staff in the leading companies reflect this. These fast-growing segments of the service sector are important for India's export profile. The direct impact on employment is small in relation to India's overall workforce, with the IT-BPO sector employing a tiny fraction, an estimated 2.2 million in 2008–09, of India's workforce. The wealth generated in this sector does have a multiplier effect and it is estimated that another 8 million jobs are created indirectly (NASSCOM, 2009a).

India remains a country of high levels of poverty despite the existence of great personal wealth for small sections of society and a growing middle class with purchasing power. Official figures show a trend of falling poverty levels since independence. Estimates suggest that in the mid 1990s the proportion of the population living in poverty was 36 per cent. In 2005 this had fallen to 27.5 per cent (World Bank, 2008: Annex B5). However, these figures almost certainly underestimate the extent of poverty.

The measurement of poverty – and especially the definition of the poverty line – has been a source of ongoing controversy. Every five years a National Sample Survey (NSS) is carried out. The consumption patterns of over 100,000 households are surveyed and the data collected are used to provide poverty estimates. The Planning Commission measures poverty in terms of the amount of income needed to buy a certain amount of food. The estimates are contested for a variety of reasons. A key issue is the price that the poor have to pay for essential goods and this can vary between states. Some have access to subsidized food through the PDS and this may keep them just above the poverty line. However, restriction of access to the PDS to the 'officially' poor hurts those who live precariously above the poverty line (Somanathan, 2007: 416). Expenditure on non-food items, including clothing and shelter, is not taken into account. Access to services like education and health also determines a person's standard of living (Swaminathan, 2003). It is quite possible to experience poverty while not being counted as poor by the Indian state.

In addition, although many people may not be categorized as falling below the poverty line, many have escaped from poverty only in a statistical sense. Their wages are above the official poverty line but they are still economically insecure. Many workers depend on casual employment. Illness or family distress could easily push those on low incomes back below the poverty line (Swaminathan, 2003: 86). A minority, mostly in the corporate sector, have had substantial wage increases since 1991. This is the group that is able to participate in the consumer boom. It was the prosperity and ambitions of this group that the BJP attempted to reflect with the slogan 'India shining' used during the 2004 general election campaign. Most workers have seen their wages increase only modestly, at only 2.5 per cent a year, while the overall economy has grown much more quickly (Jhabvala, 2005: 157–61). These increases in real wages for the majority are of course a positive development but much more is needed to improve the quality of life for the majority of the Indian population. Attention also has to be paid to factors less easy to quantify. For example, seasonal migration might improve earnings but is unlikely to improve the quality of the migrant's life. Inequality is another issue.

The very close link between social identity and poverty needs to be understood as well. Identity often determines poverty. Most women in India earn substantially less than men doing the same job. In some cases state legislation actually fixes different minimum wage rates between the sexes. Returning to the theme of caste discussed in earlier chapters also illustrates this. India has experienced social change but it is still common for caste background to determine occupational status. Thus Dalits are often kept in menial jobs because of their caste status. Poverty is about much more than a lack of income. Dalits and some members of the backward castes still experience social discrimination and hostility even when they have increased monetary income. In fact, some Dalits have experienced retribution because they are considered to have gone beyond their preordained station in life. People esteem autonomy and their freedom to act. Income-based statistics do not give a good sense of how social sanction limits these freedoms.

Another facet of poverty is the continuing use of child labour in the Indian economy. Children are paid very poorly and this enables activities with low productivity to remain profitable. The rate of participation fell between the 1991 and 2001 censuses, but the last census still recorded 12.6 million children aged 5 to 14 as being in paid employment. Rates of pay tend to be low, working conditions are often hazardous and a lack of education creates a disadvantage that will last a lifetime. Most children who work do so in agriculture, but some industries also favour child labour. The Indian state has preferred to regulate, rather than ban, child labour. This regulation has not always been effective (Swaminathan, 2007: 53–4).

Aid

Despite these high levels of poverty, the experience of colonial dominance meant that India has always had an ambivalent attitude towards foreign aid and external assistance. However, because the five-year plans were exceedingly ambitious, India could not afford to fund many planned projects out of tax revenue. This encouraged policymakers to accept aid from western states and take loans from the World Bank. As far as possible India resisted conditionality tied to overseas assistance. India also accepted aid from the USSR and this helped counter charges of dependence on western powers. The suspicions of Indian nationalists of the dangers of foreign involvement were confirmed in 1966 after the US tied food aid to policy reform and a devaluation of the rupee. The World Bank promised increased aid in return for the policy changes. Indira Gandhi's Government made the policy changes, but they proved to be deeply controversial inside India and the Prime Minister was denounced as weak. Salt was rubbed into the wound when the aid increase did not materialize.

From that point onwards India resisted external attempts to impose conditions, and the level of aid decreased. During the 1970s, 'aid barely amounted to 1 percent of Indian GNP' (Kapur, Lewis and Webb, 1997: 297).

India still receives aid but in very small quantities in relation to the overall population. It was only in 1991 that India took a conditional loan from the World Bank. After the tsunami in December 2004, India initially refused aid, and indeed the tsunami provided an opportunity to demonstrate India had the resources and the expertise to provide disaster relief to other countries. This was not an isolated incident; in 2005 after the earthquake in Kashmir, India again refused aid but offered help to Pakistan (Sengupta, 2005). Similarly, offers of outside help after the devastating floods in Bihar in August/ September 2008 were rejected. Reducing the inflow of aid is consistent with the government's desire for India to be recognized as a world power (see Chapter 8), even though such rejections may disadvantage those in most need.

India is also an aid donor. The three largest recipients of India's bilateral aid in 2008 are states where India is clearly concerned to secure political influence. India is keen to support states on its border where it fears China's influence. In 2008 the largest single recipient was Bhutan and it is estimated that India provides nearly 60 per cent of the government's budget in that state. The next largest commitment in 2008 was to Afghanistan. Nepal has received aid from India since the 1950s. In 2008, India allocated $547 million to its aid budget and made available an additional $704 million in loans. Though India's policy of giving aid is not new, the scale of aid provided has increased substantially in the last decade and it is seen as an important indicator of India's status as a world power (Dutt, 1980; Chanana, 2009: 11–12).

The Federalization of the Economy

The structure of the economy resembles, to a certain extent, India's federal political structure. This trend has been accentuated by various reforms since 1991. The institution of Indian federalism, discussed in Chapter 3, encourages this pattern beginning with the Seventh Schedule to the constitution. This Schedule lists the areas of exclusive authority for the states and areas of concurrent jurisdiction. Many of these responsibilities have economic implications. So while the central government dominates macro-economic policy-making, the states have major obligations in the areas of health, education, roads, and law and order. The states can make a direct economic impact through industrial policy, the allocation of land for development, and the taxes they levy. The states also make agricultural policy and manage labour disputes.

The planning system was designed to overcome regional imbalances in growth. It has had only limited success in this regard as some states have considerably stronger economies than others. Major industrial centres include Mumbai, Kolkata, Chennai and more recently the capital city, Delhi. Areas adjacent to the capital, including the states of Punjab, Haryana and western Uttar Pradesh, gained particular benefit from the green revolution and make a major contribution to India's agricultural output.

As the central government moved away from a state-directed model of development in the 1990s, the institutional role of the states was also changed. As discussed in Chapter 3, reforms were introduced that created more competition between states. It was hoped that states would advance their own reforms, speed up economic growth and encourage 'lagging' states to emulate the successful reforming states. For example, the central government scaled back the central regulation of investment for both domestic and foreign direct investment. State governments were much freer to negotiate with investors seeking to build new plants; for example, there have been several cases of multinational companies such as Microsoft negotiating with a number of states seeking investment. The competition between states keen to attract jobs and investment usually results in a very good deal for the company in the form of tax waivers and generous allocations of land. Declining revenue transfers to the states from the central government since 1991 have also obliged state governments to become more independent and seek alternative sources of income. The World Bank has also been involved in this process, making loans to individual states and offering advice to state governments.

The evolution of India's federalized economy has to be understood in the context of globalization and the involvement of international institutions like the WTO. One consequence of the post-1991 reforms is that states have experienced different degrees of integration with global markets. This can be explained by the quality of infrastructure, the availability of skilled labour, existing patterns of industrial development and by the willingness of state governments to accommodate investors. Towns and cities in the southern states of Andhra Pradesh, Karnataka and Tamil Nadu provide locations for a substantial amount of India's growing information technology sector and have reaped the benefits of expanding service exports. These states, along with the western states of Maharashtra and Gujarat, being well placed to attract foreign direct investment, are clear 'winners' in India's federal economy and the gap between these states and the poorer states of Bihar, Uttar Pradesh, Orissa and Madhya Pradesh is now substantial. The Government of India responded to this apprehension in 2004 by asking the World Bank to focus attention on the states, including Bihar and Orissa, where poverty rates have been high and market reform has made little impact.

The evolution of India's federal economy is part of a political process. The trend towards more autonomous policy-making at the state level has also been encouraged by the growth of regional parties since the mid 1980s. As the Congress Party has lost ground to the regional parties, these parties have emerged as the balancing force in the formation of national coalition governments since 1996. The regional parties maintain close links with regional business houses and the farming lobbies in their respective states. This has strengthened support for the principle of making certain economic policy decisions at the level of the state government, and the central government remains committed to devolved economic policy-making. The fragmentation of authority between states has had its problems but so far these tensions have been contained inside India's democratic political institutions.

Conclusion

The Indian economy has undergone important changes since 1947. India has extended its industrial capacity, developed a vibrant service economy and partially modernized agriculture. Since 1991, a process of economic liberalization has meant that India is more closely integrated with the global economy. This is not a novel situation as India was exposed to global economic forces during the colonial period. However, the contemporary engagement with the global economy is quite uneven. The ratios of exports and imports to GDP are relatively low. India is not an export economy in the sense that other developing states, highly dependent on the production of primary goods, are. As a proportion of GDP, levels of foreign direct investment are low and India is – according to some – more in danger of being bypassed by the forces of globalization. However, India has joined the WTO and has opened up its economy to imports. The agricultural economy was hit by competition from cheap imports though the emphasis is now on dealing with food shortages. Some segments of Indian industry and services have established themselves as notable producers and investors in the global economy. Overall we can say that since 1991 governments have been keen to reap the benefits of globalization and further integration with the global economy is likely.

8

India and the World

India is not content with its current international status. Indian foreign policy-makers assume that India is a unique and important state and India wants to be regarded as a leading power of equal status to world powers such as the US, Russia, and China. Ultimately India would like to see a world order in which US dominance is replaced by multi-polarity where power in the international system is shared among key states. This ambition is held in spite of the fact that India is short of some of the sources of material power, namely military capability and economic wealth, that major powers are assumed to possess. Since the mid 1990s India has changed its foreign policy profile and boosted its image. Much is made of speculation that India will emerge as one of the world's largest economies (Narlikar, 2007: 984–5). The strategic value given to India by US security planners is also taken as confirmation of India as a world power (Pant, 2007b: 57). Although for some commentators these bold ambitions represent a new departure in Indian foreign policy, we see strong continuity in policy-making. The 1998 nuclear tests and improved relations with the United States are important developments but their importance should not be overstated.

India has a long history of engagement and good global citizenship. It participates effectively in the United Nations (UN) with Nehru having begun a tradition of very active participation in the body (Cohen, 2001: 56). This continued in the 1970s as India helped coordinate the activity of the G-77 group pressing for an agenda favoured by many Third World countries (Mohan, 2003: 41). India is a notable participant in UN peacekeeping missions. In October 2009 India provided nearly 10 per cent of the military and police personnel engaged in peacekeeping and 8759 personnel were seconded to nine different missions (United Nations, 2009).

In this chapter we consider why India has generally attempted to follow an independent course in international politics. India's foreign policy orientation is related to the nationalist struggle against British colonialism. We show how the colonial legacy continues to be important even though India has defined its own policy. We chart key changes in Indian foreign policy since the end of the Cold War and give a sense of why India is seen by many as a major power. Key changes include the 1998 nuclear tests and India's attempts to gain recognition as a responsible nuclear power. We also look at the strengthened relations with the US while showing how the two states have not fully overcome the difficulties that beset their relationship during the Cold War. A key element of Indian foreign policy concerns Pakistan and we explain why so much attention focuses on the disputed region of Kashmir. We then look at India's relations with the other states of South Asia which have been less troubled but often tense. India has attempted to build better relations with states in other parts of Asia, but, as we show, the question of China overshadows this element of Indian policy. We conclude the chapter by reviewing some of the debates over the direction of Indian foreign policy.

India's Changing Place in the World

At independence India's leaders expected India to continue to be a major power in Asia. They were convinced that India was destined to play a leading role in world politics. Nehru wrote in the mid 1940s that 'India, constituted as she is, cannot play a secondary part in the world' (1946: 56). The nationalist elite were particularly galled to be excluded from the founding of the UN in 1945 (the British were still in control of India's foreign and defence policy). Nehru was strongly aware of India's rich history and the fact that India was one of the few states that encompassed an entire civilization. How could such an important state be ignored? India could also boast of political achievements. The independence struggle against the British was largely peaceful and India quickly emerged as a stable democracy. Indian nationalists expected their new state to play a progressive role in world politics. India would pursue a course independent of the western imperial powers and promote peace and cooperation. As part of this principled approach to international politics India encouraged other nationalist movements to challenge western imperialism. Indian diplomats spoke for the cause of decolonization in the newly formed

UN. If the Congress leadership did not share Gandhi's strong views on non-violence, there was at least a feeling that India should use military force only reluctantly.

The nationalist elite abandoned some of the stronger elements of the British worldview (at times expansionist and placing a premium on military security) but they did not abandon it completely. Nehru felt that India's security implied an Indian interest in the security of the region as a whole. He discouraged the presence of external powers in the region and renewed treaties with the Himalayan mountain kingdoms of Nepal and Bhutan. These treaties codified an unequal relationship between the small states and India, continuing the practice under colonial rule. The agreements also suggested that Nehru wanted to carry on with the British assumption that these kingdoms would act as buffer states between India and China (Noorani, 2000), an issue discussed in more detail below.

Nehru felt that military expenditure should be kept at modest levels so that resources would be freed up for development spending. Therefore 'his conduct of foreign policy emphasized negotiation and cooperation and he was quite unconcerned about the military aspect of India's security' (Cohen, 2001: 128). However, India's assessment of its own importance was rarely shared by major players on the international scene and, though it was a strong regional hegemon, which we discuss below, in 1962 China made its dominance of the wider region clear by invading Indian territory. Contemporary critics such as former BJP foreign minister Jaswant Singh have strongly criticized Nehru for inattention to defence policy (1999: 39). It was only in 1962 as a direct result of the Chinese invasion that the Indian military were 'given a role in the formulation' of defence policy (Pant, 2009: 257).

India's independent foreign policy was severely tested during the Cold War. The US was keen to contain the USSR and China in the 1950s through a system of alliances. Pakistan was included in two US alliances: Central Treaty Organization (CENTO) and Southeast Asia Treaty Organization (SEATO). India was keen to keep friendly relations with the US but was unwilling to enter a formal alliance, one of the benefits of non-alignment (see Box 8.1) being that India received aid from both the US and the USSR. Also, the close relationship between the US and Pakistan troubled India. For instance, in return for an emergency supply of arms during the war with China in 1962, the US put pressure on India to negotiate with Pakistan over Kashmir (Maxwell, 1972: 217, 419–20), whereas India received support from the USSR over the Kashmir issue and the willingness of the Soviets

---

Box 8.1 Non-alignment

Immediately after independence in 1947 India gained a position of leadership in international politics arguing for further decolonization and the rolling back of western imperialism. The resentment of imperial rule meant that Indian leaders wanted to avoid alliances with the existing western imperial powers and their close ally, the US. This was especially the case during the Cold War. India wanted no part of the dangerous superpower rivalry and argued for a middle way through the conflict. Nehru called this approach 'non-alignment' and he believed it would promote peace. He described his approach in a 1946 radio broadcast: 'We propose as far as possible to keep away from the power politics of groups, aligned against one another, which have led in the past to world wars and which may again lead to disaster on an even greater scale' cited in Nanda (1990: 3). Nehru did not see this as a passive approach to international politics but rather one in which India would not pre-commit to another power and would reserve the right to make its own judgment on each issue. Non-alignment was both a pragmatic policy and a clear statement of an alternative conception of international politics (Abraham, 2008: 196 and 210). This Indian worldview was very influential when the wider Non-Aligned Movement (NAM) was formed. This institution, which attracted many Third World states, gave India an opportunity to act as a leader in world politics. India gained a reputation as a seasoned negotiator in international organizations and as a representative of other Third World states at major international conferences.

---

to veto Security Council resolutions on the matter was especially useful. Therefore India developed close ties with the USSR, and even signed a treaty just prior to the Bangladesh war. It denied that these links compromised its independence and non-alignment.

The end of the Cold War obliged a foreign policy rethink. India lost a vitally important ally when the Soviet Union collapsed in 1991. As well as supporting India in the UN, the Soviet Union was the major supplier of arms for the Indian military and though Russia continued to supply arms to India, it had less influence in world politics. India was now obliged to take account of the dominant position of the US and the changed terms of global politics curtailed its ability to assert itself in South Asia. The US began to take a much closer interest in the region and it is debatable whether India could now successfully carry out an intervention, such as the invasion of East Pakistan in 1971, against the wishes of the US (Mehta, 2003). Similarly, China has been able to exert more influence in South Asia (Mohan, 2003:

145–6, 155). As we detail later in the chapter, China has close links with Pakistan and Burma (Myanmar). Indian policy-makers are somewhat intimidated by China's rapid economic growth and see themselves as having to catch up with China (Alamgir, 2009). In the absence of Cold War conflict, the concept of non-alignment lost some its meaning. The economic reforms of 1991 and changing economic circumstances also encouraged a rethink. A new emphasis on promoting exports and attracting overseas investment required Indian diplomacy to focus much more on economic issues. As well as an increase in exports, patterns of trade have also changed in important ways since the early 1990s.

Despite these changes, relations with Russia remain close. In 2001 the two countries signed the Indo-Russian Strategic Agreement, and in 2007 the two countries signed several defence agreements (Ganguly, 2008: 174). Russia remains important for India as a major arms supplier. Chenoy estimates that India depends on Russia for '70 per cent of its military hardware imports' (2008: 55). Russia also facilitates links with the Central Asian Republics, with which India does not have a land border. India's demands for energy are extremely high and many of the Central Asian Republics have oil and natural gas reserves (Chenoy, 2008: 53).

As well as retaining a close relationship because of energy and military needs (despite their rivalry in these fields), both India and Russia are part of a bloc of four countries, dubbed BRIC in a Goldman Sachs' report in 2001. The increasingly powerful economics of Brazil, Russia, India and China are seen as a potentially influential group standing apart from western alignments. In 2008, representatives from all four countries held their first formal summit in Russia. As Mortished notes, 'Brazil and India are using their economic clout to wield political influence, notably in bodies such as the World Trade Organization, in which the two often lead negotiations with the US and the EU' (2008). India is also an important member of the G20, which has effectively supplanted the G8 (CNN, 2009) and commands an important position both economically and also because of the need for global action to protect the environment.

Hard Power Routes to Influence

The BJP Government's decision to test a nuclear weapon in 1998 signalled a significant change in India's foreign policy. India's nuclear ambitions are not new. The Atomic Energy Commission

(AEC) was founded in 1948, and though Nehru opposed nuclear weapons, it was abundantly clear that technology developed for civilian use would put India in a position to develop nuclear weapons (Abraham, 1999: 48–60). China's emergence as a nuclear weapons state in the mid 1960s encouraged Indian policy-makers to consider the military applications of nuclear technology. In 1974 India conducted what it described as a 'peaceful nuclear explosion', which gave Pakistan an incentive to accelerate its nuclear programme.

Throughout the 1990s international pressure increased on India to join the non-proliferation regime and effectively opt out of the select club of nuclear weapons states. The US vigorously tried to limit India's nuclear potential and thus put India in an awkward position because US goodwill was important if India was to reap the benefits of economic globalization. Consequently the Congress administration between 1991 and 1996 exhibited restraint on nuclear issues (Perkovich, 2000: 329). Prime Minister Rao successfully promoted economic engagement with the US while stalling on Kashmir and the nuclear question. It was hoped in Washington that getting India and Pakistan to sign the Nuclear Non-Proliferation Treaty (NPT) and the Comprehensive Test Ban Treaty (CTBT) would keep South Asia free of nuclear weapons. However, Indian policy-makers, while uncertain about acquiring nuclear weapons, were adamant that they would not forgo the right to acquire them.

Unlike Congress, which had acted cautiously, the BJP proclaimed in its 1998 manifesto that 'a nation as large and capable as ourselves must make its impact felt on the world arena. A BJP Government will demand a premier position for the country in all global fora' (Bharatiya Janata Party, 1998). Unlike Nehru, the Hindu nationalists were not shy about equating power with military power. In May 1998 the BJP Government conducted five nuclear tests and declared India to be a nuclear weapons state. Nuclear tests in Pakistan shortly followed. The tests were greeted with international dismay and India was obliged to ride out a range of sanctions imposed by other states. This contrasted dramatically with the reaction inside India and of the Indian diaspora. Many Indians appeared jubilant about India's formal entry into the nuclear weapons club, although there were some prominent exceptions. The BJP, and its Hindu nationalist allies, attempted to make political capital out of the tests but it has long ceased to be a party political issue. Many of those opposed to Hindu nationalism supported the tests as confirming India's rightful place in the world, and accused the existing nuclear club of states of hypocrisy. Brajesh Mishra, a senior official in the BJP coalition government at the time of the tests, was later quoted as saying: 'I have always felt that you cannot in today's world be counted for something without going nuclear' (Chiriyankandath and Wyatt, 2005: 202). The Congress coalition governments since 2004 have not deviated significantly from the policy set in train in 1998.

Recognizing the particular danger inherent in the relationship with Pakistan, a series of Confidence Building Measures (CBMs) were agreed in 1999 to reduce the threat of nuclear confrontation (Mohan, 2003a: 19–20). Though the tests demonstrated capability, India's nuclear orientation is still somewhat ill-defined. A Draft Nuclear Doctrine was issued in 1999 which was intended to show that India was going to be a responsible nuclear power that would not rush to acquire large amounts of nuclear weaponry. India has a policy of 'no first use', keeping weapons as a deterrent in case of attack. In January 2003 India outlined the structure of its Nuclear Command Authority (Mohan, 2003b). This confirmed most of the draft doctrine. However, areas of uncertainty remain. It is not known exactly how weapons have been deployed or indeed how many warheads India possesses. India has reported successful missile tests but has not made it clear whether and when these missiles were brought into service (Rajagoplan, 2008: 201–2). Recent estimates suggested approximately 50 to 60 warheads were available (Sasikumar, 2009). India successfully tested the Agni-III missile in April 2007, showing that it had a ballistic missile which could reach targets with a 3500 km range, including Beijing and Shanghai, and bringing it closer to nuclear balance with China (Rajagoplan, 2008: 201).

India has also developed its international profile by increasing spending on conventional defence and extending the reach of its conventional forces. Unlike neighbouring Pakistan, India's army has been kept under civilian control. In part this reflects the differences in the histories of the two countries – Pakistan was insecure vis-à-vis India. Pakistan's army therefore commanded a large share of the resources of the new state, but also moved into the political vacuum left by weak and divided political parties in an insecure state (Adeney and Wyatt, 2004). Hardgrave and Kochanek's explanation for the absence of a political role for the Indian army is laid at the door of representative politics, so that the 'political system [can] respond to increasing participation and escalating demands' (2000: 123).

Although India's army has not intervened in democratic politics, it nevertheless commands a large share of resources. It is one of the largest armies in the world in terms of recruits and boasts 1.3 million serving personnel (Kundu, 2005: 226). Ongoing conflicts with Pakistan and the involvement of the army in maintaining internal order (for example in border areas where it has been deployed against autonomist and/or secessionist movements, but also in Gujarat in 2002) has ensured it will remain prominent. As an institution it has a high standing among most Indians, although its involvement in internal security operations has tarnished its reputation among certain minority groups. However, overall, 55 per cent of respondents reported a 'great deal' of trust in the army compared to 17 per cent who reported the same for the police, 18 per cent for the civil service and 27 per cent for the courts (SDSA, 2008: 248–51).

India's basic annual defence budget is augmented by amounts spent by other departments on internal security, atomic energy and space research (Kundu, 2005: 225–7). Rapid economic growth has been used to fund substantial increases in spending on defence since the late 1990s. In 2004 the defence budget, including amounts spent on internal security, was measured, using an adjustment for inflation, at $19.2 billion. This increased to $22.3 billion and $23.9 billion in 2005 and 2006 respectively (SIPRI, 2007: 314 and 336). New equipment is being purchased for the Indian armed forces that will extend its reach. The Indian Navy outlined a new doctrine in April 2004 which indicated some practical implications of India's perception of itself as a major power. Among other things, the document claimed India's security required the navy to be able to dominate a large expanse of the Indian Ocean from the Malacca Straits to the Gulf region. The Indian Navy was also expecting to make a contribution to India's nuclear deterrence (though the details were not spelt out) and in the near future will be strengthened with the purchase of new ships, submarines and the addition of two aircraft carriers. The introduction of the new Brahmos cruise missile, successfully tested in January 2009, will add to the lethal force that can be used. As a consequence of these changes the Indian Navy will be able to operate at a distance from Indian shores and support India's claim to importance in the wider Asian region.

Relations with the United States

Ironically the nuclear tests conducted in 1998 had the ultimate outcome of easing relations between India and the US. In the short

term India suffered US criticism and sanctions. The Clinton administration took a close interest in Kashmir, famously describing the
ceasefire line in 2000 as 'the most dangerous place on earth'
(Popham, 2000). This ran contrary to the Indian inclination to keep
the problem a bilateral one.

However, the US remained engaged with India. The coup carried
out by the military in Pakistan in October 1999 was a useful foil
against which India could claim to be an important power stabilized
by its democratic political system. The BJP-led NDA had few reservations about building a closer relationship with the US. It was receptive to the priorities of the Bush administration, which was likewise
very keen on a closer relationship with the world's largest democracy,
and it supported the US missile defence project. The NDA
Government offered to assist the US after 9/11 and supported the war
against the Taliban in Afghanistan. The US reciprocated by lifting
sanctions imposed on India after the 1998 tests.

The Indian shift towards the US was assisted by other long-term
developments. The Indian diaspora in the US is extremely well organized and lobbies for closer ties with India. The success of various
Indian entrepreneurs in Silicon Valley helps soften anti-American
attitudes in India. Economic ties are also important as the US absorbs
a large amount of Indian exports (Chiriyankandath, 2004: 206–8).
Exports to the US peaked at nearly $19 billion in 2006/7, but the US
is still the country that buys the largest proportion of Indian exports
(Government of India, 2009a: A97).

India's attempt to rehabilitate its reputation as a constructive participant in international regimes and gain acceptance of its status as a
nuclear power advanced rapidly during the Bush Presidency. In 2005,
Condoleezza Rice signalled that 'the Bush Administration was
willing to consider civilian nuclear cooperation with India' (Pant,
2007b: 62) and in July that year Bush and Manmohan Singh
announced 'a joint democracy initiative' (Mohan, 2007: 108). A high-
profile visit to Delhi by President Bush in March 2006 formally
signalled India's status as a nuclear power. The US confirmed the
offer of an agreement to accommodate India's nuclear ambitions and
under this deal India agreed to separate the civilian and military
elements of its nuclear programme. The civilian nuclear facilities
were to be opened for international inspection, while the military
installations remained exempt. India offered to refrain from further
nuclear tests and, in return, the US offered cooperation on civilian
nuclear projects and help with obtaining supplies of nuclear fuel.

As Pant notes, this deal has 'virtually rewritten the rules of the global nuclear regime' (2007b: 62). Although Bush justified it in the following terms: 'it's in our economic interests that India have a civilian nuclear power industry to help take the pressure off the global demand for energy' (BBC, 2006b), the deal was far from universally supported, both in India and outside. A number of political parties in India, including the Communist parties, argued that the deal compromised national sovereignty and that the US would possess too much influence over India's nuclear programme, as well as limiting India's ability to determine its own foreign policy towards Iran (Ramachandran, 2006). In July 2008 the left parties withdrew their support from the UPA over the issue and supported a no confidence vote against Manmohan Singh's Government (BBC, 2008). The Government survived the vote of confidence with support from the Samajwadi Party, indicating that the argument in favour of ratification had been won in parliament. Internationally, China criticized the deal, as India had not signed the Non-Proliferation Treaty. There were also numerous critics among US legislators. Others have noted that 'India could use the imported nuclear fuel to feed its civilian energy program while diverting its own nuclear fuel to weapons production' (Pan and Bajoria, 2008). The agreement was finally ratified by the US Congress in October 2008.

The deal meant that India's claim to be a responsible nuclear power received US endorsement. Some US commentators suggested that the deal would create a stronger India which would be a counterweight to China (VandeHei and Linzer, 2006). The agreement demonstrates the improved relations between the US and India. The US has shown it is willing to sacrifice its long-standing policy on nuclear proliferation and argue India's case: in short, the US accepts India's status as an important and nuclear-armed power.

The closeness of US relations with India is evident in joint military exercises. India also pursued closer relations with Israel to the obvious approval of the US (Chiriyankandath, 2004: 208). The trend of closer relations has continued with the Obama administration. In January 2009, the US envoy to Afghanistan and Pakistan had Kashmir removed from his portfolio, allegedly after Indian pressure. In July 2009, the US appeared to endorse India's claim that the Kashmir dispute was a bilateral one.

Relations with Pakistan

The partition of India in 1947 did not resolve tensions between the Muslim League and the Congress. Instead the enmity transferred into international politics. Pakistan emerged from the partition as the smaller state with two wings divided by India. It was therefore extremely insecure. Pakistan's military elite voiced these concerns loudly at the earliest possible stage. Congress, it was noted, had rejected the 'two-nation theory' of Muhammad Ali Jinnah and did not accept the need for a Muslim homeland in South Asia. Pakistan's generals argued that India could use its superior resources to absorb Pakistan into a greater India (Jalal, 1990: 265–6). Pakistan's civilian leaders also were not willing to trust Nehru's rejection of military diplomacy and therefore gave military expenditure top priority. The colonial legacy had left India with significant military potential and, even though some units were allocated to Pakistan as part of the partition agreement, India took control of a substantial army in 1947. India had also gained a strategic advantage as all of the armaments factories of the British Raj were based within its borders (Wainwright, 1994: 123–31). The military has never lost its prominent position in Pakistan. The consequence for India was the emergence of Pakistan as a national security state fearful for its existence and willing to use military means to protect its interests. India is proud of its democratic heritage and therefore remains suspicious of a state in which the military are so influential (Ganguly, 2002: 4). Many within Pakistan continue to fear a military attempt to forge a greater India that would erase Pakistan from the map of South Asia, however unlikely this outcome might seem to external observers.

The Kashmir Question

The tensions between India and Pakistan are epitomized by the problem of Kashmir. As discussed in Chapter 1, the British were unwilling to dictate the future of the princely states after decolonization. The princely state of Kashmir sought to determine its own destiny. The state had a Muslim majority, suggesting it might be logical for Kashmir to join Pakistan. However, its Hindu ruler, Maharajah Hari Singh, did not want to choose between the two states. It was sufficiently large and located on the edge of both Indian and Pakistani territory to make the notion of an independent Kashmir as the 'Switzerland of Asia' faintly plausible. In October 1947 the princely state proved unable to resist an armed invasion supported by Pakistan. Hari Singh appealed to India for assistance.

Nehru, from a Kashmiri Brahman family, saw his chance to force the accession issue. He agreed to send troops if the Maharajah signed an instrument of accession. India airlifted troops in once the agreement was signed. The first war with Pakistan was opened and Kashmir was claimed to be Indian territory. When it became clear that the problem could not be solved on the battlefield, Nehru was prepared to tolerate a role for the UN in mediating the dispute. In January 1949 hostilities ceased, and in July 1949 a ceasefire line was demarcated by the UN that left Pakistan holding a significant part of Kashmir. Pakistan now refers to this area as *Azad* (free) Kashmir. This was a temporary agreement under which India agreed to a plebiscite to determine the fate of the territory. The plebiscite was delayed indefinitely, India claiming that a plebiscite could not be held while part of the territory remained under foreign occupation. India became mistrustful of the UN, as the US, with its permanent seat on the Security Council, became closer to Pakistan. India reacted angrily when the US increased its military aid to Pakistan in 1954. By the end of the 1950s the role of the UN as a broker in the Kashmir dispute was over (Ganguly, 2002: 25–7).

India has regarded further attempts by Pakistan to raise the issue of Kashmir in the UN as mischief making. For a long while the USSR was willing to veto Security Council resolutions on Kashmir and thus India was able to prevent it becoming more than a regional issue. The failure of the diplomatic process encouraged Pakistan to look for military solutions. A key objective in the second Indo-Pakistan war, initiated by Pakistan in 1965, was the conquest of Kashmir. It was incorrectly assumed that the Muslim majority would welcome and assist the Pakistani 'liberators'. Even though the third war between India and Pakistan in 1971 was mainly concerned with the struggle for independence on the part of the Bengali-speaking population of East Pakistan, there was fighting on India's western border. After the ceasefire further talks were held in the Indian hill station of Simla in June 1972 to resolve outstanding issues. Inevitably the question of Kashmir was discussed, with attention focused on the 'line of control' which was the ceasefire line at the close of hostilities in December 1971. Indian participants in the talks believed that the new President of Pakistan, Zulfiqar Ali Bhutto, who had agreed to respect the line of control, would use that line as the basis for a later agreement to divide Kashmir between the two states (Frank, 2001: 346). However,

Bhutto made it clear on his return to Pakistan that he would not give up the claim to Kashmir (Wolpert, 1993: 191).

The leading political party in Kashmir, the National Conference, initially cooperated with the Government of India as the state of Jammu and Kashmir was integrated into the federal system, but in 1953 the leader of the National Conference, Sheikh Abdullah, was arrested. Under his successor, Bakshi Ghulam Mohammad, legislation was enacted that diminished Kashmiri autonomy, and formally incorporated the state into the Indian Union in 1956 (although with special status under Article 370 of the Indian constitution) (Hewitt, 1995: 140–1; Adeney, 2007: 109–10). Elections were widely believed to be rigged in favour of the National Conference and Sumantra Bose has outlined the process by which democracy was undermined within the state (1997). As well as central interference, political leaders in the state were perceived to be corrupt and incapable of administering the central development funds allocated to Kashmir. In short, many ordinary Kashmiris were not persuaded of the legitimacy of the Indian state and, once again, the possibility of an independent state began to appear desirable to disaffected elements in the Kashmir valley. The inept handling of federal relations by the central government contributed to the outbreak of an armed insurgency against the Indian state in the late 1980s (Adeney, 2007: 121).

Pakistan offered covert military and overt political support to the insurgents, which complicated a long and brutal war between the insurgents and the Indian state. The normal process of civilian rule was suspended in 1990, with Kashmir being ruled from Delhi and the Indian army deployed in large numbers. The state's economy, heavily dependent on tourism, collapsed. Many migrated out of the region to avoid the violence and seek a living elsewhere. Civilians have literally been caught in the crossfire and official figures put the death toll of civilians, military and militants at around 50,000 people. Unofficial estimates put the death toll much higher and separatist groups claim it is double (Reuters India, 2008). The Kashmir issue was the object of another major military confrontation between India and Pakistan in 1999. Pakistani forces made an incursion in the Kargil area, north of the Kashmir valley, in early 1999, to which India responded vigorously and Pakistan, under pressure from its key allies, the United States and China, was obliged to withdraw. Both armies suffered substantial casualties. The incident appeared to be an attempt by Pakistan to internationalize the issue. That the Kargil incursion followed the 1998 nuclear tests guaranteed that the incident

Illustration 8.1   The Wagah border between India and Pakistan

Wagah is the only crossing-point on the land border between India and Pakistan. It lies on the 50-mile road that links Lahore in Pakistan and the Indian city of Amritsar. Every evening there is a symbolic ceremony when the military guarding the border perform 'a choreographed routine that ends in the lowering of both flags and the slamming of the border gates' (Leithead, 2007). It is a popular tourist spectacle. Wagah is often closed at times of tension between India and Pakistan. This picture was taken from the Pakistani side of the border.

would attract international attention, but perhaps not in the way that Pakistan's military hoped.

The dispute over Kashmir has been managed more effectively since 1999, though important problems remain. In terms of India's internal policy there are some grounds for optimism as a degree of normality has returned to Kashmir. Relatively free and fair elections to the state government were held in 2002 and again in 2008, and so there is an important element of civilian administration and politics without recourse to violence. The National Conference continues to play a major role in Kashmiri politics and the grandson of Sheikh Abdullah is currently Chief Minister, in coalition with Congress. War weariness on the part of the population of Kashmir has weakened support for the insurgency even though there are still political groups that seek independence or to join Pakistan. The All Party Hurriyat Conference presents itself as an organization that advocates separatism by peaceful means. A variety of militant groups, many of whom recruit non-Kashmiris, also seek public support.

The international aspect of the Kashmir dispute has been more settled since the end of the Kargil crisis in 1999. But there have still been moments of crisis. An attack on the Indian parliament in December 2001 brought India and Pakistan close to war. The attack was attributed to a militant group, Lashkar-e-Toiba, believed to be supported by Pakistan. India mobilized in preparation for war with Pakistan in early 2002 but relations have improved since then. Pakistan has taken some steps to curb support for Kashmiri militants and former President (also army chief) Musharraf indicated that Pakistan would not press for redrawn boundaries. The new civilian administration in Pakistan headed by President Asif Ali Zardari announced in March 2008 that India and Pakistan should be allowed to disagree over Kashmir. This prompted a 'reminder' by new army chief Kayani of the 'national consensus' on Kashmir and that the army remained committed to the cause. In October that year, Zardari deviated from the usual Pakistan description of militants in Kashmir as freedom-fighters, terming them 'terrorists' instead. These moves to a more inclusive dialogue, and the opening of the border for intra-Kashmiri trade, were purposively upset by the Lashkar-e-Toiba Mumbai attacks of November 2008 that killed more than 170 people, and at the time of writing relations were still frosty. The brittle relations between the two largest states of South Asia inhibit regional integration and economic relations between India and Pakistan are underdeveloped. India's exports to Pakistan are only 0.8 per cent of its total exports (Government of India, 2009a: A95–9). The regional forum of the South Asian Association for Regional Cooperation (SAARC) has been disrupted as bilateral tensions have intruded on its proceedings, and trade with South Asia as a whole is also low.

India as a Regional Actor in South Asia

India's geographical location, the physical centre of the South Asian region, and position as the largest state in South Asia means that it has the potential to dominate the Indian Ocean. It has borders with more states in the region than any other South Asian state. India shares land borders with China, Bangladesh, Burma, Nepal, Pakistan and Bhutan and is also the largest neighbour of the island states of Sri Lanka and the Maldives. For the small Himalayan kingdoms of Nepal and Bhutan the only practical transport links for the passage of trade run through India. The size of India's population and the strength of some sectors of the economy mean that the Government of India can mobilize tax revenues to fund the largest armed forces in the region (although whether India should allocate its resources in this manner given its high levels of poverty is, of course, a matter of debate). India has a population and economic strength that over-shadow all of the other states combined. It is clearly the strongest military power in the region, though Pakistan's possession of nuclear weapons means that Indian dominance is not absolute. Despite its central position, India has not always been able to maintain construc-tive relations with other states in the region or offer leadership within the region.

During the 1970s and 1980s, India was the hegemonic power in South Asia and the smaller states in the region either feared or mistrusted India. India's perception of itself and its behaviour as a regional hegemon in the 1980s did little to alleviate such concerns (Hewitt, 1997). Military interventions in 1987 in both the Maldives and Sri Lanka suggested that India viewed itself as the regional policeman.

A more constructive approach to the region was enunciated in the 'Gujral doctrine'. Inder Kumar Gujral, then Minister of External Affairs in the newly formed United Front Government, argued in 1996 that India as the dominant power had little to fear in South Asia and therefore could afford to be magnanimous with the smaller states (Gujral, 1997). This principle has been unevenly implemented since then but the Government of India has recently returned to the spirit of the Gujral doctrine with a number of initiatives favoured by Prime Minister Manmohan Singh. Economic issues have been pushed up the agenda and the language used by senior Indian officials is much more conciliatory. The border regions within India have been encour-aged to build stronger links with their adjoining states. A small but practical step has been improvement of poor transport links that cross India's borders (Dixit, 2007). However, intra-South Asian trade remains low. In total, South Asia accounts for 5.1 per cent of Indian exports (Table 8.1) and only 0.6 per cent of its imports (Government of India, 2009a: A95–9).

Box 8.2   SAARC

The South Asian Association for Regional Cooperation (SAARC) held its first conference in 1985. The founding members of SAARC were Bangladesh, Bhutan, India, the Maldives, Nepal, Pakistan and Sri Lanka. It was agreed in November 2005 at the 13th summit that Afghanistan would become a member. Initially the heads of government of each country met for an annual conference but after 1988 meetings became less regular. A summit hosted by one of the member states occurs roughly every two years. SAARC has its secretariat in Kathmandu, the capital of Nepal. The organization arranges meetings between officials from all states and promotes various educational and cultural exchanges in the region. In recent years it has been agreed that SAARC will administer a modest development fund to assist poverty reduction in South Asia.

The rules of SAARC bear the imprint of the underlying politics of the region. The smaller states fear Indian dominance and India fears the combined opposition of the smaller states. Article X of the SAARC charter states two key principles. X.1 states that all business is transacted on the basis of unanimity. X.2 states that contentious issues are to be kept off the agenda and resolved bilaterally between individual states. Thus a mutual veto is embedded in the institution so that no state will be threatened by another. Unlike the European Union, there is no system of qualified majority voting that would enable SAARC to speed up decision making. Article X makes it very difficult for substantive business to be transacted. An example of the mutual veto is the need for all states to agree to a summit being held. The 11th summit scheduled for November 1999 and the 12th summit scheduled for January 2003 were both postponed as a result of tensions between Pakistan and India (Chiriyankandath and Wyatt, 2005: 208). The 13th summit in 2005 was held nine months late, at India's insistence, following the constitutional coup in Nepal (Cherian, 2005). Another example of tension is in the area of trade. The regional agreement on the South Asian Free Trade Area (SAFTA), after much delay, came into effect on 1 January 2006. In order to speed up integration India has signed bilateral free trade agreements with most other SAARC members but has no such agreement with Pakistan (Cherian, 2007b). Much rests on the efficacy of the SAFTA agreement, which is not due to be finally implemented until 2016. However, SAARC remains an important institution. In spite of serious tensions and conflicts between states in the region, the organization has expanded. The summits provide a useful, and discrete, opportunity for individual heads of states to meet without the heavy burden of expectation that comes with formal visits (as seen at the Colombo August 2008 summit).

Table 8.1 Volume of exports and destination April
to December 2008

	April–Dec 2008	Share
	US$ million	Per cent
Europe	30,740.3	23.5
Middle East	27,622.6	21.1
NE Asia	18,041.2	13.8
North America	16,676.8	12.8
ASEAN	13,707.8	10.5
Africa	8809.3	6.7
South Asia	6617.7	5.1
Latin America	5076.1	3.9
CIS & Baltics	1469.5	1.1
East Asia	1269.4	1.0
Unspecified regions	646.1	0.5
Total exports	**130,716.0**	**100**

Source: Adapted from Government of India (2009a).

Relations between the Government of Sri Lanka and a Tamil
minority have been the major issue in relations between India and the
island state. An outbreak of violence between the Sinhala-speaking
majority and a minority of Tamil speakers in the late 1970s was the
prelude to a long civil war. The Liberation Tigers of Tamil Eelam
(LTTE) emerged as the main anti-government force and it maintained
an insurgency against the government until 2009. India was invited
into Sri Lanka in 1987 when it provided the Indian Peacekeeping
Force, leading to a temporary truce. India wanted to be involved in a
solution for the political problems faced by Tamils in Sri Lanka
because the Government of India was anxious that the civil war
would not also destabilize India. The Tamil minority in Sri Lanka has
its origins among the Tamil population of southern India and a high
degree of sympathy is felt for the Sri Lankan Tamils in the Indian
state of Tamil Nadu. Although India entered the conflict as a peace-
keeper, the mission was a 'veritable failure' (Hewitt, 1997: 68)
because India soon found itself in armed conflict with the LTTE,
which refused to disarm. Following increasing casualties, a change of
government in India and the opposition of the Sri Lankan government, India withdrew in 1990. The reverberations of the decision to

intervene, which led to the deaths of over a thousand Indian soldiers, continued when, in 1991, former prime minister Rajiv Gandhi was assassinated by a female suicide bomber while election campaigning in Tamil Nadu. After this, India banned the LTTE and was very reluctant to become directly involved in the war. In 2008 and 2009 the Sri Lankan Government brought the civil war to a military conclusion, killing the Tamils' leader Prabhakaran in the process. Congress, led by Rajiv's widow Sonia Gandhi, 'quietly supported' this strategy, although the fate of hundreds of thousands of civilian Tamils caught up in the campaign evoked sympathy within Tamil Nadu and, indeed, around the world (*The Economist*, 2009e: 10).

India's strong presence in the region was demonstrated by its role in the Nepalese peace process. India favoured an arms embargo on Nepal following the monarchy's attempt to crack down on dissent. India, along with the US and the European Union, persuaded China to honour this (Mohan, 2007: 100). The peace process yielded an agreement in 2006. India initially favoured substantial concessions for the Maoist rebels, including their integration into the armed forces. However, India's priorities have changed. India is troubled by its own Maoist insurgency (see Chapter 5) and it is alarmed by the growing closeness of the Nepalese Maoists to the Chinese. India has offered more support to the Nepalese army, which is reluctant to integrate the Maoists, despite the dangers that backtracking on the original agreement could derail the peace process. This is because India 'regards the army as a bulwark against any radical lurch in Nepali policy' (*The Economist*, 2009d). India is also alleged to have intervened in the election held in 2008 (*The Economist*, 2008). At the same time, India is uneasy about international involvement in its sphere of influence, namely the United Nations mission in Nepal.

India has also sought closer relations with Afghanistan, a state often excluded from definitions of the South Asian region. That Afghanistan is now a member of SAARC suggests a different way of looking at the region. India offered early support to the civilian regime headed by Hamid Karzai that replaced the Taliban in late 2001 and is keen that this regime succeeds and prevents a resurgence of the Taliban. The Taliban have been backed by Pakistan's Inter-Services Intelligence (ISI), and provided support for the militants who were active in Kashmir. India has pledged a substantial amount of aid to the Karzai government and anxiety about Indian influence and a fear of 'encirclement' made it difficult for the Pakistani military to give up support for the Taliban (Adeney, 2008).

India within Asia

Although India dominates the South Asian region, the same cannot be said of Asia in general. Asia as an entity is vast – encompassing China and Japan, and the countries of South, South East Asia, Central and West Asia (or the Middle East). India imports four-fifths of its oil and much of this comes from West Asia (*The Economist*, 2009a). However, it is also important as an export market – 21 per cent of India's exports are to West Asia.

India's relations with West Asia are complex. This complexity is partially accounted for by the tensions between various states in the region with whom India seeks to retain good relations, but also because of the new policy of engagement with the US. In recent years India has sought to be more proactive in the Indian Ocean, partially to counter Chinese domination of the area. As Lavoy notes, partially in response to Chinese increased activity in the area, the Indian navy plans to acquire 42 modern ships 'to handle coastal defense and provide the blue-water capability required to protect the country's growing overseas trade and energy access' (2007: 120).

India has a large economic interest in West Asia. In addition to the region's importance as a trading partner, 5 million members of the Indian Diaspora live in the Gulf Cooperation Council (GCC) coun- tries, sending home over $4 billion of remittances each year (Lavoy, 2007: 120). Several Indian state-owned companies have pursued investments in the region – notably in Iran but also in Qatar. Another area of importance for Indian foreign policy and strategic considera- tions is relations with Israel. It is India's second largest arms supplier (after Russia), and India's Research and Analysis Wing (RAW) shares intelligence with Mossad (Lavoy, 2007: 120).

This relationship with Israel and the wish to improve relations with the US run counter to India's desire to cultivate good relations with Iran. Iran has vast energy reserves, and as India's demands for these are ever increasing, the logic of maintaining good relations is obvious. A large number of India's Muslim population are also Shia Muslims, and some have argued that this also affects India's relations as India does not want to alienate part of its Muslim population (Ganguly, 2008: 170). India and Iran also share a concern regarding Pakistan but both are committed to the gas pipeline project which would carry natural gas from Iran, through Pakistan, into India. These strategic compulsions are acknowledged by the US but India was publicly censured by several members of the US Congress for prevaricating over referring Iran to the UN Security Council because of its nuclear programme. The Bush Administration warned India that its nuclear agreement was in danger of being defeated in Congress should India fail to vote against Iran. India ultimately voted in the International Atomic Energy Agency (IAEA) to refer Iran to the UN, while strenuously denying that the status of the nuclear deal was in any way connected (Pant, 2007a: 502). Given India's varied interests in West Asia and its relations with the different states, however, a nuclear Iran is not in India's interests.

India's relations with China have complicated India's foreign policy across much of Asia. Nehru viewed China optimistically. He thought that India and China were bound together by common links including non-alignment and Third World solidarity. Under Nehru, India too readily accepted the ambitious British definition of the imprecise border between India and China (Maxwell, 1972: 73–5). China had never accepted the British maps but was too weak to resolve the issue until the 1950s. When China occupied part of the remote Aksai Chin region, Nehru failed to resolve the problem by negotiation. When war broke out in 1962, India was singularly unprepared and suffered a severe defeat. The 1962 border war with China came as a shock to Nehru, one from which he never recovered. He had not planned for such a military confrontation and assumed that he had developed good relations with China.

The 1962 war left a legacy of suspicion and tension between the two states. India accelerated its defence spending and revised its plan for any future war, such that it feels it could contain the threat of another conventional war with China (Rajagoplan, 2008: 192–3). China's acquisition of nuclear weapons in the 1960s created a new threat to India. This spurred India to seek similar weapons. China's phenomenal economic growth since the early 1980s has enabled it to be more assertive internationally and encouraged India to pursue economic growth (Alamgir, 2009). More specifically India has been discomforted by China's long-standing support for Pakistan. This has included assistance for Pakistan's nuclear and missile programme (Kapur, 2001: 330). China has also built more links with Bangladesh, Nepal and Burma – areas which India would like to think lie in its sphere of influence (Mohan, 2003a: 155).

In spite of these points of tension, India and China have improved relations in important ways since the early 1990s. Heads of government have made more frequent visits to respective capitals. In 2003 Prime Minister Vajpayee visited China, the first prime minister to do so since 1988. India seeks to position 'itself as a potential destination for China's rapidly expanding corporations' as well as to secure access to Chinese markets for Indian exports (Sáez, 2004: 31–2). China has taken a more neutral position on the Kashmir dispute, an important change from its earlier pro-Pakistan policy, though it continues to occupy part of what India considers is its territory in north-western Kashmir. China and India have also cooperated on issues like climate change and human rights in defiance of US or European priorities (Mohan, 2003a: 144–5). Unresolved (and extremely sensitive) border issues have been subject to discussion even if the process appears glacially slow. For example, in 2005 China recognized India's annexation of Sikkim. The signing of a more open treaty between India and Bhutan in 2007 was also a sign of improving relations (Dixit, 2007). As Pant notes, India and China share many interests and have been able to compartmentalize many divisive issues (2007b: 58).

Economic links between India and China have thickened though this has not been without difficulty. China is now India's largest trading partner (Government of India, 2009a: A94). This is the result of a rapid and dramatic surge in imports from China. In the nine months between April and December 2008, India imported $24.2 billion worth of goods compared to $17.5 billion for the entire 12 months of 2006–7. India would prefer a more balanced exchange with a larger volume of exports going to China. Although Indian consumers benefit from competitively priced imports, Indian producers are suspicious that goods are being dumped on the Indian market to gain market share and weaken competitors. In some sectors, such as handloom weaving, producers have been driven out of business by cheaper imports.

Despite these changes, China is still India's most powerful rival. A major Indian security concern has been China's growing strategic interest in the Indian Ocean and its involvement in the port development of Gwadar which would give it access to naval facilities on Pakistan's coast. This runs contrary to India's strategic naval doctrine, enunciated in 2004, requiring naval dominance in the Indian Ocean. Secure access to the trade lanes of the Indian Ocean will become even more important as the energy needs of both India and China rise (*The Economist*, 2009a). On India's eastern flank China has close ties with Burma. The relationship intensified after the State Law and Order Restoration Council (SLORC) seized power in Burma in 1988. China offered generous economic concessions to the

SLORC regime and also appears to have gained access to the Bay of Bengal via military facilities located on Burma's territory (Egreteau, 2003: 91–5). Indian policy towards Burma is shaped by several imperatives. Initially India supported democratic opponents of the SLORC junta and has provided shelter to refugees from Burma. However, more recently strategic considerations appear to have been given priority. India would like to counter Chinese influence, and also worries that illicit activity on this border undermines 'the security of (its) restive north-eastern provinces' (Mohan, 2007: 112). India considers getting access to gasfields in Burma a high priority. To this end, Indian commentary on democratic reform has been guarded. India has opposed sanctions and is prepared to sell military equipment to Burma. It follows a policy of 'constructive engagement' (Mohan, 2007: 112) despite US pressure to pursue a different course.

The closeness of the ties was demonstrated after the May 2008 cyclone – India was one of the few countries permitted to send aid in the early stages of the disaster. India also hopes to incorporate Burma in a network of regional economic links that include other South East Asian states (Cherian, 2007a). This is part of a larger 'Look East Policy' that seeks to build stronger relations with other Asian states which have important economic ties with India, partly as a way of countering Chinese influence in the region. The Association of South East Asian Nations (ASEAN) states accounted for just over 10 per cent of India's exports in April–December 2008. Japan, South Korea and Taiwan are important trading partners, buying 4.7 per cent of India's exports in the same period (Government of India, 2009a). India has sought closer ties with other Asian states and links to the ASEAN regional organization and in 2009 India and ASEAN finally signed a free trade agreement that will see tariffs removed on many goods by 2016. This is an important agreement given that trade between India and the ASEAN economies amounts to $40 billion and exceeds that with China. India was instrumental in forming another organization, the Bangladesh, India, Myanmar (Burma), Sri Lanka, Thailand Economic Cooperation (BIMSTEC), to strengthen a network to the immediate east of India (Egreteau, 2003: 102–6).

India's trade is now much more focused on Asia, with exports to Asia and Oceania taking a 30.4 per cent share of exports. Current trends for contemporary India are revealed in the figures for 2008/9. Potentially lucrative markets in South East Asia have encouraged closer attention to a region often neglected in Indian foreign policy. At the same time, the growing importance of Asia has been matched

Table 8.2   Volume of imports April to December 2008

	April–Dec 2008	Share
	US$ million	Per cent
Middle East	71,356.1	30.3
Europe	44,291.7	18.8
NE Asia	43,214.2	18.4
ASEAN	20,245.6	8.6
Africa	16,318.9	6.9
North America	15,648.7	6.6
East Asia	8201.2	3.5
Latin America	8143.3	3.5
CIS & Baltics	5593.2	2.4
South Asia	1407.6	0.6
Unspecified region	1000.1	0.4
Total imports	**235,420.7**	**100**

Source: Adapted from Government of India (2009a).

by a sharp decline in trade with Europe (Table 8.1). Indian exports to Europe are less than a half of their 1991 proportion, having fallen to 23.5 per cent of total exports, although Europe as a whole has the biggest share of Indian exports. Russia remains an important exporter of arms to India but is no longer a substantial consumer of Indian goods; exports to Russia were a marginal 0.6 per cent. Exports to the US have also declined over time – and now account for 12 per cent of Indian exports. The potential of the US as a major export market and a source of investment was a factor in the reorientation of Indian foreign policy away from the more ideological emphasis of non-alignment. Despite a recent decline, the US remains vitally important; it is still the largest single country that India exports to (all data from this paragraph can be found in Government of India, 2009a).

Conclusion

India successfully enhanced its influence in contemporary world politics during the last two decades. Nehru's objective of India being a major world power remains in place but the means used to obtain it have changed. India is more openly self-interested and less avowedly idealistic in its conduct of foreign policy. Increased defence spending, and expansion of the Indian navy, have underlined India's claim to be an important power in Asia.

However, India has been unable to achieve some important objectives. The push to get a permanent seat in a reformed UN Security Council has hitherto been unsuccessful. And, unlike the US, India has not been able to gain membership of the Asia Pacific Economic Cooperation (APEC) formation. India has struggled to impose its will on other powers and international institutions (Perkovich, 2003: 129) but has the potential to gain further influence in world affairs. However, tense relations with Pakistan make it impossible for India to emerge as the leader of a South Asian bloc. Relations with China have to be managed with care. India may have drawn closer to the US since the end of the Cold War but is not prepared to become a formal ally of the sole superpower. India would prefer a more balanced world order.

The methods used by India to enhance its profile have been debated. The nuclear tests were criticized by some on the left (Bidwai and Vanaik, 2001), whereas some establishment figures favour a more assertive policy (Sasikumar, 2009: 382). Some critics argue that India has been overly reliant on hard power resources, such as nuclear weapons and expanded armed forces, to extend its influence and it has been suggested that it needs to do more to develop its soft power resources (Abraham, 2007: 4209). This requires engaging more closely with other states and honing diplomatic skills. India's position as the world's largest democracy gives it a certain status in world politics as a shared set of political values is said to create a certain amount of understanding and convergence of interests between states. The relationship between India and the US is sometimes cast in these terms (Narlikar, 2007: 987–8). India can draw invidious comparisons between itself and regimes in other developing states which do not subject themselves to a process of public accountability. That said, India has not exploited its democratic orientation as much as it might have when conducting foreign policy (Mohan, 2008). This might be an unconscious acknowledgement that India's democratic credentials are not beyond reproach. Nevertheless, some commentators argue that a self-aware India which puts appropriate emphasis on positive Indian values is likely to gain respect in international politics. They see India, at its best, committed to liberal values which enhance its reputation in world politics (Mohan, 2003a: 270–2).

The soft power route raises difficult questions about Indian policy within the South Asian region. India has been reluctant to push strongly on issues such as democracy promotion that are favoured by actors such as the European Union and the US. The related issues of human rights and humanitarian intervention are sensitive ones for India. This is partly about the ongoing Kashmiri dispute, as India opposes international intervention, and is very sensitive about the issue of human rights violations in Kashmir (Mohan, 2007: 104). As we have discussed, geopolitical objectives have influenced Indian policy towards Nepal, which Delhi feels have to be balanced against straightforward support for democratic opening. Also the pursuit of geopolitical objectives, countering China's influence, and energy security have been considered more important than support for democratic reform in Burma.

India's diaspora offers another possibility for extending influence, though the Government of India was slow to recognize this (Kapur, 2003). At the very least it is an international constituency that is sympathetic to India. In some circumstances members of the diaspora have lobbied in support of India. The Indian-American population, which numbers more than a million, has begun to attract attention as a source of influence (Cohen, 2001: 307). The potential of support among the diaspora was demonstrated in the legislative battle to get the nuclear agreement through the US Congress. Members of the Indian-American lobby do not automatically support the Government of India, as they have priorities of their own and do not always support the ruling parties, but they are keen to promote closer relations between the US and India. Indian-American lobbyists worked hard to get cross-party support for controversial legislation backed by an unpopular president (Kirk, 2008: 291–5).

The debate on the orientation of Indian foreign policy and appropriate ways to gain influence is very much alive. Policy-makers continue to adhere to Nehru's idea that India is an important and distinctive participant in international politics. There is little sign of India retreating from the assertive positions taken during the 1990s.

Conclusion

Three themes have run through this book. We have discussed India's diversity, revealed areas of change and demonstrated how and why India's national identity matters. India's extreme diversity and the richness and variety that result from it create opportunities and challenges but India has long been challenged by its diversity. Contemporary India still grapples with important social and regional differences and the demand for the creation of new states and continuing violence among certain sections of religious groups in particular areas of India demonstrate this all too well. The case of Kashmir is far from resolved and violence sporadically breaks out in the Valley. Violence is also a regular occurrence in the north east of the country where calls for autonomy, separatism or statehood abound. The Naxalite violence in the 'red corridor' is also a serious challenge to the security of India's citizens. But, as we have been at pains to point out, to acknowledge that India is consumed by tensions between different groups does not mean that this is the reality of existence in contemporary India for the vast majority of Indians. The diversity of India and the existence of numerous cross-cutting cleavages such as caste, class, gender, region, religion and language is a force for stability rather than instability (Manor, 1996).

As we discussed, many social and economic changes have occurred since 1947 and these have accelerated in the last two decades. An expansion of communications, application of technology and access to international markets have changed elements of urban India beyond all recognition. The clothes that young urban middle-class Indians wear and their aspirations are markedly different to those of a decade ago. Mobile phone use has proliferated as has access to the internet. These changes (some might say opportunities) are not just confined to middle-class urbanites – poorer sections of society have also gained access to the new technologies, which have crept into rural areas as well. This has introduced tensions into society, especially along generational lines as the new aspirations of the young often do not coincide with expectations of their parents or grandparents.

The Indian political system has adapted to the caste element of India's diversity. This is not entirely new as caste became a factor in elections early in the life of the new republic. However, parties representing the lower castes and the Dalits are a newer development. Initial attempts to do this, by Ambedkar for example, were failures and Congress was easily able to contain these efforts. Nevertheless, since the 1990s a number of overtly caste-based parties have won elections. These parties have demonstrated their viability and, while they are too small to govern the country, they have made some decisive interventions. Above all they have changed the tone of Indian politics. Questions of representation and equitable treatment of Dalit and lower-caste groups cannot be ignored. Similarly India's political system has had to make adjustments in the way that the regions are accommodated. The design of the federal system gave great power to the centre. During the 1970s and 1980s these powers were overused, regional parties were bullied and several secessionist movements emerged. The rise of coalition politics has resulted in a more equitable political relationship between the states and the centre in contemporary India. While there are serious disagreements about the territorial makeup of India which we have mentioned above, the general tenor of centre–state relations is much calmer. The regional parties have endured and now they make up a sizeable chunk of the national parliament. Coalition governments cannot be formed without regional parties and this encourages the central government to be less assertive when dealing with individual states. Regional parties are key election allies that boost the number of seats won by Congress and the BJP. All this adds up to significant change in the party system, where Congress is no longer a dominant party. It may be the largest party in the current parliament but its leaders know that the smaller parties are essential for the survival of the Congress governing coalition. The prosperous metropolitan middle class may detest these regional and caste-based parties but they cannot be ignored.

Congress was slow to adapt to the necessities of the changed political situation, whereas the BJP adapted quickly to changes in the party system. The Babri Masjid issue gave the BJP a profile in all regions of India. The campaign to encourage the donation of a brick to enable the building of a temple after the demolition of the mosque was carefully designed to capture the imagination of voters across India. However, the campaign was not enough to gain substantial electoral support from those voters in the south and the east. The BJP came to power at the centre in 1998 and again in 1999 but *only* because it was allied with a large number of smaller parties. While in government the BJP failed to settle on a formula that would enable it to build a larger constituency. It was torn between the moderation preferred by its regional allies and the strong nationalist policies favoured by its activists. The need for moderation continues to be debated within the party. In the meantime the Congress Party has directed attention towards welfare issues. Substantive policies, like the NREGA, make Congress look like a party interested in the daily needs of the rural poor. The politics of secularism that dominated India in the 1990s is no longer at the top of the political agenda. However, the issue remains important, as was demonstrated by the violence unleashed against Christians in the Kandhamal district of Orissa in 2007 and 2008. A widespread consensus on how the Indian nation should be defined and the place of minorities in the national community has yet to be achieved.

India's elites always projected India as a major world player, but the politics of the Cold War and limited growth rates in the context of high population growth ensured that it was not able to fulfil its potential. After the liberalization of the economy in the early 1990s, the ending of the Cold War and the nuclear tests in 1998, India has risen in international prominence. The international media now generally speak about 'when' rather than 'if' India will become a major power. Economically and politically India has a great 'reach' – and a close relationship with the United States facilitates this.

India also influences the world in other ways. The music scene in many western countries has been enriched by Indian music – Bhangra immediately springs to mind – and the export of so-called 'Indian cuisine' continues to proliferate (although in reality many of the 'Indian' restaurants in the west are run by Pakistanis or Bangladeshis). India is not just a country of call centres, where the richer countries outsource the menial labour of answering queries; it is also a source of innovation. New growth areas include software development, animation design and production for international films as well as computer games. The Indian diaspora are becoming more assertive and are an important lobbying force in many western countries, including the UK and the United States. Many of the diaspora are also returning to India.

All the above, however, should not be taken to read that everything is rosy. The conflict between India and Pakistan will constrain India's ability to lead in the South Asia region. The dispute over Kashmir will not be resolved easily. Subordinated groups are denied some of their constitutional entitlements and they demand justice. Tensions will be generated as some of the younger generation battle against the social conservatism of earlier generations. The organizational depth of the Hindu nationalist movement and the political strength of the BJP make it likely that religious minorities will be the target of political attacks from time to time. Although millions of Indians have benefited from the process of economic liberalization, millions of others continue to live in poverty. The economic changes introduced by liberalization have increased inequalities between different states in the federation and the strength of regional identities makes this a likely point of tension in the future. Despite these challenges – most citizens of contemporary India are very proud of being 'Indian'. One thing is certain, India will continue to adapt, change and thrive *because of*, rather than *in spite of*, its diversity; tensions concerning membership of the 'Indian nation' notwithstanding.

Recommended Reading

The literature on India is vast. It is impossible to provide a comprehensive overview of all the relevant works, partially because India has changed immensely since independence and 'classic' texts often do not reflect the realities of today's India. With this in mind, our brief recommendations are concentrated on more recently published books. To follow earlier debates, the references within our text may be more appropriate, many of which also refer to journal articles and newspaper sources.

1   The Making of Modern India

For a general overview of Indian history, also covering pre-British and pre-Mughal eras, John Keay (2000) is extremely readable. Judith Brown's history of India (1994) is a clear and important introduction to the subject. On understandings of the partition of India, Ayesha Jalal (1985) and Anita Inder Singh (1990) are examples of revisionist and orthodox historiography respectively, and Mushirul Hasan (1993) provides an overview of the debates. On the making of the Indian constitution, Granville Austin (1966) provides a fascinating read. Sunil Khilnani's *Idea of India* (1997) provides an excellent overview of the founding ideas of the Indian Republic. For those wanting a different entry into the history of modern India, Judith Brown has written an accessible biography of Jawaharlal Nehru (2003), as has Katherine Frank of Indira Gandhi (2001).

2   The Diversity of India

For introductory surveys to the human geography of India, both Robert Bradnock and Glyn Williams (2002) and Stuart Corbridge *et al.* (2005) have written excellent introductions. Gavin Flood (1996) gives a useful introduction to Hinduism. Christopher Fuller (2003) shows how Hinduism is adapting to contemporary developments. John Zavos (2000) and Christophe Jaffrelot (1996) have written informative books on Hindu nationalism, including its political dimension. Mushirul Hasan (1997) and Yogindar Sikkand (2004) both provide histories of the Muslims in India since independence. The debate concerning the causes of communal violence is epitomized by three different authors: Paul Brass (2003), Ashutosh Varshney (2002) and Steven Wilkinson (2004). For an understanding of the link between language and identity politics, Katharine Adeney (2007) provides an overview of the debates in India.

3   Governing Structures

Robert Hardgrave and Stanley Kochanek (2000) provide an excellent introduction to the structures of government in India. Robert Jenkins (1999) and Aseema Sinha (2005) discuss the politics of federalism and economic reforms, while Richard Crook and James Manor (1998) provide a comparative take on the decentralization process. Katharine Adeney discusses the federal design and use of the emergency powers (2007). Alistair McMillan's book on caste reservations and electoral politics in India is a lucid account of the interaction between the two (2005). David Potter provides an excellent, if now slightly dated, account of the bureaucracy in India (1996).

4   Social Change

Francine Frankel *et al.* (2000) provide a collection of articles about the operation of India's democracy in conditions of social change. Dyson *et al.* (2004) discuss the peoples of India and the economic and social changes that affect them. Hugo Gorringe (2005) shows how Dalit activism is evolving. Leela Fernandes' work analyses the growing Indian middle class (2006), while Robert Stern (2003) provides a Marxist account of the class changes that are happening to contemporary India. Although by now slightly dated, Atul Kohli and Pranab Bardhan's (1988) collection still provides important material on the changing nature of state–society relations in India, as do Subrata Mitra and Vijay Bahadur Singh (2009). Nivedita Menon's (2001) edited collection on gender and politics in India is invaluable reading for those interested in the subject.

5   Politics and Society

For an understanding of the party system in contemporary India, the collection of articles in Hasan (2002) provides an excellent introduction. To appreciate the politics of the Hindu nationalists during their 1999–2004 rule, the edited collection by Katharine Adeney and Lawrence Sáez (2005) provides an assessment of their behaviour when constrained by coalition politics. Andrew Wyatt provides an analysis of party system change, and the ways in which leaders of political parties operate in India (2010). Pradeep Chhibber (1999) also provides an analysis of the link between society and the party system. Nivedita Menon and Aditya Nigam (2007) discuss both internal and external challenges to the Indian state.

6   Nationalism and Culture

There are a number of recent works covering the role that cricket plays within the Indian nation. These include Majumdar (2004), Anand (2003) and Bhattacharya (2006). The role that nationalism and articulation of national identity has played within India has been covered by many authors, including Adeney (2007), Khilnani (1997) and Brass (1994). Gurharpal Singh's collection (2000) provides an assessment of the Indian state's role in ethnic conflict regulation, arguing that India is best understood as an 'ethnic democracy'. The book also provides useful contributions on the conflict in Punjab. Sumantra Bose's (1997) book is now dated but covers the complexity of the conflict over Kashmir extremely well. Myron Weiner's (1978) work is even more dated but remains a classic text for appreciating the problems associated with migration within India. On Indian cinema, Rachel Dwyer is an authoritative author (2002; 2005) and Mihir Bose provides an account of the Bollywood film industry (2006). Chetan Bhagat's (2005) *One Night at a Call Centre* gives a fictional account of that industry.

7   Political Economy

India's political economy has been the subject of much change since the liberalization of the economy in 1991. Several recent books have analysed the impact of these reforms on the economy and, just as importantly, the people who have been subject to these changes and the informal economy. These include Robert Jenkins (1999), Stuart Corbridge and John Harriss (2000), Barbara Harriss-White (2003) and Kunal Sen (2009a). There are several books that compare India's performance with other economies, including Atul Kohli (2004) and Jørgen Dige Pedersen (2008). Jalal Alamgir (2009) provides an assessment of economic liberalization and its role in India's international relations. Kaushik Basu's collection (2007) provides detailed information about particular sectors of the economy. Marie Lall has written a well-informed book on the Indian diaspora and its economic role (2001).

8   India and the World

Vernon Hewitt (1997) provides a lively and interesting account of India's position and foreign policy within South Asia. C. Raja Mohan (2003a) provides a crisp overview of India's foreign policy after the Cold War and is a useful foil for the more leisured but equally informative book by Stephen Cohen (2001). Although all these books cover the conflict with Pakistan (no work on the international relations of India could be complete without doing so), Sumit Ganguly provides a focus on the conflict between the two countries (2002). Itty Abraham (1999), Praful Bidwai and Achin Vanaik (2001), as well as George Perkovich (2000) all analyse the nuclearization of South Asia.

India Online

General

The National Portal of India <http://india.gov.in/>

Society

Election Commission of India <http://eci.nic.in/>
Indian Council of Social Research <http://www.icssr.org/>
National Commission for Scheduled Castes <http://ncsc.nic.in/>
National Commission for Scheduled Tribes <http://ncst.nic.in/>

Government

Census of India <http://www.censusindia.net/>
Constitution of India <http://indiacode.nic.in/coiweb/welcome.html>
Lok Sabha <http://loksabha.nic.in/>
President of India <http://presidentofindia.nic.in/>
Prime Minister <http://pmindia.nic.in/>
Rajya Sabha <http://rajyasabha.nic.in/>

National Parties of India

Bahujan Samaj Party <http://www.bspindia.org/>
Bharatiya Janata Party <http://bjp.org/>
Communist Party of India <http://www.cpindia.org/>
Communist Party of India (Marxist) <http://cpim.org/>
Indian National Congress <http://www.aicc.org.in/>
Nationalist Congress Party <http://www.ncp.org.in/>

Economy and Politics

Business Standard <http://www.business-standard.com/>
Economic and Political Weekly <http:///www.epw.in>
Himal Southasian <http://www.himalmag.com/>
Ministry of Finance <http://finmin.nic.in/>
Reserve Bank of India <http://www.rbi.org.in/>
Seminar <http://www.india-seminar.com>

Civil Society

All India Trade Union Congress <http://aituc.org/>
Association of Rural Education and Development Service <http://www.aredsindia.org/>
Bharatiya Mazdoor Sangh <http://www.bms.org.in/>
Centre of Indian Trade Unions <http://www.citucentre.org/>
Self-Employed Women's Association <http://www.sewa.org/>

The Arts

Archaeological Survey of India (ASI) <http://asi.nic.in/>
philip's fil-ums: notes on Indian popular cinema <http://www.uiowa.edu/~incinema/index.html>
Sahitya Akademi <http://www.sahitya-akademi.gov.in/>

International

Ministry of External Affairs <http://meaindia.nic.in/>
Pakistan India & UK Friendship Forum <http://www.pakindiafriendship.com/>

Media

Asian Age <http://www.asianage.com/>
BBC <http://www.bbc.co.uk/india>
Frontline <http://www.frontlineonnet.com/>
Indian Express <http://www.indianexpress.com>
India Today <http://indiatoday.intoday.in>
Rediff.com <http://www.rediff.com/>
The Hindu <http://www.thehindu.com/>
The Week <http://www.the-week.com>
Times of India <http://timesofindia.indiatimes.com/>

Bibliography

Abraham, Itty (1999) *The Making of the Indian Atomic Bomb: Science, Secrecy and the Postcolonial State* (Hyderabad: Orient Longman).

Abraham, Itty (2007) 'The Future of Indian Foreign Policy', *Economic and Political Weekly* 42(42): 4209–11.

Abraham, Itty (2008) 'From Bandung to NAM: Non-alignment and Indian Foreign Policy, 1947–65', *Commonwealth and Comparative Politics* 46(2): 195–219.

Adams, John (2007) 'Reimaging India's Economy: Magnificent Mosaic or Maddening Mishmash?', *India Review* 7(3): 240–53.

ADB (Asian Development Bank) (2008) 'Key Indicators for Asia and the Pacific 2008: 39th Edition' (Philippines: Asian Development Bank).

Adeney, Katharine (2002) 'Constitutional Centring: Nation Formation and Consociational Federalism in India and Pakistan', *Commonwealth and Comparative Politics* 40(3): 8–33.

Adeney, Katharine (2005) 'Hindu Nationalists and Federal Structures in an Era of Regionalism', in Katharine Adeney and Lawrence Sáez (eds), *Coalition Politics and Hindu Nationalism* (Abingdon: Routledge).

Adeney, Katharine (2007) *Federalism and Ethnic Conflict Regulation in India and Pakistan* (New York, NY: Palgrave Macmillan).

Adeney, Katharine (2008) 'Bad News Makes Headlines: Security Challenges Posed by Pakistan' (London: Institute for Public Policy Research).

Adeney, Katharine and Marie Lall (2005) 'Institutional Attempts to Build a "National" Identity in India: Internal and External Dimensions', *India Review* 4(3-4): 258–86.

Adeney, Katharine and Lawrence Sáez (eds) (2005) *Coalition Politics and Hindu Nationalism* (Abingdon: Routledge).

Adeney, Katharine and Andrew Wyatt (2004) 'Democracy in South Asia: Getting Beyond the Structure-Agency Dichotomy', *Political Studies* 52(1): 1–18.

Adiga, Aravind (2008) *The White Tiger* (London: Atlantic Books).

Adivasi (2009) <http://adivasi.wordpress.com/2009/05/16/>, 16 May, accessed 2 December 2009.

Advani, Nikhil (2003) *Kal Ho Naa Ho* (Dharma Productions, Yash Raj Films).

Alamgir, Jalal (2009) *India's Open-Economy Policy: Globalism, Rivalry, Continuity* (Abingdon: Routledge).

All India Radio (nd) 'All India Radio: About us', <http://www.allindiaradio. org/about1.html>, accessed 8 October 2009.

Amin, Shimit (2007) *Chak de India* (Yash Raj Films International).

Anand, S. (ed.) (2003) *Brahmans and Cricket: Lagaan's Millennial Purana and other Myths* (Pondicherry: Navayana).

Andersen, Walter and Shridhar Damle (1987) *The Brotherhood in Saffron: The Rashtriya Swayamsevak Sangh and Hindu Revivalism* (Delhi: Vistaar).

Appadurai, Arjun (1988) 'How to Make a National Cuisine: Cookbooks in Contemporary India', *Comparative Studies in Society and History* 30(1): 3–24.

AREDS – Association of Rural Education and Development Service (2007) <http://aredsindia.org/>.

Aruna, Aladi (2002) 'An Assault on Secularism', *Frontline* 19(24), 23 November.

Asif, K. (1960) *Mughal-e-Azam* (Sterling Investment Corporation).

Austin, Granville (1966) *The Indian Constitution: Cornerstone of a Nation* (New Delhi: Oxford University Press).

Awn, Peter (1994) 'Indian Islam: The Shah Bano Affair', in John Hawley (ed.) *Fundamentalism and Gender* (New York, NY: Oxford University Press).

Bajpai, Rochana (2000) 'Constituent Assembly Debates and Minority Rights', *Economic and Political Weekly*, 27 May: 1837–45.

Balakrishnan, Pulapre (2006) 'Benign Neglect or Strategic Intent? Contested Lineage of Indian Software Industry', *Economic and Political Weekly*, 9 September.

Banerjee, A. (ed.) (1949a) *Indian Constitutional Documents 1858–1917*, Vol. II (Calcutta: A. Mukherjee & Co.).

Banerjee, A. (ed.) (1949b) *Indian Constitutional Documents 1917–1939*, Vol. III (Calcutta: A. Mukherjee & Co.).

Bardhan, Pranab K. (1988) 'Dominant Proprietary Classes and India's Democracy', in Atul Kohli and Pranab K. Bardhan (eds), *India's Democracy: An Analysis of Changing State-Society Relations* (Princeton, NJ: Princeton University Press).

Barjatya, Sooraj R. (1994) *Hum Apke Hain Koun* (Rajshri Productions).

Baru, Sanjaya (2000) 'Economic Policy and the Development of Capitalism in India: The Role of Regional Capitalists and Political Parties', in Francine Frankel, Zoya Hasan, Rajeev Bhargava and Balveer Arora (eds), *Transforming India: Social and Political Dynamics of Democracy* (New Delhi: Oxford University Press).

Basu, Kaushik (ed.) (2007) *The Oxford Companion to Economics in India* (New Delhi: Oxford University Press).

Baty, Phil (2009) 'Bombay Dreams', *Times Higher Education Supplement*, 9 July.

Bayly, Christopher (1985) 'The Pre-History of "Communalism"? Religious Conflict in India, 1700–1860', *Modern Asian Studies* 19(2): 177–203.

Bayly, Christopher (ed.) (1989) *Atlas of the British Empire* (New York, NY: Hamlyn).

Bayly, Christopher (1998) *Origins of Nationality in South Asia: Patriotism and Ethical Government in the Making of Modern India* (New Delhi: Oxford University Press).

BBC (2004) 'India PM Pledge over Suicide Farmers', BBC Online, 1 July.

BBC (2006a) 'India Sex Selection Doctor Jailed', BBC Online, 29 March.

BBC (2006b) 'US and India Seal Nuclear Accord', BBC Online, 2 March.

BBC (2008) ' Indian Government Survives Vote', BBC Online, 22 July.

BBC (2009a) 'BJP Refuses to Drop Varun Gandhi', BBC Online, 23 March.

BBC (2009b) 'India is "Losing Maoist Battle"', BBC Online, 15 September.

Benegal, Shyam (2008) *Welcome to Sajjanpur* (UTV Bindass).

Bery, Suman (2004) 'Why is India Shining?', <http://www.Rediff.com>, 9 March.

Bhagat, Chetan (2005) *One Night at a Call Centre* (New Delhi: Rupa and Co).

Bhagwati, Jagdish (1993) *India in Transition: Freeing the Economy* (Oxford: Oxford University Press).

Bharatiya Janata Party (1998) 'Vote for a Stable Government and an Able Prime Minister', <http://www.bjp.org>, accessed 8 December 2009.

Bhattacharya, Soumya (2006) *You Must Like Cricket? Memoirs of an Indian Cricket Fan* (London: Yellow Jersey Press).

Bidwai, Praful and Achin Vanaik (2001) *South Asia on a Short Fuse: Nuclear Politics and the Future of Global Disarmament* (New Delhi: Oxford University Press).

Billig, Michael (1995) *Banal Nationalism* (London: Sage).

Booth, Gregory D. (1995) 'Traditional Content and Narrative Structure in the Hindi Commercial Cinema', *Asian Folklore Studies* 54(2): 169–90.

Bose, Mihir (2002) *A History of Indian Cricket* (London: André Deutsch).

Bose, Mihir (2006) *Bollywood: A History* (Stroud: Tempus).

Bose, Sugata and Ayesha Jalal (1998) *Modern South Asia: History, Culture, Political Economy* (New Delhi: Oxford University Press).

Bose, Sumantra (1997) *The Challenge in Kashmir: Democracy, Self-Determination and a Just Peace* (New Delhi: Sage).

Boyle, Danny and Loveleen Tandan (2008) *Slumdog Millionaire* (20th Century Fox).

Bradnock, Robert W. and Glyn Williams (2002) *South Asia in a Globalising World: A Reconstructed Regional Geography* (Upper Saddle River, NJ: Prentice Hall).

Brass, Paul (1994) *The Politics of India Since Independence* (New Delhi and Cambridge: Cambridge University Press).

Brass, Paul (2003) *The Production of Hindu-Muslim Violence in Contemporary India* (New Delhi: Oxford University Press).

Brown, Judith (1994) *Modern India: The Origins of an Asian Democracy* (Oxford: Oxford University Press).

Brown, Judith (2003) *Nehru: A Political Life* (New Haven, CT; London: Yale University Press).

Buncombe, Andrew and Jaideep Hardikar (2008) 'Suicide of Farmer Poet Highlights the Poverty Trap in India', *The Independent*, 6 May.

Byala, Munish (2009) 'S.G.P.C. Elections Marred by Violence, Alcohol, and Hypocrisy', *The Sikh Times*, July.

Centre for Social Research (nd) 'Girls' education', <http://www.csrindia.org/girls%20education.htm>, accessed 27 August 2008.

Chadda, Maya (1997) *Ethnicity, Security and Separatism in India* (New York, NY: Columbia University Press).

Chakrabarti, Rakesh (2007) 'Foreign Institutional Investment', in Kaushik Basu (ed.), *The Oxford Companion to Economics in India* (New Delhi: Oxford University Press).

Chakravarty, Sumita (1993) *National Identity in Indian Popular Cinema 1947–1987* (Austin, TX: University of Texas Press).

Chanana, Dweep (2009) 'India as an Emerging Donor', *Economic and Political Weekly* 54(12): 11–14.

Chandra, B., Mridula Mukherjee, Aditya Mukherjee, Sucheta Mahajan and K.N. Panikkar (1989) *India's Struggle for Independence* (New Delhi: Penguin).

Chandra, Kanchan and David Laitin (2002) 'A Framework for Thinking about Identity Change', *LiCEP* (Stanford University).

Chandra, Smita (1991) *From Bengal to Punjab: The Cuisines of India* (Freedom, CA: Crossing Press).

Chandrasekhar, S. (1972) 'Personal Perspectives on Untouchablity', in Michael Mahar (ed.), *The Untouchables in Contemporary India* (Tuscon, AZ: University of Arizona Press).

Chatterjee, Gayatri (2002) *Mother India* (London: British Film Institute).

Chaudhuri, P. (1988) 'Origins of Modern India's Economic Development Strategy', in Mike Shepperdson and Colin Simmons (eds), *The Indian National Congress and the Political Economy of India 1885–1985* (Aldershot: Avebury).

Chenoy, Anuradha M. (2008) 'India and Russia: Allies in the International Political System', *South Asian Survey* 15(1): 49–62.

Cherian, John (2005) 'A Summit of Promise', *Frontline* 22(25): 3 December.

Cherian, John (2007a) 'Guarded Optimism', *Frontline* 24(20): 6 October.

Cherian, John (2007b) 'Miles to Go', *Frontline* 24(7): 7 April.

Chester, Lucy (2002) 'The 1947 Partition: Drawing the Indo-Pakistani Boundary', *American Diplomacy* 7(1).

Chhibber, Pradeep (1999) *Democracy without Associations: Transformation of the Party System and Social Cleavages in India* (Ann Arbor, MI: University of Michigan Press).

Chhibber, Vivek (2004) *Locked in Place: State Building and Late Industrialization in India* (Delhi: Tulika).

Chiriyankandath, James (2000) 'Creating a Secular State in a Religious Country: The Debate in the Indian Constituent Assembly', *Commonwealth and Comparative Politics* 38(2): 1–24.

Chiriyankandath, James (2004) 'Realigning India: Indian Foreign Policy after the Cold War', *Roundtable* 93(374): 199–211.

Chiriyankandath, James and Andrew Wyatt (2005) 'The NDA and Indian Foreign Policy', in Katharine Adeney and Lawrence Sáez (eds), *Coalition Politics and Hindu Nationalism* (Abingdon: Routledge).

Chopra, Yash (1975) *Deewaar* (Trimurti Films).

Chu, Henry (2007) 'Wedded to Greed in India', *LA Times*, 22 September.

CNN (2009) 'Officials: G-20 to supplant G-8 as international economic council', <http://www.cnn.com>, 24 September.

Cohen, Stephen (1990) *The Indian Army: Its Contribution to the Development of a Nation* (New Delhi: Oxford University Press).

Cohen, Stephen (2001) *India: Emerging Power* (Washington, DC: Brookings).

Commonwealth Human Rights Initiative (2008) 'Supreme Court Creates a Monitoring Committee in Prakash Singh Police Reforms Case', <http://www.humanrightsinitiative.org/default.htm>, accessed 2 October 2009.

Commonwealth Human Rights Initiative (nd) 'Police Reforms: India. Police Reforms: Too Important to Neglect, Too Urgent to Delay', <http://www.humanrightsinitiative.org/default.htm>, accessed 2 October 2009.

Coorlawala, Uttara Asha (1992) 'Illustrating Kathak', *Dance Chronicle* 15(1): 88–93.

Copland, Ian (1997) *The Princes of India in the Endgame of Empire, 1917–1947* (Cambridge: Cambridge University Press).

Corbridge, Stuart (2000) 'Competing Inequalities: The Scheduled Tribes and the Reservations System in India's Jharkhand', *Journal of Asian Studies* 59(1): 62–85.

Corbridge, Stuart and John Harriss (2000) *Reinventing India: Liberalization, Hindu Nationalism and Popular Democracy* (Cambridge: Polity).

Corbridge, Stuart, Glyn Williams, René Véron and Manoj Srivastava (2005) *Seeing the State: Governance and Governmentality in India* (Cambridge: Cambridge University Press).

Crook, Richard and James Manor (1998) *Democracy and Decentralisation in South Asia and West Africa: Participation, Accountability and Performance* (Cambridge: Cambridge University Press).

Dangle, Arjun (1992) *Poisoned Bread: Translations from Modern Marathi Dalit Literature* (London: Sangam).

Davis, Richard H. (1996) 'The Iconography of Rama's Chariot', in David Ludden (ed.), *Contesting the Nation: Religion, Community, and the Politics of Democracy in India* (Philadelphia, PA: University of Pennsylvania Press).

Desai, Anita (1999) *Fasting, Feasting* (London: Chatto & Windus).

Desai, Kiran (2006) *The Inheritance of Loss* (London: Hamish Hamilton).

Deshpande, Sudhanva (2001) 'Hindi Films: The Rise of the Consumable Hero', *Himal*: <http://www.himalmag.com>, August.

Deshpande, Sudhanva (2003) 'What's so Great about Lagaan?', in Geeti Sen (ed.), *India: A National Culture?* (New Delhi: Sage).

Dixit, K.M. (2007) 'India Realizing Southasia', *Himal*, March.

Dutt, Srikant (1980) 'Indian Aid to Co-developing Countries', *Economic and Political Weekly* 15(14): 672–8.

Duverger, Maurice (1964) *Political Parties: Their Organisation and Activity in the Modern State* (London: Methuen).

Dwyer, Rachel (2002) *Yash Chopra* (London: BFI).

Dwyer, Rachel (2005) *100 Bollywood Films* (London: BFI).

Dwyer, Rachel and Divia Patel (2002) *Cinema India: The Visual Culture of Hindi Film* (London: Reaktion Books).

Dyson, Tim, Robert Cassen and Léela Visaria (eds) (2004) *Twenty-first Century India: Population, Economy, Human Development, and the Environment* (Oxford: Oxford University Press).

Dyson, Tim and Léela Visaria (2004) 'Migration and Urbanization: Retrospect and Prospects', in Tim Dyson, Robert Cassen and Léela Visaria (eds), *Twenty-first Century India: Population, Economy, Human Development, and the Environment* (Oxford: Oxford University Press).

Egreteau, Renaud (2003) *Wooing the Generals: India's New Burma Policy* (Delhi: Authors Press).

Election Commission of India (1952–2004) 'Statistical Reports of General Elections' <www.eci.gov.in/ElectionResults/ElectionResults_fs.htm>.

Election Commission of India (2007) 'Model Code of Conduct for the Guidance of Political Parties and Candidates', <http://eci.nic.in/faq/faq_mcc.pdf>, accessed 3 October 2009.

Express India (2008) 'Uniform Civil Code, Article 370 Back on BJP Agenda', *Express India*, 1 June.

Farmer, B. H. (1983) *An Introduction to South Asia* (London: Methuen).

Farmer, Victoria (1996) 'Mass Media: Images, Mobilization, and Communalism', in David Ludden (ed.) *Contesting the Nation: Religion, Community, and the Politics of Democracy in India* (Philadelphia, PA: University of Pennsylvania Press).

Farrell, Gerry (1990) *Indian Music in Education* (Cambridge: Cambridge University Press).

Fernandes, Leela (2006) *India's New Middle Class: Democratic Politics in an Era of Economic Reform* (Minneapolis, MN: University of Minnesota Press).

Fernandes, Leela and Patrick Heller (2006) 'Hegemonic Aspirations: New Middle Class Politics and India's Democracy in Comparative Perspective', *Critical Asian Studies* 38(4): 495–522.

Financial Express (2009) 'Haryana Govt's Move to Create Separate SGPC Rocks Rajya Sabha', *Financial Express*, 7 August.

Flood, Gavin (1996) *An Introduction to Hinduism* (Cambridge: Cambridge University Press).

Frank, Katherine (2001) *Indira: The Life of Indira Nehru Gandhi* (London: HarperCollins).

Frankel, Francine R. (2000) *Transforming India: Social and Political Dynamics of Democracy* (New Delhi: Oxford University Press).

Fuchs, Martin (2005) 'Slum as Achievement: Governmentality and the Agency of Slum Dwellers', in Evelin Hust and Michael Mann (eds), *Urbanization and Governance in India* (Delhi: Manohar).

Fuller, Christopher J. (2003) *The Renewal of the Priesthood: Modernity and Traditionalism in a South Indian Temple* (Princeton, NJ: Princeton University Press).

Gadgil, Madhav and Ramachandra Guha (1992) *This Fissured Land: An Ecological History of India* (New Delhi: Oxford University Press).

Galanter, Marc (1997) 'Pursuing Equality: An Assessment of India's Policy of Compensatory Discrimination for Disadvantaged Groups', in Sudipta Kaviraj (ed.), *Politics in India* (New Delhi: Oxford University Press).

Ganguly, Sumit (2002) *Conflict Unending: India-Pakistan Tensions since 1947* (New Delhi: Oxford University Press).

Ganguly, Sumit (2008) 'India in 2007: A Year of Opportunities and Disappointments', *Asian Survey* 48(1): 164–76.

Ghosh, Amitav (2000) *The Glass Palace* (New Delhi: Ravi Dayal).

Ghosh, Jayati and C. P. Chandrasekhar (2009) 'The Costs of 'Coupling': The Global Crisis and the Indian Economy', *Cambridge Journal of Economics* 33: 725–39.

Ghosh, Swati (2009) 'Fragmented Labour and Elusive Solidarity: The Brickfields of Bengal', Third Critical Studies Conference: Empires, States & Migration, Kolkata, unpublished conference paper.

Ghurye, Govind S. (1980) *The Scheduled Tribes of India* (New Brunswick, NJ: Transaction Books).

Gorringe, Hugo (2005) *Untouchable Citizens: Dalit Movements and Democratisation in Tamil Nadu* (New Delhi: Sage).

Gorringe, Hugo (2008) 'The Caste of the Nation: Untouchability and Citizenship in South India', *Contributions to Indian Sociology* 42(1): 123–49.

Gough, Kathleen (1989) *Rural Change in Southeast India, 1950s to 1980s* (New Delhi: Oxford University Press).

Government of India (1947) *Constituent Assembly of India (Legislative) Debates: Official Report Vol. IV (7) 14th July–31st July 1947* (Delhi: Government of India Press).

Government of India (1953) *Census of India Paper No. 2: Religion – 1951 Census* (Delhi: Manager of Publications, Government of India Press).

Government of India (2001a) 'Abstract of Speakers' Strength of Languages and Mother Tongues – 2001', <http://censusindia.gov.in/>, accessed 2 December 2009.

Government of India (2001b) 'India at a Glance', Census of India <http://censusindia.gov.in/>, accessed 14 October 2009.

Government of India (2007) 'Report of the Expert Group on Agricultural Indebtedness', Banking Division, Department of Economic Affairs (New Delhi: Ministry of Finance).

Government of India (2009a) 'Economic Survey 2008–2009', <http://indiabudget.nic.in/es2008-09/esmain.htm>, accessed 5 November 2009.

Government of India (2009b) 'Fact Sheet on Foreign Direct Investment (FDI), From August 1991 to September 2009', Ministry of Commerce and Industry, <http://dipp.nic.in/fdi_statistics/india_FDI_September2009.pdf>, accessed 25 November 2009.

Government of India (2009c) 'Monthly Economic Report, December 2009', Ministry of Finance, <http://finmin.nic.in/stats_data/monthly_economic_report/inddec09.pdf>, accessed 1 March 2010.

Government of India (nd-a) 'All India Radio', in <http://india.gov.in/knowindia/radio.php>, accessed 8 October 2009.

Government of India (nd-b) 'National Symbols', <http://india.gov.in/knowindia/national_symbols.php>, accessed 8 October 2009.

Government of India (nd-c) 'Television – Doordarshan', in <http://india.gov.in/knowindia/television.php>, accessed 8 October 2009.

Gowariker, Ashutosh (2001) *Lagaan* (Aamir Khan Productions).

Gowariker, Ashutosh (2008) *Jodhaa-Akbar* (Ashutosh Gowariker Productions).

Gujral, Inder Kumar (1997) 'India in a Changing World', *Frontline* 14(16): 9 August.

Gupta, Dipankar (2004) *Whither the Indian Village? Culture and Agriculture in 'Rural' India* (Chennai: Madras Institute of Development Studies).

Gwatkin, Davidson R. (1979) 'Political Will and Family Planning: The Implications of India's Emergency Experience', *Population and Development Review* 5(1): 29–59.

Hardgrave, Robert and Stanley Kochanek (2000) *India: Government and Politics in a Developing Nation* (Fort Worth, TX: Harcourt Brace Jovanovich Publishers).

Hardgrave, Robert (1970) 'The Congress in India – Crisis and Split', *Asian Survey* 10(3): 256–62.

Harding, Luke (2001) 'Census-Takers Prepare to Map India's Millions', *Guardian*, 9 February.

Harriss, John (1991) 'The Green Revolution in North Arcot: Economic Trends, Household Mobility, and the Politics of an 'Awkward Class'', in Peter Hazell and C. Ramasamy (eds), *The Green Revolution Reconsidered: The Impact of High-Yielding Rice Varieties in South India* (Baltimore, MD: Johns Hopkins University Press).

Harriss, John (2003) 'The Great Tradition Globalizes: Reflections on Two Studies of "The Industrial Leaders" of Madras', *Modern Asian Studies* 37(2): 327–62.

Harriss, John (2007) 'Antinomies of Empowerment: Observations on Civil Society, Politics and Urban Governance in India', *Economic and Political Weekly* 37: 2716–24.

Harriss-White, Barbara (2001) 'Gender Cleansing', in Rajeswari Sunder Rajan (ed.), *Signposts: Gender Issues in Post-Independence India* (New Brunswick, NJ: Rutgers University Press).

Harriss-White, Barbara (2003) *India Working: Essays on Society and Economy* (Cambridge: Cambridge University Press).

Harriss-White, Barbara and Nandini Gooptu (2001) 'Mapping India's World of Unorganized Labour', *Socialist Register* 37: 89–118.

Hasan, Mushirul (1993) *India's Partition: Process, Strategy and Mobilisation* (New Delhi: Oxford University Press).

Hasan, Mushirul (1997) *Legacy of a Divided Nation: India's Muslims since Independence* (London: Hurst).

Hasan, Zoya (1998) *Quest for Power: Oppositional Movements and Post-Congress Politics in Uttar Pradesh* (New Delhi: Oxford University Press).

Hasan, Zoya (ed.) (2002) *Parties and Party Politics in India* (New Delhi: Oxford University Press).

Hewitt, Vernon (1995) *Reclaiming the Past? The Search for Political and Cultural Unity in Contemporary Jammu and Kashmir* (London: Portland).

Hewitt, Vernon (1997) *The New International Politics of South Asia* (Manchester: Manchester University Press).

Hewitt, Vernon and Shirin Rai (2010) 'The Indian Parliament', in Niraja Jayal and Pratap Bhanu Mehta (eds), *The Oxford Companion to Politics in India* (New Delhi: Oxford University Press).

Human Rights Watch (2002) '"We Have No Orders to Save You", State Participation and Complicity in Communal Violence in Gujarat', <http://www.hrw.org/legacy/reports/2002/india/>.

Human Rights Watch (2007) 'Hidden Apartheid: Caste Discrimination against India's "Untouchables"', <http://www.hrw.org/sites/default/files/reports/india0207webwcover_0.pdf>.

Hust, Evelin (2005) 'Introduction: Problems of Urbanization and Urban Governance in India', in Evelin Hust and Michael Mann (eds), *Urbanization and Governance in India* (Delhi: Manohar).

Illaiah, Kancha (1998) *Why I am Not a Hindu* (Calcutta: Samaya).

Inder Singh, Anita (1990) *The Origins of the Partition of India, 1936–1947* (New Delhi: Oxford University Press).

Irving, Robert Grant (1982) 'Architecture for Empire's Sake: Lutyens's Palace for Delhi', *Perspecta* 18: 7–23.

Irwin, Kathryn (2009) 'The World's Worst Job', *Christian Aid News* 44: 12–13.

Jaffrelot, Christophe (1996) *The Hindu Nationalist Movement and Indian Politics, 1925 to the 1990s: Strategies of Identity-Building, Implantation and Mobilisation (with Special Reference to Central India)* (London: Hurst).

Jaffrelot, Christophe (2009) 'Introduction', in Christophe Jaffrelot and Sanjay Kumar (eds), *Rise of the Plebeians? The Changing Face of Indian Legislative Assemblies* (New Delhi: Routledge).

Jalal, Ayesha (1985) *The Sole Spokesman: Jinnah, the Muslim League and the Demand for Pakistan* (Cambridge: Cambridge University Press).

Jalal, Ayesha (1990) 'State-Building in the Post-War World: Britain's Colonial Legacy, American Futures and Pakistan', in Sugata Bose (ed.), *South Asia and World Capitalism* (Delhi: Oxford University Press).

Jayal, Niraja (2007) 'The Role of Civil Society', in Sumit Ganguly (ed.), *The State of India's Democracy* (Baltimore, MD: Johns Hopkins University Press).

Jeffrey, Robin (2006) 'The Mahatma Didn't Like the Movies and Why it Matters: Indian Broadcasting Policy, 1920s–1990s', *Global Media and Communication* 2(2): 204–24.

Jenkins, Robert (1999) *Democratic Politics and Economic Reform in India* (Cambridge: Cambridge University Press).

Jenkins, Robert (2007) 'Civil Society Versus Corruption', *Journal of Democracy* 18(2): 55–69.

Jenkins, Robert (2005) 'India's Civil Society', in Peter Burnell and Vicky Randall (eds), *Politics in the Developing World* (Oxford: Oxford University Press).

Jha, Prabhat, Rajesh Kumar and Neeraj Dhingra (2006) 'Low Male-to-Female Sex Ratio of Children Born in India: National Survey of 1.1 Million Households', *The Lancet* 367(9506): 211–18.

Jhabvala, Renana (2005) 'Work and Wealth', in Alyssa Ayres and Philip Oldenburg (eds), *India Briefing: Takeoff at Last?* (Armonk, NY: ME Sharpe).

Johar, Karan (1998) *Kuch Kuch Hota Hai* (Dharma Productions).

Johar, Karan (2006) *Kabhi Alvida Naa Kehna* (Dharma Productions).

John, J. (2007) 'Overall Increase and Sectoral Setbacks: Lessons from Central Trade Union Verification 2002 Data', Labour File, <http://www.labourfile.org/ArticleMore.aspx?Id=900>, accessed 18 January 2010.

John, Mary (2001) 'Gender, Development and the Women's Movement', in R. Sunder Rajan (ed.), *Signposts: Gender in Post-Independence India* (New Brunswick, NJ: Rutgers University Press).

Joshi, Barbara (ed.) (1986) *Untouchable! Voices of the Dalit Liberation Movement* (London: Zed Books).

Juluri, Vamsee (2002) 'Music Television and the Invention of Youth Culture in India', *Television and New Media* 3(4): 367–86.

Kabir, M. (2001) *Bollywood: The Indian Cinema Story* (London: Channel 4 Books).

Kailash, K. K. (2009) 'Alliances and Lessons of Elections 2009', *Economic and Political Weekly* 44(39): 52–7.

Kanda, K. C. (1992) *Masterpieces of Urdu Ghazal: From 17th to 20th Century* (New Delhi: Sterling).

Kapoor, Raj (1955) *Shree 420* (R.K. Films).

Kapur, Ashok (2001) 'Pokhran II and After: Consequences of the Indian Nuclear Tests of 1998', in Amita Shastri and A. Jeyaratnam Wilson (eds), *The Post-Colonial States of South Asia: Democracy, Development and Identity* (Richmond: Curzon).

Kapur, Devesh (2003) 'Indian Diaspora as a Strategic Asset', *Economic and Political Weekly* 38(5): 445–8.

Kapur, Devesh, John Lewis and Richard Webb (1997) *The World Bank: Its First Half Century, Volume 1 – History* (Washington, DC: Brookings).

Karat, Brinda (2006) 'The PDS and Eroding Food Security', *The Hindu*, 6 June.

Keay, John (2000) *India: A History* (London: HarperCollins).

Keith, A. B. (1936) *A Constitutional History of India 1600–1935* (London: Methuen).

Khan, Mehboob (1957) *Mother India* (Mehboob Productions).

Khilnani, Sunil (1997) *The Idea of India* (London: Hamish Hamilton).

Khosla, Gopal Das (1949) *Stern Reckoning: A Survey of the Events Leading up to and Following the Partition of India* (New Delhi: Bhawnani).

Kirk, Jason A. (2008) 'Indian-Americans and the U.S.–India Nuclear Agreement: Consolidation of an Ethnic Lobby?', *Foreign Policy Analysis* 4(3): 275–300.

Kohli, Atul (2004) *State-Directed Development: Political Power and Industrialization in the Global Periphery* (Cambridge: Cambridge University Press).

Kohli, Atul (2006) 'Politics of Economic Growth in India, 1980–2005, Part I: The 1980s', *Economic and Political Weekly* April 1: 1251–9.

Kohli, Atul and Pranab K. Bardhan (1988) *India's Democracy: An Analysis of Changing State-Society Relations* (Princeton, NJ: Princeton University Press).

Kothari, Rajni (1964) 'The Congress "System" in India', *Asian Survey* 4(12): 1161–73.

Kukunoor, Nagesh (2005) *Iqbal* (Mukta Searchlight Films).

Kumar, Nagesh (1996) 'India: Industrialization, Liberalization and Inward and Outward Foreign Direct Investment', in John Dunning and Rajneesh Narula (eds), *Foreign Direct Investment and Governments: Catalysts for Economic Restructuring* (London: Routledge).

Kumar, S. Nagesh (2010) 'Talking Peace', *Frontline* 27(2): January 16.

Kumari, Abhilasha and Sabina Kidwai (1998) *Crossing the Sacred Line: Women's Search for Political Power* (Hyderabad: Orient Longman).

Kundu, Apurba (2005) 'The NDA and National Security', in Katharine Adeney and Lawrence Sáez (eds), *Coalition Politics and Hindu Nationalism* (Abingdon: Routledge).

Lahiri, Jhumpa (1999) *Interpreter of Maladies* (London: Flamingo).

Lahiri, Jhumpa (2004) *The Namesake* (London: Flamingo).

Lahiri, Jhumpa (2009) *Unaccustomed Earth* (London: Bloomsbury).

Lall, Marie C. (2001) *India's Missed Opportunity: India's Relationship with the Non-resident Indians* (Aldershot: Ashgate).

Larsson, Marie (2006) '"When Women Unite!": The Making of the Anti-Liquor Movement in Andhra Pradesh, India', Ph.D Thesis, Stockholm University.

Lavoy, Peter R. (2007) 'India in 2006: A New Emphasis on Engagement', *Asian Survey* 47(1): 113–24.

Leithead, Alistair (2007) 'Mixed Feelings on India-Pakistan Border', BBC Online, 14 August.

Luce, Edward (2007) *In Spite of the Gods: The Strange Rise of Modern India* (London: Abacus).

Ludden, David E. (1996) *Contesting the Nation: Religion, Community, and the Politics of Democracy in India* (Philadelphia, PA: University of Pennsylvania Press).

Mahaprashasta, Ajoy Ashirwad (2009) 'SAD-BJP Dusting Out Old Issues in Punjab', *Business Line*, 4 April.

Majumdar, Boria (2004) *Twenty Yards to Freedom: A Social History of Indian Cricket* (New Delhi: Viking).

Manor, James (1990) 'How and Why Liberal and Representative Politics Emerged in India', *Political Studies* 38(1): 20–38.

Manor, James (1995) 'Regional Parties in Federal Systems', in Douglas Verney and Balveer Arora (eds), *Multiple Identities in a Single State: Indian Federalism in Comparative Perspective* (Delhi: Konark Publishers Ltd).

Manor, James (1996) 'Ethnicity and Politics in India', *International Affairs* 72(1): 459–75.

Manuel, Peter (1988) 'A Historical Survey of the Urdu Gazal-Song in India', *Asian Music* 20(1): 93–113.

Mathur, O. P. (2002) *India: Evaluating Bank Assistance for Urban Development* (Washington, DC: World Bank – Operations Evaluation Department).

Maxwell, Neville (1972) *India's China War* (Harmondsworth: Penguin).

Mayaram, Shail (1993) 'Communal Violence in Jaipur', *Economic and Political Weekly*, 13 November.

Mayaram, Shail (2002) 'New Modes of Violence: The Backlash against Women in the Panchayat System', in Karin Kapadia (ed.), *The Violence of Development: The Politics of Identity, Gender and Social Inequalities in India* (Delhi: Kali for Women).

McMillan, Alistair (2001) 'Population Change and the Democratic Structure', *Seminar* 506.

McMillan, Alistair (2005) *Standing at the Margins: Representation and Electoral Reservation in India* (New Delhi: Oxford University Press).

McMillin, Divya C. (2001) 'Localizing the Global: Television and Hybrid Programming in India', *International Journal of Cultural Studies* 4(1): 45–68.

Meduri, Avanthi (1988) 'Bharatha Natyam-What Are You?', *Asian Theatre Journal* 5(1): 1–22.

Mehta, Pratap Bhanu (2003) 'A New Foreign Policy?', *Economic and Political Weekly* 38(30): 3173–4.

Mehta, Pratap Bhanu (2007) 'The Rise of Judicial Sovereignty', *Journal of Democracy* 18(2): 70–83.

Menon, Nivedita (1998) 'Women and Citizenship', in Partha Chatterjee (ed.), *Wages of Freedom: Fifty Years of the Indian Nation-State* (New Delhi: Oxford University Press).

Menon, Nivedita (2001) *Gender and Politics in India* (New Delhi: Oxford University Press).

Menon, Nivedita and Aditya Nigam (2007) *Power and Contestation: India since 1989* (London: Zed).

Michelutti, Lucia (2004) '"We (Yadavs) are a Caste of Politicians": Caste and Modern Politics in a North Indian Town', *Contributions to Indian Sociology* 38(1&2): 43–71.

Ministry of Home Affairs (2009) 'Overseas Citizenship of India (OCI)' <http://www.mha.nic.in>, accessed September 2009.

Misra, B.B. (1961) *The Indian Middle Classes: Their Growth in Modern Times* (Oxford: Oxford University Press).

Mistry, Rohinton (1987) *Tales from Firozsha Baagh* (Harmondsworth: Penguin).

Mistry, Rohinton (1995) *A Fine Balance* (Toronto: McClelland & Stewart).

Mitra, Barbara (2009) Personal communication.

Mitra, Subrata K. and Vijay Bahadur Singh (2009) *When Rebels Become Stakeholders: Democracy, Agency and Social Change in India* (New Delhi: Sage).

Mitra, Subrata K. and Vijay Bahadur Singh (1999) *Democracy and Social Change in India: A Cross-Sectional Analysis of the National Electorate* (New Delhi: Sage).

Mohan, C. Raja (2003a) *Crossing the Rubicon: The Shaping of India's New Foreign Policy* (Delhi: Penguin).

Mohan, C. Raja (2003b) 'Nuclear Command Authority Comes into Being', *The Hindu*, 5 January.

Mohan, C. Raja (2007) 'Balancing Interests and Values: India's Struggle with Democracy Promotion', *The Washington Quarterly* 303: 99–115.

Mohan, C. Raja (2008) 'India's Great Power Burdens', *Seminar* 581.

Morcom, Anna (2001) 'An Understanding between Bollywood and Hollywood? The Meaning of Hollywood-Style Music in Hindi Films', *British Journal of Ethnomusicology* 10(1): 63–84.

Morris, Robert (2001) 'Variation and Process in South Indian Music: Some "Kritis" and Their "Sangatis"', *Music Theory Spectrum* 23(1): 74–89.

Mortimer-Franklyn, H. (1887) *The Unit of Imperial Federation: A Solution of the Problem* (London: Swan Sonnerchein, Lowrey and Co.).

Mortished, Carl (2008) 'Russia Shows its Political Clout by Hosting Bric Summit', The Times Online, 16 May.

MTV India (2009) 'Non stop hits', <http://www.mtvindia.com/tvschedule/>, accessed October 21 2009.

Mukerjee, Sutapa (2005) 'India's Muslims Face up to Rifts', BBC Online, 9 February.

Nanda, B.R. (1990) 'Introduction', in B.R. Nanda (ed.), *Indian Foreign Policy: The Nehru Years* (London: Sangam).

Nandy, Ashis (2004) 'The Changing Popular Culture of Indian Food: Preliminary Notes', *South Asia Research* 24(1): 9–20.

Narayana Murthy, N.R. (2007) 'Software Exports', in Kaushik Basu (ed.), *The Oxford Companion to Economics in India* (New Delhi: Oxford University Press).

Narlikar, Amrita (2007) 'All that Glitters is Not Gold: India's Rise to Power', *Third World Quarterly* 28(5): 983–96.

Narmada Valley Development Authority (nd) 'Resettlement and Rehabilitation', in <http://www.mp.gov.in/nvda/statistics.htm>, accessed 26 January 2008.

NASSCOM (2009a) 'The IT-BPO Sector in India, Strategic Review 2009', <http://www.nasscom.in/upload/60452/Executive_summary.pdf>, accessed December 2009.

NASSCOM (2009b) 'NASSCOM Releases Indian IT Software and Services – FY09 Performance and Future Trends', <http://www.nasscom.in/Nasscom/templates/NormalPage.aspx?id=55739>, accessed December 2009.

National Election Watch and Association for Democratic Reforms (2009) 'Analysis of the MPs of 15th Lok Sabha (2009)-High Level Summary', <http://nationalelectionwatch.org/files/new/pdfs/Lok%20Sabha%20high%20level%20analysis.pdf>, accessed September 2009.

Nayar, Baldev Raj (1966) *Minority Politics in the Punjab* (Princeton, NJ: Princeton University Press).

NCAER (2005) 'The Great Indian Market: Results from the NCAER's Market Information Survey of Households', <http://www.ncaer.org/downloads/PPT/TheGreatIndianMarket.pdf>, accessed 2 December 2009.

Nehru, Jawaharlal (1938) *Nehru-Jinnah Correspondence: Including Gandhi-Jinnah and Nehru-Nawab Ismail Correspondence* (Allahabad: J.B. Kripalani, AICC).

Nehru, Jawaharlal (1946) *The Discovery of India* (London: Meridian Books Ltd).

Noorani, A. (1999) 'How Secular is Vande Mataram?', *Frontline* 16(1) 2 January.

Noorani, A. (2000) 'Nehru: A Democratic Curzon?', *Frontline* 17(26): 23 December.

Nunnenkamp, Peter and Rudi Stracke (2008) 'Foreign Direct Investment in Post-reform India: Likely to Work Wonders for Regional Development', *Journal of Economic Development* 33 (2): 55–84.

O'Shea, Janet (1998) '"Traditional" Indian Dance and the Making of Interpretive Communities', *Asian Theatre Journal* 15(1): 45–63.

Omvedt, Gail (1993) *Reinventing Revolution: New Social Movements and the Socialist Tradition in India* (Armonk, NY: M.E. Sharpe).

Oommen, T.K. (1984) *Social Transformation in Rural India: Mobilization and State Intervention* (Delhi: Vikas).

Pan, Esther and Jayshree Bajoria (2008) 'The US-India Nuclear Deal', Council on Foreign Relations, <http://www.cfr.org/publication/9663/#p9665>, accessed 13 November 2009.

Pant, Harsh V. (2007a) 'A Fine Balance: India Walks a Tightrope between Iran and the United States', *Orbis* 51(3): 495–509.

Pant, Harsh V. (2007b) 'India in the Asia-Pacific: Rising Ambitions with an Eye on China', *Asia-Pacific Review* 14(1): 5–71.

Pant, Harsh V. (2009) 'A Rising India's Search for a Foreign Policy', *Orbis* 53(2): 250–64.

Parry, Jonathan (2000) '"The Crisis of Corruption" and the "idea of India": A Worm's Eye View', in Italo Pardo (ed.), *The Morals of Legitimacy: Between Agency and System* (Oxford: Berghahn Books).

Pedersen, Jørgen Dige (2000) 'Explaining Economic Liberalization in India: State and Society Perspectives', *World Development* 28(2): 265–82.

Pedersen, Jørgen Dige (2008) *Globalization, Development and the State: The Performance of India and Brazil since 1990* (Basingstoke: Palgrave Macmillan).

Peiris, G. L. (1991) 'Public Interest Litigation in the Indian Subcontinent: Current Dimensions', *The International and Comparative Law Quarterly* 40(1): 66–90.

Perkovich, George (2000) *India's Nuclear Bomb: The Impact on Global Proliferation* (New Delhi: Oxford University Press).

Perkovich, George (2003) 'Is India a Major Power?' *The Washington Quarterly* 27(1): 129–44.

Popham, Peter (2000) '"The World's Most Dangerous Place" is Already at War', *The Independent*, March 18.

Potter, David (1996) *India's Political Administrators: From ICS to IAS* (New Delhi: Oxford University Press).

Press Information Bureau (2009), 'National Tally – Party-Wise', <http://pib.nic.in/release/release.asp?relid=48763>, accessed 8 April 2010.

Price, Gareth (1997) 'The Assam Movement and the Construction of Assamese Identity', unpublished thesis, University of Bristol.

Qureshi, Regula (1992) '"Muslim Devotional": Popular Religious Music and Muslim Identity under British, Indian and Pakistani Hegemony', *Asian Music* 24(1): 111–21.

Raghavan, R. K. (2003) 'The Indian Police: Problems and Prospects', *Publius* 33(4): 119–33.

Rahman, Faizur (2003) 'Uniform Civil Code and National Integration', *The Hindu*, 19 August.

Rai, Alok (2002) 'Representing India: Indian Literature on the World Stage', in Alyssa Ayres and Philip Oldenburg (eds), *India Briefing: Quickening the Pace of Change* (Armonk, NY: M.E. Sharpe).

Rajagopalan, Rajesh (2008) 'India: The Logic of Assured Retaliation', in Muthiah Alagappa (ed.), *The Long Shadow: Nuclear Weapons and Security in 21st Century Asia* (Stanford, CA: Stanford University Press).

Ramachandran, R. (2006) 'Shifting of Goalposts', *Frontline* 23(25): 16 December.

Ramaswamy, E. A. (1995) 'Organized Labor and Economic Reform', in Philip Oldenburg (ed.), *India Briefing: Staying the Course* (Armonk, NY: M.E. Sharpe).

Randall, Vicky (2006) 'Legislative Gender Quotas and Indian Exceptionalism: The Travails of the Women's Reservation Bill', *Comparative Politics* 39(1): 63–82.

Ratnam, Mani (1992) *Roja* (Kavithalaya Productions).

Ratnam, Mani (1995) *Bombay* (Amitabh Bachchan Corporation).

Rediff.com (2006) 'Singing of Vande Mataram Optional in Most States', <http://www.Rediff.com>, 6 September.

Rediff.com (2009) 'CPI-Maoist Banned to Avoid Ambiguity: Chidambaram', <http://www.Rediff.com>, 22 June.

Renouf, Renee (1978) 'Review: Folk Dances of India', *Dance Chronicle* 2(4): 327–34.

Reuters India (2008) 'India Revises Kashmir Death Toll to 47,000', <http://in.reuters.com>, 21 November.

Robinson, Francis (1993) *Separatism among Indian Muslims: The Politics of the United Provinces' Muslims 1860–1923* (New Delhi: Oxford University Press).

Robinson, H. (1972) *Monsoon Asia* (London: MacDonald).

Roy, Arundhati (1997) *The God of Small Things* (New Delhi: IndiaInk).

Roy, Arundhati (1999) 'The Greater Common Good', *Frontline* 16(11): May 22.

Roy, Asim (1993) 'The High Politics of India's Partition: The Revisionist Perspective', in Mushirul Hasan (ed.), *India's Partition: Process, Strategy and Mobilisation* (New Delhi: Oxford University Press).

Roy, Srirupa (2006) '"A Symbol of Freedom": The Indian Flag and the Transformations of Nationalism, 1906–2002', *The Journal of Asian Studies* 65(3): 495–527.

Rudolph, Lloyd I. and Susanne Hoeber Rudolph (1967) *The Modernity of Tradition: Political Development in India* (Chicago, IL: University of Chicago Press).

Rudolph, Lloyd I. and Susanne Hoeber Rudolph (1981) 'Judicial Review versus Parliamentary Sovereignty: The Struggle over Stateness in India', *Journal of Commonwealth and Comparative Politics* 19(3): 231–56.

Rudolph, Lloyd I. and Susanne Hoeber Rudolph (1987) *In Pursuit of Lakshmi: The Political Economy of the Indian State* (Chicago, IL: London: University of Chicago Press).

Rushdie, Salman (1981) *Midnight's Children* (London: Jonathan Cape).

Rushdie, Salman (1995) *The Moor's Last Sigh* (London: Jonathan Cape).

Sáez, Lawrence (2004) 'India in 2003: Pre-Electoral Maneuvering and the Prospects for Regional Peace', *Asian Survey* 44(1): 23–35.

Sainath, P. (2004) 'McMedia and Market Jihad ', *The Hindu*, 1 June.

Sanghavi, Prachi, K. Bhalla and V. Das (2009) 'Fire-Related Deaths in India in 2001: A Retrospective Analysis of Data', *The Lancet* 373(9671): 1282–8.

Sarrazin, Natalie (2006) 'India's Music: Popular Film Songs in the Classroom', *Music Educators Journal* 93(1): 26–32.

Sasikumar, Karthika (2009) 'India's Debated Nuclear Policy', *India Review* 8(3): 375–84.

SATPO – South Asia Terrorism Portal (2009) '2009 Fatalities in Left-wing Extremism', <http://www.satp.org/satporgtp/countries/india/maoist/data_sheets/fatalitiesnaxal.htm>, accessed 8 October 2009.

SATPO – South Asia Terrorism Portal (nd) 'Left Wing Extremist Group: Communist Party of India-Maoist (CPI-Maoist)', <http://www.satp.org/satporgtp/countries/india/terroristoutfits/CPI_M.htm>, accessed September 2009.

Savarkar, Vinayak D. (1999) *Hindutva: Who is a Hindu?* (Mumbai: Swatantryaveer Savarkar Rashtriya Smarak).

Schulze, Brigitte (2002) 'The Cinematic "Discovery of India": Mehboob's Re-Invention of the Nation in Mother India', *Social Scientist* 30(9/10): 72–87.

Schwartzberg, Joseph (ed.) (1978) *An Historical Atlas of South Asia* (Chicago, IL: University of Chicago Press).

Scott, James M. and Carie A. Steele (2005) 'Assisting Democrats or Resisting Dictators? The Nature and Impact of Democracy Support by the United States National Endowment for Democracy, 1990–99', *Democratization* 12(4): 439–60.

SDSA (2008) *State of Democracy in South Asia* (New Delhi: Oxford University Press).

Sen, Aparna (2002) *Mr and Mrs Iyer* (Triplecom Media Production).

Sen, Geeti (2003) 'Iconising the Nation: Political Agendas', in Geeti Sen (ed.), *India: A National Culture?* (New Delhi: Sage).

Sen, Kunal (2009a) *Trade Policy, Inequality and Performance in Indian Manufacturing* (Abingdon: Routledge).

Sen, Kunal (2009b) 'What a Long, Strange Trip it's Been: Reflections on India's Economic Growth in the Twentieth Century', *Heidelberg Papers in South Asian and Comparative Politics*, 47 (April), <http://www.ub.uni-heidelberg.de/archiv/9444>.

Sen, Ronojoy (2009) 'Walking a Tightrope: Judicial Activism and Indian Democracy', *India Review* 8(1): 63–80.

Sengupta, Somini (2005) 'Pride and Politics: India Rejects Quake Aid', *New York Times*, 19 October.

Seth, Vikram (1994) *A Suitable Boy* (London: Penguin).

SEWA – Self Employed Women's Association (2006) 'Annual Report <http://www.sewa.org/Annual_Report/AnnualReport2006/index.html>, accessed September 2009.

SGPC (2009) 'Shiromani Gurdwara Parbandhak Committee', <http://www.sgpc.net/the-sgpc/index.asp>, accessed 7 October 2009.

Shankar, S. (2007) *Sijavi: The Boss* (A.V.M Productions).

Sharma, Shalendra D. (1999) *Development and Democracy in India* (Boulder, CO: Lynne Rienner Publishers).

Sharma, Ursula (1999) *Caste* (Buckingham: Open University Press).

Sikkand, Yogindar (2004) *Muslims in India since 1947: Islamic Perspectives on Inter-faith Relations* (London: RoutledgeCurzon).

Singh, Gurharpal (2000) *Ethnic Conflict in India* (Basingstoke and London: Macmillan).

Singh, Jaswant (1999) *Defending India* (New Delhi: Macmillan).

Singh, Onkar (2008) 'Centre Recommends President's Rule in Nagaland', <http://www.Rediff.com.>, 2 January.

Singh, S. (2000) 'Secularist Faith in Salman Rushdie's Midnight's Children', *New Formations* 41(Autumn): 158–72.

Sinha, Aseema (2005) *The Regional Roots of Developmental Politics in India: A Divided Leviathan* (Bloomington, IN: Indiana University Press).

Sinha, Pravin (2002) 'Issues before the Indian Trade Union Movement', unpublished paper, Friedrich Ebert Stiftung (India), <http://library.fes.de/pdf-files/iez/01963.pdf>, accessed 18 January 2010.

Sippy, Ramesh (1975) *Sholay* (Sippy Films).

SIPRI (2007) *SIPRI Yearbook 2007: Armament, Disarmament and International Security* (Oxford: Oxford University Press).

Somanathan, Rohini (2007) 'Poverty and Exclusion', in Kaushik Basu (ed.), *The Oxford Companion to Economics in India* (New Delhi: Oxford University Press).

Sonwalkar, Prasun (2002) '"Murdochization" of the Indian Press: From By-line to Bottom Line', *Media, Culture and Society* 24(6): 821–34.

Spary, Carole (2007) 'Female Political Leadership in India'', *Commonwealth and Comparative Politics* 45(3): 253–77.

Spary, Carole (2008) 'Mainstreaming Gender in Development Policy: A Comparative Analysis of Tamil Nadu and Andhra Pradesh, India', unpublished thesis, University of Bristol.

Spary, Carole (2009) Personal communication.

Spodek, Howard (1990) 'Review of Shramshakti: Report of the National Commission of Self Employed Women and Women in the Informal Sector', *Economic Development and Cultural Change* 38(4): 896–901.

Spodek, Howard (1994) 'The Self-Employed Women's Association (SEWA) in India: Feminist, Gandhian Power in Development', *Economic Development and Cultural Change* 43(1): 193–202.

Sridharan, E (2002) 'The Fragmentation of the Indian Party System,

1952–1999; Seven Competing Explanations', in Zoya Hasan (ed.), *Parties and Party Politics in India* (New Delhi: Oxford University Press).

Sridharan, E. and Ashutosh Varshney (2001) 'Towards Moderate Pluralism: Political Parties in India', in Larry Diamond and Richard Gunther (eds), *Political Parties and Democracy* (Baltimore, MD; London: Johns Hopkins University Press).

Srinivas, A. (2005) *Ambani vs Ambani: Storms in the Sea Wind* (Delhi: Roli Books).

Srinivas, S. V. (2000) 'Devotion and Defiance in Fan Activity', in Ravi Vasudevan (ed.), *Making Meaning in Indian Cinema* (New Delhi: Oxford University Press).

Srinivasan, T. N. (2000) *Eight Lectures on India's Economic Reforms* (New Delhi: Oxford University Press).

Srinivasan, T. N. (1990) 'External Sector in Development: China and India, 1950–89', *The American Economic Review* 80(2): 113–17.

Stern, Robert W. (2003) *Changing India: Bourgeois Revolution on the Subcontinent* (Cambridge: Cambridge University Press).

Sundaram, Krishnamurthy (2007) 'Employment and Poverty in India, 2000–2005', *Economic and Political Weekly* 42(30): 3121–31.

Supreme Court of India (2006) *Prakash Singh & Ors. Versus Union of India and Ors.*, Writ Petition (Civil) No. 310 of 1996, September 22, 2006.

Swaminathan, Madhura (2003) 'Aspects of Poverty and Living Standards', in Sujata Patel and Jim Masselos (eds), *Bombay and Mumbai: The City in Transition* (New Delhi: Oxford University Press).

Swaminathan, Madhura (2007) 'Child Labour', in Kaushik Basu (ed.), *The Oxford Companion to Economics in India* (New Delhi: Oxford University Press).

Swaminathan, Padmini (2002) 'The Violence of Gender-Biased Development', in Karin Kapadia (ed.), *The Violence of Development: the Politics of Identity, Gender and Social Inequalities in India* (Delhi: Kali for Women).

Talbot, Ian (1990) *Provincial Politics and the Pakistan Movement: The Growth of the Muslim League in North-West and North-East India 1937–47* (Karachi: Oxford University Press).

Thapar, Romila (1985) 'Syndicated Moksha?', *Seminar* 313.

The Economist (2006) 'India's Naxalites: A Spectre Haunting India', *The Economist*, 17 August.

The Economist (2007) 'Home Truths', *The Economist*, 5 July.

The Economist (2008) 'A Special Report on India: India Elsewhere', *The Economist*, 13 December: 68.

The Economist (2009a) 'Banyan: Chasing Ghosts', *The Economist*, 13 June: 5.

The Economist (2009b) 'India's Cheap Housing Boom: The Nano Home', *The Economist*, 13 June: 92.

The Economist (2009c) 'Global Migration and the Downturn: The People Crunch', *The Economist*, 17 January: 46.

The Economist (2009d) 'Nepal and the United Nations: Another Fine Mission', *The Economist*, 17 January: 8.

The Economist (2009e) 'Tamil Nadu and Sri Lanka: Stoking the Flames', *The Economist*, 28 February: 10.

The Hindu (2003) 'Disrespect to Tricolour: Nod for Bill Spelling Out Punishment', *The Hindu*, 24 April.

The Independent (2008) 'Mayawati Kumari: Untouchable and Unstoppable', The Independent Online, 4 February.

The Telegraph (2009) 'Outlaw Prescription Hasn't Cured Red Corridor', *The Telegraph*, 23 June.

Thorat, Sukhadeo (2005) 'Why Reservation is Necessary', *Seminar* 549.

Thoraval, Yves (2000) *The Cinemas of India* (New Delhi: Macmillan).

Thornton, A. P. (1985) *The Imperial Idea and its Enemies: A Study in British Power* (London: Macmillan).

Thussu, Daya Kishan (1999) 'Privatizing the Airwaves: The Impact of Globalization on Broadcasting in India', *Media Culture and Society* 21(1): 125–31.

Thussu, Daya Kishan (2007) 'The "Murdochization" of News? The Case of Star TV in India', *Media Culture Society* 29(4): 593–611.

Times of India (2004) 'Muslim Growth Rate up by 1.5 pc', Times of India Online, 7 September.

Transparency International (2009a) '2009 Global Corruption Barometer': <http://www.transparency.org/publications/publications/gcb2009>.

Transparency International (2009b) 'Full GCB Results' <http://www.transparency.org/policy_research/surveys_indices/gcb/2009>, accessed 2 October 2009.

Tripathi, Dwijendra (2004) *The Oxford History of Indian Business* (New Delhi: Oxford University Press).

United Nations (2009) 'Monthly Summary of Contributors of Military and Police Personnel', Department of Peacekeeping Operations, <http://www.un.org/en/peacekeeping/contributors/>, accessed 20 November 2009.

VandeHei, Jim and Dafna Linzer (2006) 'U.S., India Reach Deal on Nuclear Cooperation', *Washington Post*, 3 March.

Varshney, Ashutosh (1998) 'Why Democracy Survives', *Journal of Democracy* 9(3): 36–50.

Varshney, Ashutosh (2000) 'Is India Becoming More Democratic?', *Journal of Asian Studies* 59(1): 3–25.

Varshney, Ashutosh (2002) *Ethnic Conflict and Civic Life* (New Haven, CT and London: Yale University Press).

Vaswani, Karishma (2007) 'Subsidised Fuel Weighs on India's Budget', BBC Online, 23 November.

Vaswani, Karishma (2009) 'Satyam Scandal Shocks India', BBC Online, 8 January.

Velayutham, S. (2008) 'Introduction: The Cultural History and Politics of South Indian Tamil Cinema', in S. Velayutham (ed.), *Tamil Cinema: The Cultural Politics of India's Other Film Industry* (Abingdon: Routledge).

Vijayabaskar, M. and Andrew Wyatt (2007) 'Many Messages of Sivaji', *Economic and Political Weekly* 42(44): 29–32.

Viswanathan, S. (2005) 'Disempowering Dalits', *Frontline* 22(10): 7 May.

Wade, Bonnie (1987) 'Introduction: Performing Arts in India: Essays on Music, Dance and Drama', *Asian Music* 18(2): 1–13.

Waghorne, J. P. (1981) 'The Case of the Missing Autobiography', *Journal of the American Academy of Religion* 49(4): 589–603.

Wainwright, Martin A. (1994) *Inheritance of Empire: Britain, India, and the Balance of Power in Asia, 1938–55* (Westport, CT: Praeger).

Washbrook, David (1997) 'The Rhetoric of Democracy and Development in Late Colonial India', in Sugata Bose and Ayesha Jalal (eds), *Nationalism, Democracy and Development: State and Politics in India* (New Delhi: Oxford University Press).

Waters, Anne (1997) 'Enduring Stereotypes: The Status of Women in South Asia', *Education about Asia* 2(2): 21–5.

Weiner, Myron (1957) *Party Politics in India: The Development of a Multi-Party System* (Princeton, NJ: Princeton University Press).

Weiner, Myron (1978) *Sons of the Soil: Migration and Ethnic Conflict in India* (Princeton, NJ; Guildford: Princeton University Press).

Whitehead, Lawrence (1997) 'Bowling in the Bronx: The Uncivil Interstices between Civil and Political Society', *Democratization* 4(1): 94–114.

Wilkinson, Steven (2004) *Votes and Violence: Electoral Competition and Ethnic Riots in India* (Cambridge: Cambridge University Press).

Williams, Glyn and Emma Mawdsley (2006) 'Postcolonial Environmental Justice: Government and Governance in India', *Geoforum* 37(5): 660–70.

Wolpert, Stanley (1993) *Zulfi Bhutto of Pakistan: His Life and Times* (New York, NY: Oxford University Press).

World Bank (2007) *World Development Report 2008: Agriculture for Development* (Washington, DC: World Bank).

World Bank (2008) *Country Strategy for the Republic of India for the Period FY 2009–2012* (New Delhi: World Bank).

World Bank (2009a) 'Data Finder: Life Expectancy at Birth', http://datafinder.worldbank.org/world-bank-data-finder, accessed 2 December 2009.

World Bank (2009b) 'World Development Report 2009: Reshaping Economic Geography' (Washington, DC: World Bank).

World Bank (2009c) *World Development Report 2010: Development and Climate Change* (Washington, DC: World Bank).

Wyatt, Andrew (1998) 'Dalit Christians and Identity Politics in India', *Bulletin of Concerned Asian Scholars* 30(4): 16–23.

Wyatt, Andrew (1999) 'The Limitations on Coalition Politics in India: The Case of Electoral Alliances in Uttar Pradesh', *Commonwealth and Comparative Politics* 37(2): 1–21.

Wyatt, Andrew (2005a) 'Do Our Stamps Evoke Nationalism?', *The Hindu*, 30 October.

Wyatt, Andrew (2005b) '(Re)imagining the Indian (Inter)national Economy', *New Political Economy* 10(2): 163–79.

Wyatt, Andrew (2005c) 'Building the Temples of Postmodern India: Economic Constructions of National Identity', *Contemporary South Asia* 14(4): 465–80.

Wyatt, Andrew (2010) *Party System Change in South India: Political Entrepreneurs, Patterns and Processes* (Abingdon: Routledge).

Xaxa, V. (2003) 'Tribes in India', in Veena Das (ed.), *The Oxford India Companion to Sociology and Social Anthropology* (New Delhi: Oxford University Press).

Yadav, Yogendra and Suhas Palshikar (2009) 'Between Fortuna and Virtu: Explaining the Congress' Ambiguous Victory in 2009', *Economic and Political Weekly* 44(39): 33–46.

Zavos, John (2000) *The Emergence of Hindu Nationalism in India* (New Delhi: Oxford University Press).

Zavos, John (2001) 'Conversion and the Assertive Margins: An Analysis of Hindu Nationalist Discourse and the Recent Attacks on Indian Christians', *South Asia: Journal of South Asian Studies* 24(2): 73–89.

Zavos, John (2005) 'The Shapes of Hindu Nationalism', in Katharine Adeney and Lawrence Sáez (eds), *Coalition Politics and Hindu Nationalism* (Abingdon: Routledge).

Index